POLICING CHINA

Studies of the Weatherhead East Asian Institute, Columbia University

The Studies of the Weatherhead East Asian Institute of Columbia University were inaugurated in 1962 to bring to a wider public the results of significant new research on modern and contemporary East Asia.

POLICING CHINA

Street-Level Cops in the Shadow of Protest

Suzanne E. Scoggins

CORNELL UNIVERSITY PRESS ITHACA AND LONDON

First published 2021 by Cornell University Press

Library of Congress Cataloging-in-Publication Data

Names: Scoggins, Suzanne E., 1979– author.
Title: Policing China: street-level cops in the shadow of protest / Suzanne E. Scoggins.
Description: Ithaca [New York]: Cornell University Press, 2021. | Series: Studies of the Weatherhead East Asian Institute, Columbia University | Includes bibliographical references and index. |
Identifiers: LCCN 2020037659 (print) | LCCN 2020037660 (ebook) | ISBN 9781501755583 (hardcover) | ISBN 9781501755606 (pdf) | ISBN 9781501755590 (epub)
Subjects: LCSH: Police administration—China. | Police—Political aspects—China.
Classification: LCC HV7935.S333 2021 (print) | LCC HV7935 (ebook) | DDC 363.20951—dc23
LC record available at https://lccn.loc.gov/2020037659
LC ebook record available at https://lccn.loc.gov/2020037660

Contents

Acknowledgments

As is often the case with research of this nature, I am unable to properly thank the respondents who helped make this project a reality. There would be no book without the Chinese police officers and ministry officials who were willing to sit down and talk with me about their jobs. I am truly grateful for their friendship and candor.

The research and writing for this book span a decade, and there are many who were there for its duration. Kevin O'Brien, whom I will forever refer to as the best adviser in the business, was an invaluable resource who guided me through failed starts, poorly fleshed-out ideas, and many, many drafts. I am glad he fully recovered from choking on a dish I ordered in a Xi'an restaurant toward the end of my fieldwork. Despite a rocky start, our conversation that day was the beginning of the paper "China's Unhappy Police" and marks the first point at which I realized I had enough material for this book.

A great debt is owed to others at Berkeley. Laura Stoker—never known for sugarcoating advice—was unequivocal that I had to get back into the field and talk to "police officers, any police officers" after my first fieldwork trip revealed that I would have trouble following my original research design. I am glad she struck down the possibility that I could simply go to the archives in Hong Kong and make do. Peter Lorentzen was a tireless supporter of the project, and while in the field I often returned to his advice that I find out how a police station in China works, which seemed like a manageable goal and kept me going. I am also grateful to Rachel Stern for her pointed questions and suggestions. This book is better for them.

Researching the police in China was at times a nerve-racking experience. I was lucky to have the company of my roommate and fellow researcher Alexsia Chan for much of that time. She kept me sane and curious about the world around me when things fell apart. Jianhua Xu, Jeffery Martin, Hualing Fu, and everyone at the Policing Studies Forum at the University of Hong Kong were also an intellectual lifeline during fieldwork. They helped me figure out which questions to ask and how to relate my observations back to other policing developments both in China and beyond. I am also grateful for my lifelong friends in China who made a challenging time fun: Lili Blum, Jacky Guan, Alicia Anderson, Katherine Sun and the Sun family, Leo Wang, Luna Zhou, and Kevin Woo, who still complains that I spilled coffee on his notebook fifteen years ago in Chinese class but who nevertheless went on to become one of this project's biggest supporters.

Writing the book turned out to be just barely easier than researching it. A special thanks goes to Ben Allen and Chris Chambers-Ju for their weekly check-ins. Our little accountability group has become a ritual, and I am lucky to have their collective encouragement. The keen eyes and encouragement of Yanilda Gonzalez, Sheena Greitens, Lauren McCarthy, and Nicholas Smith were also instrumental to the final product and my trajectory as a scholar more generally. I inadvertently crashed their APSA panel shortly upon returning from the field, and the informal policing group and friendship that resulted from that conference have become invaluable assets. A huge thank you also goes to my A-Team: Abby Wood, Akasemi Newsome, and Alexsia Chan. There are few friendships like graduate school friendships, and they have supported the writing of this book on a near daily basis, often one pomodoro at a time over group text or video chat.

Many others offered comments and assistance along the way. Thanks are due to Rachel Bernhard, Margaret Boittin, Meina Cai, Jennifer Choo, Julia Choucair Vizoso, Julia Chuang, Aileen Cruz, Rongbin Han, Lina Hu, Xian Huang, Francesca Jensenius, Charlotte Lee, Carl Minzner, Dann Naseemullah, Seung-Youn Oh, Youjeong Oh, David Sklansky, Albert Wu, John Yasuda, and the community of scholars at Stanford University's Center on Democracy, Development, and the Rule of Law (CDDRL) and the Berkeley Empirical Legal Studies (BELS) group. This project has benefited greatly from their time, insights, and suggestions.

I am also privileged to have wonderful colleagues at Clark University. A special thanks goes to Heather Silber Mohamed for answering all kinds of questions at all hours of the day over text, to Valerie Sperling for her early insights into the book publishing process, to Nina Kushner for helping me work through a critical last-minute question, and to Lex Jing Lu for his good humor and camaraderie in the process of finishing up the book manuscript. Last but certainly not least, I am grateful for the stellar skills and tireless enthusiasm of my research assistant, William Chen.

Of course, none of this happens without my editor at Cornell, Roger Haydon. I was fortunate to have approached Roger before I knew too much about his reputation, particularly his predilection for the word "no." Roger's insights and support through the review process have made the final product much better, and I am grateful to the entire team at Cornell University Press for their work on the book. A special thanks goes to Ariana King and the Weatherhead East Asian Institute at Columbia University for reviewing and including the book in their series. The three anonymous reviewers commissioned by Cornell and Weatherhead were instrumental to refining the argument and flow of the manuscript, as were the detailed insights of Sheena Greitens, Andrew Mertha, and Jianhua Xu, who were kind enough to provide detailed comments on earlier drafts.

The project was fieldwork intensive, and I am grateful for the financial support of the Boren Fellowship, the Smith Richardson Foundation, the University of California–Berkeley, the China Times Cultural Foundation, the Association for Asian Studies, and the Foreign Language and Area Studies (FLAS) Fellowship. I also owe a special thanks to UC Berkeley's Center for Chinese Studies, which supported my fieldwork from infancy to completion through a series of grants, and to CDDRL, which supported me financially and intellectually as I worked through my findings and wrote up the results.

This book is dedicated to my family. My parents, Jim and Anne Scoggins, gave me the great gift of their tireless love and support in the way that only parents can. I will forever be shaped by their guidance. Their influence is matched only by that of my husband, Edward Hung. I could not have invented a better partner. He has weathered many a trip to China, moved his legal practice and our family across the country so I could pursue my academic career, and proofread far too many papers and versions of this manuscript. He did all of this gladly, and I doubt I could have finished anything without his love or the boundless joy of our three little girls. Thank you, Octavia, Katerina, and Zelda. You are my inspiration.

Introduction

THE DEATH OF XIAO HU

In late summer 2013, police officers in Bengbu, China, came under scathing criticism because they failed to stop a murder. Seventeen-year-old Xiao Hu had begun her shift that day by walking from her grandmother's home to her job at a local supermarket. Before the afternoon was out, the young cashier was dead—stabbed to death in the store's entryway by a man purported to be a boyfriend she met online. News of her murder spread quickly, and critics soon began pointing fingers at the local police when newspapers and netizens learned that the attack unfolded while two local cops stood by and watched, unable to stop it.

Security footage of the crime revealed in detail a scene that was just as tragic as eyewitnesses reported. It all began when the suspect entered the store and began acting strangely. According to one employee, the man loitered in the aisles and eventually purchased two knives, leading her to call the police because she feared the man might use the knives to rob the market. Local police were dispatched, but by the time they arrived, the man was gone. When he later returned, the employee again called the police. Two officers arrived just in time to see the suspect grab Xiao Hu by the neck.

The security video released by the *People's Daily* Anhui shows Xiao Hu as she is pulled from behind the checkout counter and dragged to the floor by a man in a white shirt. The footage—still available online—is not easy to watch. As the perpetrator stabs Xiao Hu repeatedly with a knife, the officers stand in the entryway even as another employee urges them forward to stop the attack. Xiao Hu struggles alone until one officer finally throws an empty cardboard box at the attacker and—seconds later—a blue plastic stool. Both are immediately tossed aside, as the perpetrator pauses only momentarily before continuing his attack. In the interim, the second officer moves cautiously toward the fray with what appears to be a can of pepper spray, but his efforts produce no response.

It is only after the attacker turns the knife repeatedly on himself and falls to the floor that the officers finally move in and drag him away from the victim. Unfortunately, it comes too late. In the video, Xiao Hu lies motionless as two coworkers rush to her side, dialing cell phones and shooing away unknowing customers who try to enter the store. The publicly available footage ends as the officers pull the grievously self-injured perpetrator out of the camera's line of sight.

News of the attack and the accompanying video spread quickly online. Family members told reporters, "The two policemen are just two or three meters away. How can they bear to watch a child fall to the ground and be slashed? Why don't they come forward?" Xiao Hu's mother is said to have asked over and over, "The poor child. Why didn't you go save [her]? Why not?" Headlines in state-run media sources across the country told the tragic story in single sentences: "Police Witness Young Girl's Death Yet Fail to Stop It," and "Young Girl Stabbed Ten Times While Police Stand within Arm's Reach but Don't Stop It."[1] Online commentators also expressed outrage.[2] One netizen wrote, "A failure to do their duty! They were afraid of losing their own lives, and yet they are paid by taxpayers' salaries! What do we need this kind of policeman for!" Another asked, "So this is the character of the people's police??? Just how did these two get into the public security system?"

Shortly after the video went public, the local head of police issued a statement that admitted a slow response on the part of the officers but ultimately defended them, claiming that the officers were not afraid to die and at least took some action.[3] This response provoked additional ire, as did the report that one of the officers had at least twenty years' experience on the job and had even served as a training instructor for the local station. "The police are still making excuses," read one comment; "[they are] truly without integrity, without humanity."[4] Another read, "Trash! That police chief should be immediately fired," and yet another compared the incident to other police failures: "This is nothing, policemen in Foshan Xiqiao [a town in Foshan city] watched two brothers being stabbed to death. They only dared to fire six shots into the sky. The killer was not hurt at all."

Policing in the Shadow of Protest

This is a book about police failure. Xiao Hu's death demonstrates in heartbreaking detail the inability of two officers to do their jobs, but the case is also emblematic of more systemic problems facing policing in today's China. Front-line forces across the country far too often lack the equipment, training, and human resources they need to adequately respond to attacks like the one that ended Xiao Hu's life. This portrait of failure runs counter to many of our prior expectations about policing in China, which are shaped in no small part by news coverage of heavily armed officers forcibly subduing protesters, the militarization of policing in China's western Xinjiang Province, and the use of artificial intelligence to identify faces on the street or track a suspect's whereabouts.[5] These comparative strengths in the area of social control have overshadowed the everyday problems exemplified by the Xiao Hu case.

Despite projecting the appearance of a strong security state, the police bureaucracy in China is weak and plagued by problems of resources, enforcement, and oversight in virtually every area of policing except protest response. The central government and the Ministry of Public Security (MPS) have prioritized what is euphemistically referred to as "stability maintenance" (*weiwen*) to the detriment of nearly everything else, and the result is a hollowed-out and ineffective police force that struggles to deal with everyday crime. To analyze the true extent of these failures, we must go down to the ground level and talk to police officers on the front lines to gain a better understanding of the challenges they face and the specific ways in which success in the area of protest comes at the expense of other areas of policing. Ultimately, these conversations reveal that ground-level problems—present in one of the county's more powerful bureaucracies—compromise security on the ground for the Chinese public and bode poorly for regime resilience, police legitimacy, and other street-level bureaucrats in China.

This was never supposed to be a story about police failure. I originally planned to write about effective policing practices. After all, policing in China appears—at least from the outside—to be fairly effective. In addition to the police excelling at protest management, official crime statistics are low, the streets feel safe, and many cities seem to maintain a decent police presence on the street. Notably, public security departments in China have achieved this apparent success despite reports in the literature that the organization has long been underfunded and understaffed (Fu and Choy 2003; Fu 2005). As such, many signs point to good policies and innovative practices at the ground level—phenomena that others have also observed in studies of the local Chinese state (Heilmann and Perry 2011; Teets and Hurst 2014). More generally, effective policing matters for people's lives and well-being (Skogan and Frydl 2004), and for those studying China more specifically, the topic of effective policing is less politically sensitive than other issues related to the police—an unavoidable consideration for any researcher seeking to understand the inner workings of the Chinese state. But this is not a story about effective policing practices in China. It is, in fact, the opposite.

Talking to police officers on the street reveals an entirely different world, one in which cops say the official statistics systematically underreport crime, stations continue to lack adequate resources and officers, and no one has anything to say about effective policing.

"What?"—Shenme?—responded a frontline officer when I asked him about effective practices in one of the first interviews I conducted for this research in 2011. "What do you mean?" (Shenme yisi?). I tried another approach, this time asking about new techniques, then innovation, then improved response, only to get nowhere.[6] Subsequent interviewees had similar reactions. No one had anything to say about better practices or effective response. Instead, officers told story after story about resource constraints, counterproductive reporting requirements, and reforms that made their work harder. Often, they gave examples showcasing the sheer exhaustion of life on the front lines. Perhaps these officers were just disgruntled employees like other unhappy workers anywhere else. But their reports were too detailed, too focused, and in some cases too shocking to dismiss. The more that officers talked, the more the police bureaucracy began to look less and less like the well-oiled machine I had expected to find.

Patterns quickly emerged, and it was soon apparent that the issues officers reported were not isolated stories about low morale or inefficiency; they also revealed cracks in the bureaucracy that held larger political significance. These interviews with frontline cops and their superiors at the Ministry of Public Security unearthed challenges to local security capacity that even a well-organized central ministry is, for the most part, unable to resolve. Frontline police report that the local state has difficulty responding to most types of crime. From dealing with thefts to handling drug crimes, officers say they struggle under heavy workloads and lack the proper guidance and training to solve cases. Yet many of the same local police who complain about problems with everyday crime response also report achieving relative success in the area of protest control. Such differences raise many questions. Why, if the security state is strong, do local police have so much trouble on the ground? In what areas do they struggle the most? Perhaps most importantly, why have they not replicated the model of protest response to address other types of crime management?

Policing Protest in China

To fully understand policing in China, it is necessary to begin with the observation that success in the area of protest response brings challenges to other areas of policing. We typically think of the Chinese security state as strong and robust because the Communist Party (CCP) is adept at jailing or silencing dissidents and quashing rising protests at nearly every turn.[7] But the policing of social unrest in China was not always so successful. Officers recall that protests in the 1980s were handled haphazardly and with little guidance from above.[8] More generally, criticism and other displays of dissent tended to crop up in waves or "political cycles" as the CCP fell into a pattern of opening up space for political expression and then cracking down when criticism spiraled out of control (Lorentzen, n.d.).

All this changed in the aftermath of the 1989 Tiananmen Square protests. Fearful that another Tiananmen-size uprising might unseat the CCP's rule, central government leaders directed police and military officials to develop a more unified approach to dealing with social unrest. The resulting new best practices were ultimately codified in the 1995 Police Law. Efforts further intensified in 2005 when President Hu Jintao called on provincial and ministerial-level cadres to build a "socialist harmonious society."[9] In response, government leaders at all levels made a strong commitment to stability maintenance. This was mostly because their jobs depended on it. Performance measures for economic development and *weiwen*—which includes controlling protests, riots, and other forms of dissent—became the two key determinants of local cadre promotion, punishment, and dismissal. Cadres could be fired if they failed to "maintain public order," regardless of whether or not they performed well in other areas.[10] With new attention from government leaders, protest response became more standardized, and resources such as funding and manpower began to flow into stability maintenance from the local, provincial, and central levels at a higher rate, giving rise to the coordinated and sometimes militarized responses we read about in the news today.

Unsurprisingly, the police are on the front lines of this battle for stability maintenance. Local police are expected to respond to protest events, track and detain dissidents, and retrieve petitioners who attempt to lodge complaints at higher levels of government. The job is not easy, and by most accounts, the workload is increasing. The annual number of "mass incidents"—a vaguely defined term that can encompass anything from a few peaceful protesters to a violent riot—is generally believed to be rising. Widely cited MPS figures put the total number of incidents in 1993 at 8,706, but as table 1 demonstrates, that estimate rose dramatically until 2005, when the government stopped reporting figures.[11] The number is now estimated to be somewhere around 180,000, and probably higher.[12] Local police do not handle the large-scale riots, but they deal with nearly everything else, right down to small displays of dissent (*shangfang*) that sometimes involve only single individuals. When a situation becomes too large or violent, local governments and police leaders have the option to call in the People's Armed Police (PAP), a paramilitary force that is specially equipped for such tasks.

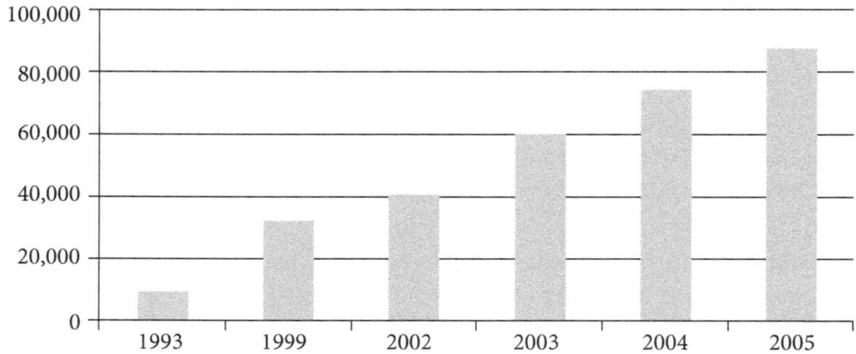

FIGURE 1. Official MPS estimate of mass incidents in China Chart by author.

Though the work can be challenging, frontline police do report satisfaction in their station's ability to manage protest-related tasks, largely because they say they have the requisite skills, resources, and interagency coordination they need to perform the work (Scoggins 2021). As a result, the police bureaucracy's response to protests is highly coordinated and swift. One government report released by the *Legal Daily* in 2012 detailed the causes of mass incidents by issue area and provided some insight into the success ground-level forces have in containing incidents of unrest.[13] The report found that 75.6 percent of the protests analyzed were resolved within a single day, 20.0 percent in two to seven days, and 4.4 percent in seven days to three months. Numbers like these, along with the absence of regime-destabilizing protests and sustained social movements in China, speak to the success of the local police and the PAP in containing China's social unrest.

Policing Everything Else

Given the frequency of reports about rising protests in the international news and the highly developed protest literature within China studies, it is easy to form the impression that much of what Chinese police officers do on a daily basis is related to protest and dissent.[14] This is inaccurate. Outside of politically sensitive areas like Xinjiang or Tibet, most city and county stations are filled with officers who rarely deal with protests. Details about how the police spend their time are not public information, but among the cities where I conducted research, even police in the city that experienced the most social unrest said their station spends approximately 30 percent of its time on the issue.[15] In other areas with fewer minority groups and less economic development, many officers said that they personally never deal with such issues, although some officers in their stations did. Thus before we get carried away with the implications of police strength in stability maintenance, it is important to note that much of police work in China is not protest related.

What does everyday policing look like? The bulk of police work involves managing incidents such as traffic accidents, burglaries, petty thefts, white-collar crime, rapes, murders, and other violent offenses. The size of police stations can vary dramatically, and a small local station (*paichusuo*) has as few as five employees. Frontline officers are primarily recruited locally, while station leaders may be appointed by local officials or sent in from other locales by the provincial ministry. New officer recruits who are city residents are often required to start their careers in nearby county stations or as contract officers. Officers who have social connections might secure a position in a city station directly. In county stations, officers on duty may share responsibility for handling all the crimes that occur in their jurisdiction, although who does what depends on seniority and social connections. In larger cities, caseloads are divided among specialized departments. Criminal investigation divisions, for example, handle murder, violent crime, and rape cases, while traffic divisions deal with any and all street activity. Patrol divisions primarily manage petty theft and other public order violations, although patrol officers are also the first responders for a wide variety of cases, given the nature of their presence on the street. All officers are expected to manage their caseload in accordance with the regulations set forth by the ministry in the criminal procedure code. Local police are also expected to file case reports that document each and every crime, police action taken, and any admission of guilt by the offending parties.

The job is neither glamorous nor particularly appreciated by the public. As Kevin O'Brien and I have documented elsewhere, police work can be exhausting for frontline agents, as officers labor under heavy caseloads, low pay, and administrative drudgery (Scoggins and O'Brien 2016). The work itself can vary, even for officers in the same position. Sometimes the job is excruciatingly boring, as evidenced by the patrol officers I often observed sleeping in squad cars parked on the side of the road at busy intersections. In the summer, they typically sit two or four per car with the windows down, feet up, and heads back, catching rest any way they can in the smoggy heat; in the winter, they hunch down under heavy coats and gloves as they wait. When a call comes in, however, these same officers must shift on a dime, since patrol work can also be demanding and dangerous. Office work is typically more consistent, but almost all officers report working long hours with frequent overtime.[16]

In addition to the physical and mental hardships of the job, officers say they are poorly prepared to do their jobs and struggle to manage their caseloads. Interviews reveal that police face problems of limited resources, poorly devised or executed reforms, and insufficient assistance from higher-ups. Frontline stories about worthless training programs, police officers looking the other way when they see criminal wrongdoing, or cops making deals with victims to make cases go away all provide critical insight into the day-to-day struggles of local police. Their caseloads are also higher than official statistics might lead casual observers to believe. The Chinese government is selective in the information it releases about crime rates, and more importantly, no frontline officer I spoke with expressed confidence in the reliability of official figures.[17] "You cannot trust any of the crime statistics," explained one officer.[18] "Crime in China is not nearly as low as they say it is." These heavy caseloads, limited resources, and inadequate training make it difficult for officers to respond to everyday crime.

The Argument

Reports from frontline officers raise questions about how discrepancies between the policing of protest and the policing of everything else affect public security and the party-state more broadly. Because policing—even in authoritarian states—is about so much more than keeping dissidents at bay, these observations about the ineffectiveness of everyday crime response show the folly of characterizing China as a strong security state. If the police are failing at basic tasks such as crime control, these problems indicate weakness in the bureaucracy that has widespread implications for public safety. Moreover, such problems may ultimately compromise regime stability and police legitimacy and bode poorly for other legal institutions. By prioritizing protest control and stability maintenance over other types of crime control, the party-state has opened itself up to a world of contradictions and vulnerability.

The roots for this focus on stability maintenance in China run deep. The People's Republic of China is a single-party state that has experienced a wide range of political change over the course of its seventy-year history. It transformed from a large, poorly unified country crippled by wars on two fronts into a communist state punctuated by the chaos of the Cultural Revolution. Since 1978, China has become an economic powerhouse dedicated to reforms that prioritize growth but not political participation. Although experimentation with economic reform created both winners and losers and caused income inequality to skyrocket, the Chinese government continued to push for economic development, pulling the nation further away from its earlier communist ideals even as officials continued to espouse socialist language and norms. This whipsaw of contradictory ideologies and political change opens up the regime to the risk of popular challenge to its authority. Leaders have watched the former Soviet states and Arab Spring countries closely, determined not to fall victim to similar winds of change.

Their answer—particularly in the wake of the Tiananmen protests and the instability of other authoritarian states around the globe—was to double down on stability maintenance. By most accounts, the party-state has excelled in this arena, demonstrating the strength of what it can do when resources are mustered and local power holders brought into line. Recent developments in stability maintenance seek to perfect the system by making use of both old and new techniques. In Xinjiang, fear over social unrest from the Uighur minority group has led to the internment of somewhere between eight hundred thousand and two million people in "reeducation"-style camps that Chinese leaders have used since the communist era to control targeted groups.[19] And although the Chinese regime did not invent facial recognition software, it is taking the technology to the next level by installing millions of cameras across the country to better assist social control in the age of digital surveillance (X. Xu 2020). Whatever one may think about the politics of these decisions, the scope of capabilities is impressive.

But the decision to prioritize stability maintenance comes at the expense of everyday policing. Interviews with frontline police officers reveal the ways in which the focus on *weiwen* receives the lion's share of the Ministry of Public Security's attention and resources while leaving the policing of other types of crime behind. Stories of poorly devised protocols, inadequate training, onerous reporting requirements, and limited manpower permeate conversations with frontline police. Given the low pay, high expectations, and the frequency with which overtime work goes unpaid, police morale is low, and officers say that they have a hard time doing their jobs.

To assess these claims, inquiry into three areas—resource allocation, police reforms, and structural patterns of control—provides insight into the ways in which failures in everyday policing manifest themselves in a systematic fashion. While the police bureaucracy is able to allocate sufficient resources such as training and manpower for the control of social unrest, comparable accommodations for other areas of policing are lacking. Similarly with regard to police reform, ministerial efforts often fall short of helping police manage ground-level problems and even undermine efforts at effective policing by placing limitations on the use of force or imposing difficult-to-achieve reporting requirements. In contrast, reforms in the area of protest policing are more practice oriented and successful in achieving desirable outcomes for the state. Finally, the ministry exercises different patterns of control over local stations in ways that vary by issue area. For the policing of protest and dissent, the ministry centralizes control by streamlining the process of responding to unrest; but with most other types of police activity, central-level officials either share control with local governments or provide superficial control over local station activities.

Interviews with ministerial officials indicate that the upper levels of the police bureaucracy are aware of the inconsistencies but ill equipped to address them. Everyday policing failures are deeply rooted in both the nature of police work and the structural patterns of control that have emerged as a result of the central government's influence over matters of political policing. By emphasizing the control of social unrest and dissent through calls for stability maintenance and the establishment of a "harmonious society," central government officials set the stage for discrepancies in police response. More directly, the central government also created institutions and mandated interagency coordination efforts that further ensured the success of *weiwen* efforts. As resources were directed toward unrest, however, other areas of policing were not developed at the same rate, bringing unintended consequences for the bureaucracy and the public at large.

The problems of everyday policing remain hidden because of the successes in protest control and the widespread use of inaccurate crime statistics to suppress the truth about crime rates (J. Xu 2018), but that does not make the failures any less troubling. There is much to learn from and about a state that does well with the political elements of policing like protest control yet struggles with everyday crime management. This is not an idle discussion about bureaucratic functioning; these are issues that matter fundamentally for ground-level security and members of the Chinese public. Police are the cornerstone of order in society, and individuals everywhere—including those living under authoritarian regimes—expect the police to protect them from the Hobbesian ills of the world. When the police are unable to do so, their failures have widespread consequences for personal security, police legitimacy, and state stability more broadly.

Implications

Perhaps the most important function of police in any society is to provide the essential public good of security. How and whether or not they are able to do that job matters for individual members of the public and the society at large. In the Chinese case, systematic problems with police training, order maintenance, and compliance with state directives diminish the effectiveness of ground-level agents struggling to manage basic tasks like crime fighting. When police do not know what to do or are not willing to act when they witness a crime in progress, this is a public security problem. When police would rather fix someone's broken lock in exchange for a callback saying a burglary was reported by mistake, this is a public security problem. When police classify a murder as a suicide just so they can avoid reporting a difficult-to-solve case, this too is a public security problem. In the aggregate, these problems reported by frontline police demonstrate the tenuousness of the local state's grasp on public security and may contribute to feelings of insecurity among residents.

Failures of policing on the ground also undermine perceptions of police legitimacy that may bleed into broader beliefs about the state's legitimacy (Bradford et al. 2014). Most members of the public care very little about the ability of the state to put down a protest. People are far more interested in whether or not the police can help them when they or their loved ones encounter a problem. There is of course a possibility that leaders in Beijing have made a calculated decision to prioritize stability maintenance over other types of policing because they believe ineffective local policing is not a threat to the regime's legitimacy, but the evidence for this is not clear-cut. Failures of everyday policing can lead to a slow erosion of public trust in the organization, as officers fail to engage in effective practices or neglect to provide procedural justice in case after case. Ineffective policing can also feed into public protest and other types of social unrest. Public perceptions of these deficiencies may be one reason why reports of protests and attacks against the police are on the rise, reflecting dissatisfaction with the way officers do their jobs and interact with the public. In the final chapter, I discuss how these concerns of the public are actually feeding back into a loop of protest, creating more instability—and more work—for the stability maintenance organs.

By studying a wider range of frontline police functions, we can make more accurate assessments about the durability of the Chinese regime. Scholars studying authoritarian resilience both in and beyond China studies have recently turned to institutional mechanisms to rectify a lack of attention to the lower rungs of state control, shifting our focus to the people and processes that actually undergird state power and away from top-down approaches to understanding regime resilience that once dominated the literature.[20] The critical next step is to turn our attention to the workhorse of state control: the coercive apparatus. Here, scholars have already begun the important job of analyzing protest response capacity, but police—that core institution of state coercion—do so much more than control dissent.[21] The management of public uprisings is an essential part of authoritarian policing and regime resilience, but coercive institutions have a broad range of functions (Greitens 2017). For the police, everyday activities like responding to a call when someone's house is broken into or stepping in to stop illegal activities from taking place are also measures of whether or not frontline government agents are able to enforce goals of local security and stability. If police are struggling with everyday functions, then those failures have consequences for larger assessments of security capabilities and, ultimately, regime longevity. This book thus adopts a broader definition of coercive capacity to consider everyday crime management as a measure of authoritarian resilience and argues that the day-to-day activities of coercive institutions like the police and their regular interactions with the public are a critical and overlooked part of regime resilience. By focusing squarely on the ground-level forces and institutions, I find that the security state in China is far more fragile than accounts of protest response would have us believe.

As a strategy, the Chinese government's attention to controlling social unrest is risky to the extent that it overshadows everyday policing concerns. It is important to note that the problems with everyday policing do not constitute a strategy so much as they do the unintended consequences of the state's increasingly myopic focus on protest control. If protest and dissent are the wildfire that the stability maintenance regime is trying to put out, then everyday crime management is the vulnerable dry vegetation, sitting far enough in the distance to pose little immediate threat but nevertheless constituting a vulnerability if the winds change. Interviews with mid-level ministry officials indicate that individuals within the power structure are aware of these problems but unable to solve them without more resources and institutional reform.

Structurally, the problems with frontline policing in China also have important implications for studies of governance. By design, the Public Security Bureau (PSB) is relatively centralized in comparison to some of the other Chinese bureaucracies, as well as to police systems in the United States and Australia. Like many security institutions in authoritarian states elsewhere (Bayley 1985), the Chinese leadership has clear motivations for pursuing policies that promote centralization in the police bureaucracy. A streamlined system is more likely to ensure uniformity of policy implementation during times of crisis and to be more adept at communicating ground-level issues to central leaders; and problems of control emerge when overlapping organizations operate in similar spaces (Greitens 2016). Interviews with frontline officers reveal that the degree of centralization is not uniform across issue area—nor does it always serve the provision of security—and those differences negatively affect crime management and safety on the ground. Because control over the bureaucracy is highly centralized, and successful, in the area of social unrest but relatively decentralized, and unsuccessful, when it comes to handling other types of crime, this pattern has implications for the way we think about decentralization and ground-level service provision. Decentralization is often cited as a benefit because of the discretion it can afford ground-level agents to do their jobs (Lipsky 1971; Maynard-Moody, Musheno, and Palumbo 1990), but the case of policing in China demonstrates the harms of decentralization, especially when manpower is low, caseloads are high, and time is limited. Failures of everyday policing also provide insight into the study of decentralization in security bureaucracies elsewhere. If the police bureaucracy in China is having trouble, then institutions in other authoritarian or "hybrid" regimes like Russia may also be facing similar challenges.[22]

Finally, problems with everyday policing signal broad trouble for other legal organs and street-level bureaucrats. In China, the legal institutions remain far less independent and influential than the police bureaucracy. Because these institutions sit farther down the supply line, the court system's enforcement of laws is necessarily dependent on the input of cases from the police. If the police are not sending all cases to the court system, or if the police are providing the court system with imperfect or inaccurate information, this compromises the institutions charged with upholding legal norms and practices. Furthermore, if the relatively powerful police bureaucracy is unable to resolve its own ground-level issues and problems associated with decentralization, then the less powerful courts, procuratorates, and other street-level bureaucracies like the Urban Administrative Law Enforcement Agency (*chengguan*) or the tax administration are likely to face similar if not more pronounced constraints, especially when the degree of decentralization is high. Both these trends lead to poorer outcomes for local state governance in Chinese society.

Sources

This book takes frontline police seriously. Much of the existing literature on reform-era policing in China focuses on higher-level concerns such as protest response (M. S. Tanner 2004; Xie 2012), practices known as strike-hard campaigns (Trevaskes 2010; M. S. Tanner 2000), leadership selection (Y. Wang 2014), or structural reform (Wong 2011; Fu 2005; Dutton 1995). Far less attention has been paid to the front lines of Chinese policing, although a handful of scholars are probing the depths of local police involvement with crime campaigns (J. Xu 2012, 2014), business ties (J. Xu 2013), and social service provision (X. Wang 2015; Wang and Wong 2012). More often, ground-level police are presented as abstract opponents of protesters, even though local police play a key role in shaping narratives of resistance. This sidelining of police and their lived experience is not unique to the Chinese case; scholars of comparative politics also tend to overlook the importance of policing in studies of the political world (Powell 2014). Although the state of the field has improved since David Bayley wrote in 1971 that "police are rarely viewed from perspectives natural to political science," some of the best scholarship remains in criminology, sociology, and legal studies (Bayley 1971).[23]

The absence of frontline police perspectives is more than just an unfortunate omission. Police constitute an important class of street-level bureaucrats who stand at the intersection of state and society, carrying out government policies and interacting with citizens on a daily basis. Police officers in particular are charged with enforcing laws and other security-related policies on the ground; thus, they are a key source for understanding the processes that undergird state presence and power.[24] When we lack the perspectives of local police on these issues, we miss much about the daily functions of the local state. Notable failures in everyday policing and success in the area of protest control are thus not just an interesting idiosyncrasy of policing in China; they have also led to a mischaracterization of the strength of the security state. This book aims to rectify that misperception.

We know little about the front lines of China's domestic security apparatus because doing research on the police in China presents many logistical challenges. Like individuals in security apparatuses elsewhere, Chinese police officers are hard to reach, and some are wary of or unwilling to speak with foreigners.[25] China opened its doors to social science researchers from around the world over thirty years ago, but concerns about secrecy continue to limit access. In Chinese, the term *mingan* (sensitive) can signal a nonstarter for research projects,[26] and studies on the police are fairly sensitive across the board. Yet as scholars working around political sensitivities in China note, what gets branded sensitive often varies across time, locale, and issue area (Hsing 2010, 16–17; Spires 2011, 18). This opens up room to pursue topics that might otherwise or elsewhere be inaccessible.

About the Interviews

To get to the heart of frontline policing in China, I conducted 112 interviews with fifty-six police officers. Over a period of twenty-two months between 2009 and 2015, I interviewed officers up and down the hierarchy of the PSB. I also conducted follow-up interviews in 2017, 2018, and 2019 with a handful of these officers. The majority of interviewees worked on the front lines as local station officers, detectives, patrol cops, emergency call workers, household registration officers, traffic police, and PAP officers. A small number of those interviewees were mid-level supervisors, and I also interviewed one station chief, one assistant station chief, and one PAP squad leader. The age and experience level of the respondents ranged from new hires in their early to mid-twenties to soon-to-be retirees in their late fifties. All but six of the frontline officers were men. Further up the chain of command, I interviewed provincial bureau officers in two provinces, as well as a handful of central ministry officials. In order to ensure confidentiality of all sources, references to interviews throughout the chapters are intentionally vague and in some cases have been slightly altered to conceal the identity of interviewees.

Gaining access to these individuals required time, persistence, and a bit of luck. As a former English teacher and language student in Beijing, I drew upon contacts I made in the years before beginning my PhD—appealing to friends as well as former students and colleagues in my bid to gain entry into the world of local policing. Even with a relatively large network of contacts, I ran into difficulties. Many of my contacts were unable or unwilling to help me. On several occasions, an officer backed out of an interview at the last minute, presumably because he or she was afraid there might be consequences for speaking to a foreign researcher. On more than one occasion, contacts gently—and not so gently—suggested I focus on another topic or bureaucracy. But not everyone found the prospect of a foreigner researching the police in China ill-advised. Other respondents were eager to talk about their work. One long-term contact even banged his hand on the table in excitement when I told him about my plans to focus on the police. "That's great!" he enthused. "We Chinese police are very important, but too many people do not pay attention to us."[27]

Interviewees such as the one above notwithstanding, my research proceeded in fits and starts as I worked with and around my own identity as a Caucasian female foreigner with no firsthand policing experience (Scoggins 2014). Police officers can be a fairly inscrutable lot, and it typically required multiple meetings in order to establish trust and legitimacy with officers before they were willing to share details of their working lives. To ease the way with new interviewees, I relied on mutual contacts and conducted interviews in social settings such as restaurants, teahouses, and the occasional karaoke club or bar. I found that the length of time I had known someone, as well as our ability to find commonalties, improved the probability of a frank and productive conversation. Sometimes female or younger officers opened up more quickly, but sometimes other frontline officers—many of whom had little or no previous direct contact with a foreigner—were eager to learn more about policing in America and contrast it with their own experiences. For most, the process of trust building unfolded gradually, so I made multiple trips to research sites and spent time getting to know the officers and sometimes their friends and families.

These interviews give voice to a group of individuals who are often ignored for a reason beyond access limitations: police officers have a bad reputation. Reports of police brutality and misuse of power are just as common in China as they are everywhere else. But to characterize all police as little more than lazy and corrupt or as marionettes of state repression reduces the individuals behind the uniforms to simple caricatures that belie the complexity of the people they are and the jobs they do. Those who have spent time with police officers know this all too well and have written about the dilemmas confronting police, the vulnerabilities that officers feel, and the coping strategies they adopt to manage the many difficult tasks they face.[28] The job is not easy. One interviewee who later left his post as an officer said his decision to pursue other work was made out of consideration for his family. Although he loved being a cop, he said he knew all too well the type of mind-set that police officers must adopt after being in such close contact with the worst elements of society. "I don't want my children to grow up in that environment," he said.[29] This research thus aims to understand political society from the standpoint of the police, but it simultaneously seeks to acknowledge the complexity of their work and to humanize them as individuals. By taking the experiences and accounts of police seriously, we are able to gain a deeper understanding of the roles they play in society.

About the Research Sites

My selection of research sites was necessarily constrained by the political sensitivity of the topic and the need to rely on social contacts for access to interviewees. Nevertheless, I conducted research in areas that vary by size, economic development, and geographic location. In total, I conducted fieldwork in eight Chinese cities. The bulk of the observations come from five of those cities, which were located in three different provinces. One city was well-off in terms of economic development, three were middle of the road, and one was poor. Of the remaining three cities, one was poor, and the other two were well-off. To make these characterizations, I rely on city GDP, which also roughly corresponds with more police-specific signs of development such as publicly available budget reports, officer statements about equipment, stations' physical appearances, and the ability of stations to pay overtime or offer a salary that is higher than the national standard. Table 1 shows how the cities compare in terms of size, development level, and location.

Scholars traditionally characterize the Chinese bureaucratic system as a loosely centralized entity composed of five distinct layers: central, provincial, city, county, and village. The Ministry of Public Security controls agents at the provincial, city, and county levels but typically does not maintain a dedicated presence at the village level.[30] All research sites were in areas classified as cities, although I also interviewed county officers near those cities. Moreover, many of the interviewees had experience working at the county level, which is one level below the city. Since I evaluate police response to protest throughout the study, it is also important to note that all cities reported some degree of social unrest, with one of the most developed cities experiencing the most protests.

TABLE 1 Research site size and development levels

	POPULATION SIZE[1]	LEVEL OF DEVELOPMENT	LOCATION
City 1	Small	Low	Northern China
City 2	Small	Medium	Northern China
City 3	Large	Medium	Northern China
City 4	Large	High	Northern China
City 5	Large	High	Central China
City 6	Medium	Medium	Southern China
City 7	Large	High	Southern China
City 8	Medium	Low	Southern China

[1] "Large" indicates cities with population over four million, "medium" indicates cities between one and three million, and "small" indicates cities of less than a million. All estimates are based on 2010 census data.

The ultimate findings of the study do not vary across research sites, despite differences in economic development. But such uniformity raises another important point about the scope of the research: this book represents one particular slice of policing in China. It is not, so to speak, "policing at its best," since that would require interviewing officers in the heavily developed "top tier" cities such as Beijing, Shanghai, or Guangzhou. It is also not "policing at its worst," which is what we would expect to find in the poorest counties or perhaps along the borders. While I conducted a few interviews on either end of this spectrum, I was unable to gain the type of access that would allow me to make conclusive statements about policing in these areas. This is, instead, a book about policing "in between." In some ways, that makes the findings more widely applicable than they would have been had I focused on the polar ends of the spectrum or on special-case areas like Xinjiang and Tibet, but it is nevertheless a limitation of the research.

Triangulating Data

To round out the data collection, I use information obtained from policing journals, public or semipublic handbooks and other publications, online documents, news reports, and social media postings. Policing journal articles are an excellent source of information about frontline issues such as overtime frequency, protest response, and equipment usage. They often contain references to studies and other figures that are not readily available anywhere else. I spent two months going through older issues of select publications and additional materials held by the Universities Service Centre at the Chinese University of Hong Kong. Many articles are also available through China Knowledge Infrastructure (CNKI), and a surprising amount of additional information about Chinese policing is available online. In addition to documents published by the Ministry of Public Security, city police bureaus and local governments often maintain their own websites and social media accounts with information about police station infrastructure, budget reports, and recent incidents. Individual officers also post work-related information online through social media accounts. Moreover, news reports, when available, provide insight into local crime issues or particular high-profile cases. I use these sources throughout the book to cross-check interviews and further strengthen the findings.

Beyond the Police Perspective

To fully understand the institutionalized challenges that arise when prioritization of policing dissent overshadows the policing of everything else, this book takes policing and the perspectives of officers seriously. But for all the benefits of looking closely at frontline police, there are also disadvantages. Absent from this account is the perspective of local government officials. Absent, too, is an in-depth discussion of how the public experiences crime management and social control. Police officers do not operate in a vacuum, and the perspectives of local leaders and members of the public are critical dimensions of public security that provide insight into police legitimacy and the handling of crime. Nevertheless, interviews with frontline officers reveal much about their perceptions of interactions with local government officials and the public. For example, many officers believe that the public's respect for and perhaps fear of the police have steadily declined since the start of the reform period. One oft-repeated bit of police lore sums this up nicely: "In the 1980s," explained a detective, "one police officer could catch ten bad guys simply by walking into a restaurant and yelling 'halt!' These days, it takes ten of us to catch a single criminal."[31] Unfortunately, the public's reaction to these and other observations shared by informants in the police bureaucracy lies beyond the scope of this book, a limitation that is in no small part due to the research challenges that are inherently baked into any study of policing in an authoritarian regime.

Frontline Insights

Conversations with police officers and their superiors in the ministry provide an unparalleled window into the realities of life on the front lines for the Chinese security state, showing in detail the ways in which police in China struggle with everyday crime management and excel at protest control. By analyzing differences in how limited resources are allocated, how reforms are crafted and received, and how influence from different types of higher authorities can affect outcomes, this book presents a damning portrait of everyday crime management even as it provides insight into why the Chinese police bureaucracy is so very good at stability maintenance. With regard to the latter, scholars of contentious politics may be especially interested in tactics used by the bureaucracy to redirect limited resources, implement reforms that overcome institutionalized biases, and enforce coordination between different police forces to keep protesters in line.

The implications of these failures are both social and political. Issues with everyday crime management are exacerbated by de facto decentralization and raise questions for other Chinese bureaucracies that provide ground-level services, but there are also broader implications for assessments of authoritarian durability and state legitimacy. Most pressing, some evidence suggests that failures of everyday policing are actually feeding public dissatisfaction and dissent, thereby creating a loop of protest that ultimately undermines the stability maintenance regime. In the aggregate, these observations tell a story of weakness in one of the strongest branches in the Chinese bureaucracy, a weakness that hits everyday crime management the hardest but to which stability maintenance work is also not immune. Such weakness makes the issue of regime resilience particularly salient because reports of police-society conflict are on the rise.

From the standpoint of frontline enforcement, the police bureaucracy in China is an institution in distress. Many of the problems facing the ground level are deeply rooted in the institutional culture or structure of the police bureaucracy and are issues that more money or even a change in the priorities of the bureaucracy's leaders will be hard pressed to solve. Although the research for this book was collected over nearly a decade, follow-up interviews conducted in 2018 and 2019 reveal that little has changed for everyday policing, even as the growth of the stability maintenance regime has further improved protest response. Evidence for the intractability of frontline policing problems abounds. Training programs are undermined by the ministry's arguably outdated need to instill political ideology in officers who would rather be learning how to collect forensic evidence. Local government leaders circumvent the ministry and exert their power over police stations by forcing them to ignore ministry regulations so that these local leaders can protect their own private interests. And the institutional culture of social connections (*guanxi*) leaves station offices stocked with well-connected and senior police officers, even though patrol leaders do not have enough men to send out on the beat. These cultural and institutional impediments make reform difficult and quick fixes impossible, especially in a conservative bureaucracy that is by nature adverse to change.[32] Filled with inefficiency, frustration, mismanagement, and competing interests, this is the world of frontline police in China.

1

POLICING CHINA

Demographics, Mission, and Funding

Who are the Chinese police? How does policing in China work? Who oversees the police, and how are the police funded? Before diving into a deeper investigation of how the police in China excel at managing protest while falling short with regard to almost everything else, we must first answer the who, what, and how questions of policing in today's China. Unfortunately, much of this information is scattered and sometimes contradictory. The academic literature remains underdeveloped, leaving gaps in our knowledge about how frontline policing actually functions, and media or scholarly accounts of single events in specific locations can be misleading. Sometimes the Chinese police appear remarkably strong, as they did in foreign media reports about a broad-sweeping order for the police to monitor nearly seven thousand foreign organizations.[1] News coverage of this change gave the impression of a powerful, coherent public security force that was capable of implementing such an endeavor, focusing on the far-reaching effects of the policy on foreign organizations while ignoring questions of whether or not local forces beyond major metropolitan zones such as Beijing would actually have the manpower and organizational wherewithal to meet the law's requirements. At other times, the police in China appear hopelessly feckless. In one tragic example that made international news, a Shanghai traffic officer was dragged to his death after trying to stop a driver from making an illegal turn.[2] Although the driver was heavily criticized, netizens also questioned why the police officer refused to let go of the moving vehicle until it was too late. With such disparate accounts, it is hard to know what to think about the Chinese police and their enforcement capacity.

The literature on frontline policing in China gives us insight into the jobs, motivations, and institutional constraints of the police, but it remains a developing subfield. Scholars have told us much about local crime prevention campaigns (J. Xu 2015, 2014, 2012, 2009), station relationships with businesses (J. Xu 2013), frontline dissatisfaction (Scoggins and O'Brien 2016), and police tactics for managing groups like petitioners (Deng and O'Brien 2013) or prostitutes (Boittin 2013). There is also a growing body of literature on frontline police perceptions, such as how officers view police culture and their role in society (Z. Chen 2016a, 2016b, 2016c), how police perceive and manage expectations about social service provision (X. Wang 2015, 2014), and how station supervisors view their work and report job satisfaction (Sun, Liu, and Farmer 2016). Moreover, several studies have analyzed the occupational attitudes of police cadets (Sun et al. 2009; Sun et al. 2010; Wu, Sun, and Cretacci 2009; Cuvelier, Jia, and Cheng 2015). In the more distant past, Fredrick Wakeman's *Policing Shanghai* provided a detail-rich description of police activity in the city over a ten-year period between 1927 and 1937 (Wakeman 1995). These works have opened up the world of frontline policing in China and given insight into officer motivations, frustrations, and expectations, but there is still much to be said about how police work influences and is shaped by broader political phenomena.[3] A wealth of information about the issues that the police bureaucracy faces can be found in Chinese-language materials in national journals like *Gongan yanjiu* (Policing studies) and regional police college journals. Chinese policing scholars cover a wide range of topics related to frontline work, including stability maintenance (Ye, Xiao, and Liu 2006; P. Li 2008; J. Liu 2005), psychological health and distress of frontline officers (Zhang, Zou, and Tong 2012; Wei 2011; Hu 2009; Hu and Ren 2006), corruption (Yin 2013; Lu and Qiao 2006; Guo 2003; G. Wang 2002), crisis management (X. Meng 2013), self-defense (W. Meng 2006; Ding 2002), and frontline police training (Zhou 2010), to name a few. Available only in Chinese, these articles tend to be more practice-oriented than theoretical and often focus on policy recommendations or editorial assessments. They nevertheless remain excellent sources of empirical information for specific topics.[4]

To fully understand the Chinese police, however, we must piece together the existing literature with accounts from actual police officers as well as other publicly available data from the Ministry of Public Security, individual stations, social media accounts, and reports in the popular press. From there, we gain a more comprehensive picture of who the Chinese police are, to whom they answer, and what they do on a daily basis. Doing so systematically addresses common misconceptions about issues such as police funding or the command structure. These essential facts are important for evaluating frontline policing efforts in China, and they set the stage for larger discussions about how resource constraints, ministerial reforms, and variation in control over the local police weaken security response on the ground in nearly every area of policing except response to public protest.

Who Are the Chinese Police?

Descriptions of the Chinese police can vary dramatically. Sometimes frontline police are depicted as automatons of the Chinese state and local governments.[5] Sometimes they are seen as protest crushers and fearsome enforcers of state control.[6] And sometimes they are described as corrupt, brutish thugs who demand bribes and mete out justice with little regard to national laws or basic human rights.[7] Yet at other times, Chinese police are portrayed as incompetent dolts, whose ignorance can be both humorous and alarming.[8] Often these reports raise more questions than they answer about China's frontline agents of state control. Who are the Chinese police?

Starting with basic factual data: the Ministry of Public Security employs approximately two million officers nationwide.[9] By global comparison, this is a relatively small per capita force, and those numbers, which are especially low in less populated areas, often cause trouble for enforcement efforts on the ground.[10] All police officers within the PSB are part of the Chinese civil service (*gongwuyuan*), a distinction that affords officers a higher social status and is sometimes referred to as an "iron rice bowl" for frontline officers, "silver rice bowl" for provincial level officials, and "golden rice bowl" for central police officials. With civil servant status come more desirable benefits than those available to other frontline security forces such as the auxiliary police (*xiejing*) or urban law enforcement management officers (*chengguan*). These benefits include higher salaries, pensions, health care, and—for some officers—housing. Official police also carry a badge and can be identified by their police number (*jinghao*). The vast majority of officers in China do not carry guns unless they are taking part in a special mission that has been authorized by both their station leaders and the relevant city or county officials. Regarding demographics, police officers enter the force as early as age eighteen and retire at sixty; but much like other civil servants in China, older officers begin reducing their workloads around age fifty-five, even though they collect a paycheck until age sixty.[11] There is a distinct divide between older officers, many of whom cut their teeth as PLA soldiers in the 1970s and 1980s, and younger officers, who often have little or no military experience.

This generation gap is the result of professionalization reforms that began in the 1990s as a move to improve recruitment standards and attract more-qualified individuals. At that time, the force was mostly stocked with men who had military backgrounds but little formal police training or education. Higher-ups were concerned that a lack of standardization allowed unqualified individuals to don the uniform, leading to problems of corruption, misconduct, and abuse of power (Ma 1997, 119). Article 26 of the 1995 Police Law was the first major step to improve recruitment and set basic qualification standards for incoming officers.[12] These new standards have changed the face of frontline police and resulted in a more educated force with less military training. Police leaders have mostly welcomed the changes, but professionalization of the force has come with certain costs. One official from the provincial ministry who was serving as an assistant county station chief at the time of our interview noted that many of the younger officers lack the real-world experience of older generations, much to the chagrin of station leaders.[13] "The officers born after 1980 are only children who are used to being served by their parents and grandparents," he explained. "These workers are more difficult to deal with and often look down on certain types of work.... Their lack of experience makes it hard for them to do their jobs."

Policing in China is also a highly gendered profession. The overall proportion of female officers working in the PSB is at least 10 percent or higher, but the distribution varies dramatically across divisions.[14] Patrol work is generally not considered suitable for female officers in the areas where I conducted research. Instead, women tend to work in the stations, answering calls or managing household registration (*hukou*) duties. Often women working in police stations in smaller cities are young, and many eventually quit their positions once they marry or have children, resulting in a high turnover rate.[15] Women in larger cities with a higher cost of living are more likely to continue working and gain some seniority, but they rarely get the opportunity to work outside the office.[16] A smattering of cities in China maintain female horseback patrols. The phenomenon began in 1994 in Dalian, where the city's program has grown to over sixty-five officers with one hundred horses, and subsequently spread to other cities.[17] The patrol forces are not charged with catching criminals, and one ministry official explained that stations like to send female officers out on patrol because police leaders believe women are "better at resolving disputes" than their male counterparts.[18] At the provincial level, women make up roughly 30 percent of the force, but they too are more likely to work in internal positions (*neibu*) and take fewer trips to the field.[19]

Official police are sometimes confused with other frontline workers who wear similar uniforms or perform overlapping functions. This book focuses solely on official frontline police and their superiors, but it is nevertheless important to outline the differences between police and other frontlines agents, since even seasoned China hands get confused over who is a police officer and who is not. An article in the *Atlantic*, for example, referred to *chengguan* officers from the City Urban Administrative Law Enforcement Bureau as "police" and "cops," despite the fact that the much-hated *chengguan* are not police.[20] While some functions of the *chengguan*, such as dealing with unlicensed street vendors, may be similar to jobs police elsewhere perform, the *chengguan* are a distinctly separate security force.[21]

Xiejing also cause confusion. *Xiejing* are a class of auxiliary police sometimes referred to as *fujing*, which can be translated as assistant or supplemental police.[22] *Xiejing* are not official police, even though they work alongside official police and often perform the same functions. One duty for some *xiejing* is watching dissidents. These are the hired "thugs" who receive media attention for beating, harassing, and detaining activists and their families.[23] But most *xiejing* are involved in more mundane matters. The older men with the words "POLICE" or "警察" (*jingcha*) emblazoned across poorly constructed uniforms who are sitting or standing on the side of the road at busy intersections urging pedestrians not to cross illegally are usually *xiejing*, as are many of the men stationed at the small, temporary police sheds erected on the streets of some Chinese cities. *Xiejing* wear the characteristic light blue shirts and dark slacks that are the uniform of China's police, but most do not have badges.

Finally, there are the People's Armed Police, which are no longer official police but instead a paramilitary force composed of somewhere between 660,000 and 1.5 million men and women.[24] The PAP is most famous for riot control, but it also protects the borders, national forests, and state-owned gold mines. Teams can travel in detachments of up to five hundred men, although they usually go out in groups from one hundred to two hundred.[25] In addition to responding to riots, the PAP also handles terrorist situations and other violent altercations. Depending on the city, a PAP officer explained, they may also be brought in for small demonstrations if the protesters "have a conflict with another group . . . have become violent . . . [or if] local police do not have enough people to manage the problem." At the time of data collection for this book, the PAP was jointly governed by the Ministry of Public Security and the People's Liberation Army, but on January 1, 2018, President Xi Jinping brought the PAP under his control as chairman of the Central Military Commission, just two months before the constitution was changed to abolish presidential term limits. This move centralized Xi Jinping's power over all armed forces, put to bed concerns that the PAP might one day be used against him, and diminished the power of both the Ministry of Public Security and Li Keqiang, China's premier and leader of the State Council.[26]

A handful of additional law enforcement officers are also sometimes confused with official police but are not attached to the MPS. Judicial Police are housed within both the courts and procuratorates; Prison Police are administered by

FIGURE 2. Summer police uniforms. Courtesy of Shutterstock.

FIGURE 3. Long-sleeve uniform with coat. Courtesy of Shutterstock.

FIGURE 4. A reporter is stopped by security personnel outside the compound where dissident Zeng Jinyan is under house arrest. Because of the relatively high profile of Zeng, it is possible these men are official police from the local station or the Domestic Security Department. Photo credit: Frederic J. Brown, Getty Images.

the Ministry of Justice; and State Security Police handle foreign espionage, sabotage, and conspiracies (Ma 1997, 117). Figures 2 through 7 illustrate the similarities between frontline forces. Visual ambiguities make it difficult to distinguish between official police and other frontline security agents. Figures 2 and 3 show official police uniforms. Anyone working at the local *paichusuo* is most certainly a police officer, but what of the plainclothes men guarding the gate in figure 4? Or the security forces dressed in black handling protest control in figure 6? And what of the uniformed older man in figure 7, or the official-looking officers in figure 5? Since the PAP detached from the MPS in 2018, none of these security forces in figures 4 through 7 are official Chinese police, although real officers are sometimes dispatched to handle dissident control instead of *xiejing*. Sometimes it is almost impossible to know if someone is an official police officer without asking him or her directly. *Chengguan* often look similar to police, but their uniforms are typically marked "*chengguan*" on the sleeve. *Xiejing* can be tougher to identify, since their uniforms are marked "police."[27] One officer offered the

FIGURE 5. Two *chengguan* officers observe street vendors in Suzhou. Photo credit: Chinanews.com. Courtesy of Getty Images.

FIGURE 6. Riot police in Shifang guard a street against protesters. Photo credit: Weibo user 3483416086. Courtesy of Shutterstock.

FIGURE 7. An older man, most likely a *xiejing*, stands on the side of the road supervising traffic. Author's photo.

following advice: "Look at their feet. Real officers wear police shoes."[28] Looking at the images presented here, the *chengguan* officers in figure 5 are clearly wearing soft shoes that indicate their status, although this does not hold true for every city. The security personnel guarding the dissident's residence in figure 4 are wearing a more formal type of shoe, leading to ambiguity about whether or not they are real officers or just wearing a common black shoe popular among Chinese men working in a variety of professions.

Who Oversees the Police?

Policing in China is ostensibly centralized and governed from the top down. In contrast to decentralized systems such as in the United States where police stations work with city officials to set priorities and adopt locally tailored rules and regulations, even the most far-flung county stations in China are required to follow national directives and are ultimately held accountable to the Ministry of Public Security in Beijing. The National People's Congress officially sets general policies and legal priorities, and the ministry uses these directives to devise more specific laws and regulations that local stations must follow. The central ministry oversees training programs for local police, affording it considerable influence over policing practices such as how to use new technology or respond to certain crimes. To further ensure compliance, local police bureaus are required to file reports with higher-ups in the bureaucracy, and representatives of the ministry may periodically make trips to the local level to observe operations firsthand. A chart mapping the chain of command is outlined in figure 8.

In practice, control over the police is far more complicated. As the box to the far right indicates, the ministry must also share control over the lower levels with local governments. Ties between the central and local state in China have always been fraught, and the proverb "Heaven is high and the emperor is far away" (*Tian gao huangdi yuan*) is often used to describe the weak connection between the two, implying that distance as well as local autonomy drives the tendency of

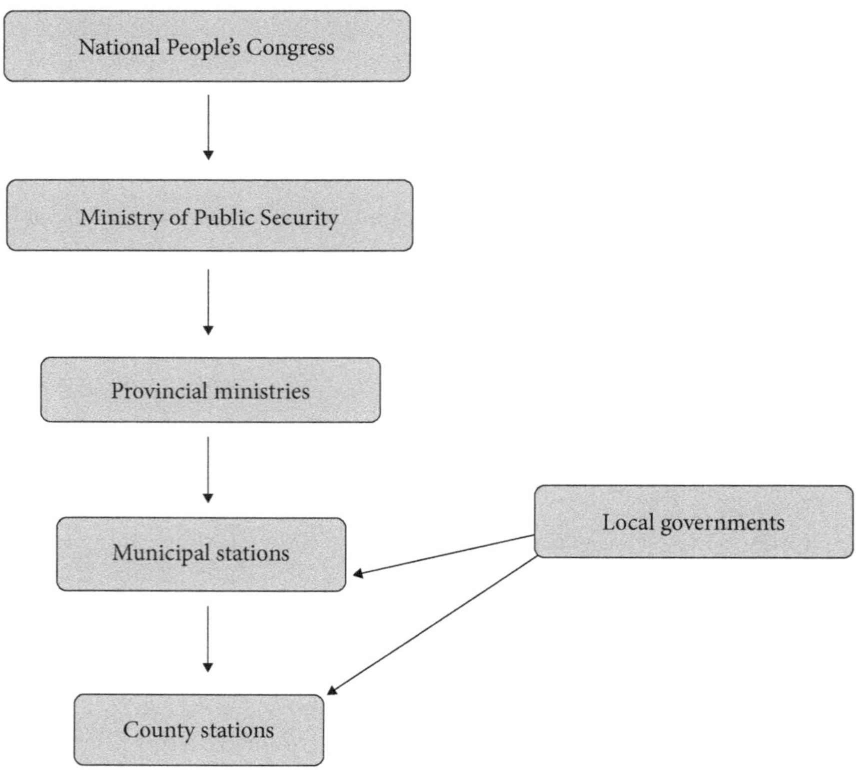

FIGURE 8. Public security chain of command

municipal and county officials to ignore the center. Both are issues for the police bureaucracy. The sheer variety of local and street-level actors—frontline police, station leaders, and city and county-level government officials—complicates the ministry's enforcement of rules, as does the physical remove of counties and cities from the center.

Moreover, the Ministry of Public Security is a vast organization that does much more than oversee local police. In total, the MPS has at least thirty-six departments that manage a host of public security concerns such as criminal investigations, economic crimes, internet security, customs, border control, prison administration, transportation, and narcotics. The list goes on: departments are devoted to domestic security protection, counterterrorism, forestry services, and civil aviation. It even has departments charged with overseeing dangerous cults and mobile technology. This is in addition to a small group of departments that manage matters such as public relations, internal auditing, and political concerns.[29]

Many of these departments do not involve frontline police. Internet activism and the online spread of misinformation, for example, are a growing concern for the ministry, and it maintains a large team of officers in Beijing and elsewhere who work around the clock to monitor email, social media, and other web-based communications.[30] Because blanket censorship is no longer feasible given the number of internet users and the possibilities that the creative use of homonyms provides, programmers within the ministry are working to find better solutions that allow a certain amount of dissent.[31] "We have the Water Army [*wangluo shuijun*—an online group of commentators] to spread information," explained one provincial bureau official, "but we are most concerned with the rise of misinformation. Four or five years ago, unfounded rumors were a big problem in our province, but now we have better methods to shut them down."[32] Such efforts to police the internet require technical expertise and have little to no involvement with frontline police or local stations.

Other political concerns also occupy the attention of the ministry. Many such matters involve the Domestic Security Department (DSD, Guonei anquan baohu zhidui) and have slightly more frontline police involvement. The DSD is a special branch of the Chinese police force that maintains departments all the way down to the municipal level and is charged with protecting and strengthening the rule of the Chinese Communist Party. It is one of the most secretive branches within the ministry, since it specializes in intelligence collection, political dissident control, and response to a wide range of activities deemed subversive to the regime. Limited information about DSD activity is publicly available, but scholars occasionally get critical glimpses into the inner workings of the organization. Two recent collections of essays penned by individuals detained by the DSD and the

Ministry of State Security (a separate administrative organization that focuses on national security threats) shed light on the tactics used by officers during detention as well as on how the DSD cooperates with other law enforcement groups to apprehend, hold, and release individuals suspected of crimes against the state (Xu and Hua 2013; Caster 2017). Internal documents from the DSD have also surfaced. One such document confirmed that the DSD's number one priority is to protect social and political stability and provided some insight into the party committee leadership's control over DSD activities.[33] Because of its proximity to the party and focus on national security issues, the DSD remains separate from other police forces and enjoys a high priority in the MPS.[34] The local police are subordinate to the DSD and expected to assist the DSD officers when necessary, but none of my respondents reported such an experience.

Frontline police are thus controlled or influenced by several different types of higher-ranking authorities, the two most important of which are the Ministry of Public Security and local governments. Chapter 4 explores these relationships in greater detail and shows how and under what conditions the two exert control over the local station's crime response. For now, it is sufficient to say that control over local police is divided, and variations in how control is wielded can influence response outcomes on the ground, especially when central ministry officials decide to get directly involved in frontline affairs.

What Is the Mission of the Police?

What does police work in China look like? Frontline officers are formally charged with serving the Communist Party and the public (*weile renmin fuwu*). In practice, this means they must deal with crime, handle stability maintenance, and pursue any additional tasks that advance the interests of the government in the area of public security. Since the bulk of police work in China involves managing everyday crimes, these activities occupy the majority of officers' time as they respond to crimes that have been committed or are in progress and work on measures to reduce the frequency with which subsequent crimes might occur. The police in China are also charged with pursuing political work, and because of the central government's emphasis on stability maintenance, efforts in this area often take precedence over everyday policing.[35] The relationship between political policing and everyday crime-fighting can be better understood by looking at how the Public Security Bureau has developed over time.

Policing in China, much like policing everywhere else, has a comparatively short history, but the profession has come a long way since the 1890s when urban areas began replacing the constabulary—a coterie of guards charged with defending city gates and in possession of some powers of arrest—with the law enforcement agents that more closely resemble the police we know today. Crime nevertheless flourished throughout the late Qing and Republican eras as a result of the expansion of cities and certain administrative weaknesses of those governments. When the Communist Party took over in 1949, it inherited a weakly connected system of police departments that were struggling to cope with criminal gangs, prostitutes, kidnappers, murderers, drug lords, and run-of-the-mill robbers and bandits. With new class consciousness, the CCP also added counterrevolutionaries to that list.

The next steps of the party-state significantly influenced the institution we know today. A new Ministry of Public Security was created in October 1949 under the paternalistic eye of the CCP and charged with strengthening ideological education work and reducing crime. Through the use of campaign-style policing, the PSB set off on a mission to supervise and eliminate counterrevolutionaries, which was no small task, given that in 1957 activities labeled as "counterrevolutionary crime" made up almost half of all reported crimes (Bakken 1993, 29). Official statistics (figure 9) indicate that significant progress was made in controlling crime during this time period, but all efforts were disrupted when the turmoil of the Cultural Revolution hit the agency in 1966. Local police officers were no match for an emboldened Red Guard, especially after MPS leaders were purged and replaced by the new Ministry of Public Security Cultural Revolution Group. Officers around the country began defecting en masse, and

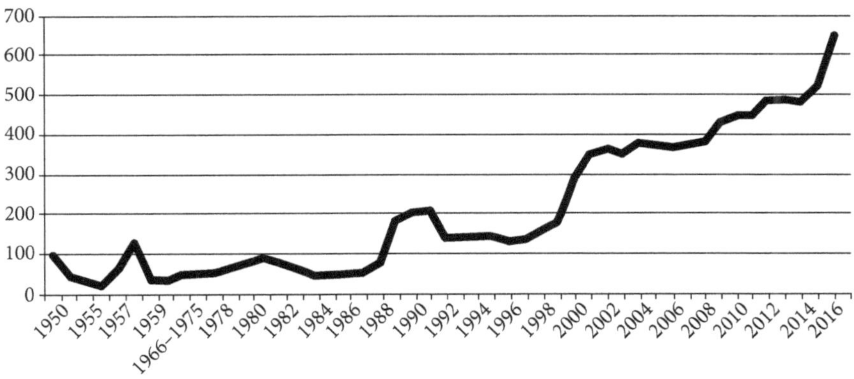

FIGURE 9. Criminal cases per 100,000 (population), 1950–2016

Source: Adapted from Bakken 1993, Liang 2005, and the *Law Yearbook of China*.

* Reflects the average. Annual crime rates during the Cultural Revolution ranged between forty and sixty cases per one hundred thousand population.

the organization effectively disbanded, resulting in what Kam Wong (2004a) has termed the "lawless era" of policing that lasted until the Cultural Revolution ended in 1976. During this time, many cities were policed by the Red Guards rather than the police themselves. The accuracy of reported crime figures at this time must thus be considered in light of this disruption.

When Deng Xiaoping seized the reins of reform in 1978, the public security institution was in disarray. Ministry officials faced the daunting task of expanding and adapting a reconstructed police bureaucracy, which meant recruiting officers and adapting to the new rules set forth by the Criminal Law and Criminal Procedure Law of 1980. This is not to say, however, that police reformers were starting from scratch. Reformers fell back on many of the old elements of political policing, including the use of campaigns to address various societal problems and continued dependence on the urban street and neighborhood committee system that originated under communist-era "Mass Line" policing (Bo and Dai 1990). For all the ministry's new talk about the rule of law and strict adherence to procedure, the Chinese police continued to operate in a politicized, authoritarian environment. Although the police are more independent from the Communist Party in the reform era than they were under Mao (Fu 1994), their relationship with the party remains strong at all levels, and local stations are still held accountable to local CCP Committees.[36] One officer I interviewed explained this relationship simply: "The party is still the most important [authority for local police]."[37] Specific elements of present-day political policing include the protest and dissident control work of stability maintenance practices but also more mundane activities such as monitoring population movement through the household registration system or using police power to carry out activities in the service of the party that are technically illegal.[38]

Even as the ministry was adopting past practices of political policing and developing new responses to political problems such as the growing number of mass incidents, the police bureaucracy was also coming head to head with rising crime rates and new types of crime such as human trafficking, drug smuggling, arms trading (Ma 1997), and information-age crimes. As figure 9 indicates, the early 1980s were marked by a crime wave that briefly abated but soon returned with a vengeance, bringing with it increases in public concerns about safety (Dutton and Lee 1993, 319–22). It is important to note that these are official crime statistics provided by the government and must be treated with caution; but they are nevertheless the best figures we have and show a dramatic increase in overall crime during the reform era. As market reforms were enacted, newly mobile populations flocked to the cities and the old social control structures fell, creating more opportunities for crime as well as more types of economic activities deemed illegal (Dutton 2005, 256; Liu and Messner 2001). Under economic reform it was now harder for the police to monitor and control this variable population, especially in comparison to the static cities they had once policed (Dutton and Lee 1993; Ma 1997; M. S. Tanner 2005a). As crime spiraled upward and the utility of old social control tools floundered, the new name of the game was stopping crime with punitive policing (Dutton and Lee 1993). Police in the reform era doubled down on past practices while simultaneously turning outward to other models of policing in an attempt to stem the crime wave. "Hard strike" campaigns targeting criminal activities were launched beginning in 1983, even though their success was debatable. Local governments also increased the number of neighborhood committees in urban areas during this period.[39] Around the same time, police leaders moved quickly to adopt the patrol model, which had not been a feature of policing in China prior to the 1980s (Fu 1990).

The mission of the Chinese police thus expanded greatly during the reform era, as frontline officers and ministry officials faced new and growing challenges with regard to both political policing and everyday crime management. How the PSB responds to these challenges is fundamentally influenced by the priorities set forth by the party-state, which values both social stability and a reduction in crime. But with limited resources, police leaders up and down the bureaucracy have been forced to make difficult decisions about how to prioritize their efforts.

How Are Chinese Police Funded?

Local police need money to carry out their mission of handling crime, conducting stability maintenance work, and serving the political directives of the party. Much has been made of national budget figures showing that China spends more on internal security than it does on national defense, but a breakdown demonstrates that the figures do not translate into a financial windfall for ground-level police.[40] If we only look at the numbers, the budget for China's internal security looks impressive. In 2013, the Twelfth National People's Congress allocated RMB 769.1 billion (approximately US$117 billion) to public security. Yet the reported budget fell to just RMB 205 billion (US$31 billion) in 2014 and RMB 212 billion (US$32 billion) in 2015. These lower figures reflect not a decrease in the actual budget but rather a change in how it is reported. The new, lower figures only detail central government spending on internal security, omitting local and provincial government contributions. Officially, the Ministry of Finance changed the reporting practice because data collection at the lower levels was still in progress. But the decision is most likely related to concerns over international press coverage and the political sensitivity of stability maintenance work, which many believe is driving the increase in domestic security funds.[41] The budget from 2017 further confirms these suspicions. In that year, the internal security figure was obscured in the Ministry of Finance's budget report, appearing not as an actual number but as a percentage figure in a chart on total government spending.[42] Though the new budgets are incomplete, we can assume that the total remains somewhere in the neighborhood of 2013's RMB 769 billion, if not higher.[43] Domestic security spending has risen rapidly every year since 2006 (Greitens 2017).[44]

What does the internal security budget mean in comparative perspective? Given that the Chinese budget funds a range of legal entities across the politics and law system (*zhengfa xitong*), precise comparisons are difficult; but if we take the last available Chinese figure from 2013 (US$117 billion) and look at spending on policing in similar time periods elsewhere, China's 2013 budget would have been roughly on par with the next big spender on policing: the United States.[45] This is more than in heavily policed[46] Russia (US$22 billion)[47] or Turkey (US$3.4 billion),[48] and it outstrips the budgets of similarly sized India (US$19.7 billion)[49] and neighboring Japan (US$3.1 billion).[50] Per capita, however, China's US$86 per person spending is less conspicuous, since the nation spends half of what Russia does per capita (US$154) and less than a quarter of what is spent on US policing (US$401).[51] China's per capita budget for 2013 is nevertheless four times what Japan spends (US$24), six times India's spending (US$16), and nearly twice as much as Turkey (US$49).

The problem with comparing China's internal security budget with the police spending of other countries is of course that not everything in the budget goes to the police. Though the specifics of how the entire suspected RMB 769 billion is distributed remain unclear, we know that in 2014, the People's Armed Police received RMB 107.4 billion, Public Security was allocated RMB 16.5 billion, the Anti-smuggling Police received RMB 1.8 billion, and the Procuratorate, Courts, and Judiciary respectively received RMB 373 million, RMB 528 million, and RMB 194 million.[52] This budget also included RMB 66 billion in transfer payments to the local level, and we can assume that at least another RMB 560 billion was expected in contributions from the lower-level governments, given what we know about the 2013 budget. How high are these figures, given the needs of the legal system? Analyzing domestic security spending between 1992 and 2012, Sheena Greitens argues that even the RMB 769 billion figure is not historically unprecedented or unnecessarily high, given the growing challenges faced by the broader coercive apparatus (Greitens 2017). She further finds that spending across provinces is uneven, and additional research on more recent police spending in high-conflict areas such as Xinjiang confirms this trend (Zenz 2018).

How much of this money makes it to the ground level? Contributions from local and provincial governments can be fraught, since not every government has the ability to meet the central government's expectations (Xie 2013). Combined with central government transfer payments, a portion of this money supports the local police, but funds are also earmarked for stability preservation offices at all levels of government, offices that are separate and distinct from the police (Feng 2013, 3), as well as local courts, jails, prisons, and other public works.[53] Detailed budget reports at these levels are not generally available to the public, but in 2012, Gangcha County in Qinghai Province released an uncharacteristically specific account.[54] In addition to spending on the categories listed above in the central budget, the county uses internal security funds for national security, prisons, and reeducation through labor. Such documents reveal that even the internal security budget at the local level supports more departments than Public Security.

Given these budget breakdowns, how much of the approximately RMB 630 billion (transfer payments + locally provided funds) in public security funds actually makes it to the front lines where the bulk of police work is done? Unfortunately, there is no easy answer. In Gangcha County, half of the reported RMB 15.17 million (US$2.5 million) total funds for public security went to the local police. For other cities, the percentage ranged from 30 percent to 60 percent.[55] In Harbin, the local police received 40 percent of public security funds in 2013.[56] Based on these figures, local police funding is likely somewhere between one-third and one-half of the RMB 630 billion, but even this approximation may not reflect actual spending. In 2003, government leaders designed budget reforms to increase cash flow to ground-level stations by making counties contribute a higher percentage of their budgets to public security; but without the necessary funds, many cash-strapped local governments were saddled with funding expectations they could not meet (Xie 2013, 87). Even when funds are available, reports of station expenditures in four provinces (Guangdong, Jiangsu, Qinghai, and Ningxia) showed that much of the money was used to pay down old debts, not support operations (86). The central government is trying to increase transfer payments to ensure funding at the local level, but progress is slow.

This breakdown presents a far slimmer budget for policing than casual consumers of the RMB 769 billion figure might suspect. Some bureaus in large cities nevertheless appear well funded. In Beijing, the municipal public security budget for 2019 was RMB 24.42 billion (US$3.6 billion), or US$180 per capita for that year. Although a complete breakdown was not available, the public announcement noted that the funds would be used for equipment purchases, video surveillance, and improvements for the courts.[57] This figure, to the extent that it is accurate, paints an impressive picture of local funding, but Beijing is atypical. As the capital city and site of mass incidents like the 1989 Tiananmen Square protest, Beijing is a politically important location that the leadership wishes to safeguard against social unrest and crime. Other cities are not as well funded. Even the boomtown of Shenzhen—an economic powerhouse bordering Hong Kong with a manufacturing sector that employs more than seven million migrant workers—spent just RMB 1.19 billion (US$176 million) in 2017 on police officer salaries, operations, special projects, and social insurance fund contributions.[58] While any comparison should be cautious, given the lack of detail provided in both budgets, this comes out to approximately US$15 per capita, assuming the budget figures are close to actual spending on policing.

Yet the majority of local police stations in China are not located in major cities or politically contentious regions. Historically, these cities and counties cannot turn to rich local governments or national public security funds, and their chronic budget shortages are well documented (Fu and Choy 2003). Interviews reveal that many bureaus do not have enough funds to purchase proper equipment, making everyday tasks more challenging and time consuming. Most local stations are left to cope with budget shortfalls by resorting to catch-as-catch-can strategies in order to keep their bureaus running. Money-making activities include tried-and-true methods like levying fines,[59] but stations also pursue more innovative means such as teaming up with businesses—both local and foreign—to generate profits, a widespread practice that is not without controversy in policing circles because it publicly exposes the symbiotic relationship between the police and corporations (J. Xu 2013). Notably, follow-up interviews that I conducted in 2018 and 2019 reveal that the budget situation for some stations has improved in the last few years.[60] In cities in Hebei and Hunan Provinces, officers report that transfer payments from the central government have increased, allowing their stations to update equipment and add new technologies such as body cameras. But the improvements have also been uneven. In Hunan, for example, the local governments are still responsible for salaries and remain unable to pay overtime to officers even though the physical state of their stations has improved.[61]

Local Police Corruption and Misconduct

Corruption and misconduct are also issues for the local police, but unfortunately, data on the prevalence of these issues is limited. We know the ministry has enacted an increasingly developed system of laws and procedures to curb individualized police power and mold the local force in a lawful image. In the 1980s, central government officials were concerned that the unchecked authority of local police was eroding state legitimacy. To curb individualized power, the ministry enacted reforms such as professionalization standards to address concerns. These reforms were also joined by efforts to increase supervision over the police and require greater adherence to the rule of law. More-targeted campaigns such as the 2003 Five Prohibitions campaign led by the minister of public security at the time, Zhou Yongkang, were also enacted, although Zhou's efforts to fight corruption in the ministry were somewhat ironic, given the charges of high-level corruption that were later levied against him. A senior official in a Beijing municipal bureau explained the shift in the ministry during the reform era: "[In the 1980s], the police had a lot of power because there were no real laws. . . . Police could do whatever they wanted, but this was bad for the country. Now, the law is more important than individuals."[62] By promoting rule-following and professionalization of the force, police reforms have made some headway, but as continued reports of corruption and misconduct demonstrate, the process is far from over.

Ministry officials say that centralization efforts are necessary to bring ground-level officers in line. Chinese police, much like police elsewhere, are known to engage in a wide range of misconduct, including beating suspects, taking bribes, and engaging in illegal activities.[63] Some of the most egregious and well-publicized violence is actually carried out by the *chengguan*, but there is no shortage of evidence that police officers also engage in violent and unlawful activities.[64] Moreover, government leaders are not averse to letting state media sources report on police corruption and misconduct. China's system of internet censorship and state media control is complex, but stories of bad behavior on the part of the police regularly appear in media outlets.[65] The most famous such story in recent memory is the corruption case of the former police chief and vice mayor of Chongqing Wang Lijun, who in 2012 fled to the American consulate to seek protection from then-Politburo member Bo Xilai.[66] But other examples abound. In 2015, police shot and killed an unarmed petitioner, and in 2010 a police chief was found guilty of rape and taking bribes in excess of US$2.6 million.[67] In the age of digital media and citizen journalism, damning visual evidence against local police is also mounting. Disturbing footage has emerged of local police engaging in brazen hit-and-runs and beating residents at demolition sites.[68]

Standout stories such as those above are only a taste of the bad behavior that occurs in public security bureaus around the country. Even more common is the acceptance of gifts from individuals hoping to curry favor with police officers and leaders. In interviews, officers may discuss the misconduct of their peers and sometimes speak of their own acceptance of small gifts, but the subject is largely taboo. Companies and individuals alike may provide gifts to the police, both as an annual tradition during holidays and on an as-needed basis. This topic is very sensitive, and only respondents in Hebei were willing to discuss it in any meaningful way. According to these sources, gifts are presented to both leaders and lower-level officers alike, although higher-ranking officers tend to receive more. One officer in Hebei reported that he was offered a vast array of gifts over the course of his thirty-year career. He said that he mostly turned down cash but often accepted valuable gifts such as food products and other household items. Many of the gifts were proffered by the families who were victims of the crime he was investigating, and sometimes they were given to show appreciation for his help after the case was resolved. Often, persons who had already been charged with a crime offered up cash gifts. He said he was less willing to take such gifts because he often could do nothing to help those individuals. This particular officer was quite open in discussing the process of gift giving. As a self-identified villager he explained that his needs were simple, making him far more interested in solving cases than profiting financially. His wife, now a successful businesswoman, corroborated this explanation by complaining about how much money they could have made off of the gifts her husband turned down. She even compared him to some of his colleagues who profited financially in this manner from their posts.

Most recently with the anticorruption efforts led by the Xi Jinping administration, public security reforms have begun to target internal corruption head-on, unseating officials at all levels of the bureaucracy who have been deemed to engage in inappropriate behavior, and strengthening supervisory capabilities of the procuratorate over public security (Greitens 2019). Data from interviews with ministry officials also reveals concern over local police malfeasance as a motivating factor for efforts to increase centralized control. "Corruption is a very big problem," said one official.[69] "It is perhaps the biggest challenge the ministry faces." "We must curb local police power," said another police leader.[70] Whether or not such efforts will be successful is unclear. There is some evidence to suggest that headway has been made in larger cities. "The standards for Beijing police are much higher," explained another official; "[officers in Beijing] have a greater understanding of the law. If you compare them with other areas, you can clearly see the difference. The character of local officers [elsewhere] is lower quality. . . . This causes problems for the ministry."[71] But others say that much work remains to be done. "The anticorruption campaign has not resulted in significantly more resources to fight corruption at the local level," said one ministry official. "The results are largely concentrated at the higher levels and target the associates of former minister Zhou Yongkang."[72]

The issues of police corruption and misconduct are important. We know that the Chinese public is concerned about police corruption and that a growing body of literature in Chinese policing journals has developed in response to the administration's concern for prevention and management of corruption (Yin 2013; Liu and Li 2013; Lu and Qiao 2006).[73] Yet because the subject of misconduct is inherently taboo and politically sensitive under the current administration, it is difficult to research in depth (Scoggins 2018, 107–8). One notable exception is the work of Wang Peng, whose examination of the "red mafia" details how police jobs under Wen Qiang—the now disgraced deputy head of the Chongqing Public Security Bureau—were bought and sold (P. Wang 2017, 2014, 2013). Wang's work shows how some lower- and middle-level police officers engage in corrupt behavior through involvement with local criminal networks and illegal entrepreneurs. Using focus groups, semi-structured interviews, and archival research, Wang helpfully tells readers what he was able to accomplish as well as what he was not, and his example serves as a model for other scholars going forward. Beyond the discussion of gift giving outlined above, respondents for the present study were largely unwilling to discuss the issue, citing "sensitivity" (*mingan*) as the reason. Even the discussions of corruption published in policing journals are high on prescriptive suggestions and low on concrete information about the extent or even specific nature of the problem. Because of such difficulties, this study addresses corruption and misconduct where applicable and when information is available, but the issues are not the focus of analysis.

Although both corruption and police violence are undeniable problems, they are not the only important issues facing Chinese policing today. Moving beyond stereotypes of police as nothing more than corrupt, brutish thugs enables meaningful questions about what police actually do on a daily basis and how they rate their own work performance as well as that of their peers. The Chinese police inhabit a rich and colorful world filled with danger, boredom, frustration, and occasional bursts of joy when a difficult case is solved or a promotion granted. Understanding who they are and what they do as street-level bureaucrats is essential for understanding how the Chinese security state operates. Their accounts about neglected overtime pay, station leadership appointments, ridiculous service calls, and resentment of well-connected officers do more than just give body to a poorly understood and often maligned profession; they also reveal the complexities of law enforcement on the ground in Chinese cities. The chapters that follow lend voice to frontline stories and interpret them with the intent of establishing a more complete picture of what policing in China is, as well as what it is not.

Starting at the ground from the worm's-eye view, flaws and strengths of the local policing system emerge that we are likely to miss if we focus only on high-level reforms or conduct narrow investigations of police activity in certain locales or on specific issues like protest control. This study aims to correct misperceptions and demonstrate the ways in which police work in China is languishing, especially in comparison to protest control. One of the major misperceptions that this chapter has challenged is the belief that an eye-popping internal security budget translates into well-funded frontline police stations. The next chapter looks more deeply at the effects of budget and other resource limitations to argue that many areas of policing fall short, even as protest control excels.

2

UNEVEN RESOURCES AND MANPOWER CONCERNS

Resource limitations make life on the ground difficult for officers in ways that compromise police response. Interviews reveal that pay is low, overtime goes unpaid, and stations do not have enough qualified officers on the front lines to manage current workloads. With insufficient financial support, street-level police say they struggle to do their jobs well, and many further complain that the way stations allocate scarce resources can make life on the ground even harder. These reports come at a time when things should be getting better for local police. Yet improvements in funding, training, and technology have failed to keep pace with increases in crime, citizen demands, and central government hiring limits for civil service employees. While some might dismiss dissatisfaction over resources as the kind of grumbling so often seen among people at the bottom of any hierarchy, complaints also highlight core institutional problems that we might miss if we did not talk to people on the front lines.

What do resource limitations look like on the ground? One young officer explained his station's situation over dinner one night with his girlfriend and a few mutual contacts.[1] "I like my job, but the work is unsafe, and the pay is not enough [to make up for the lack of safe working conditions]. I'm happier now because I'm no longer at the *paichusuo*. When I was there, I sometimes had to work thirty-six hours straight without sleep. The work was just too tiring. Now I still work a lot of overtime but never thirty-six hours." When the officer began speaking about overtime work, his girlfriend interrupted him, explaining how frequently he was away from home and how much she worried about him when he was out on patrol. The officer went on to admit that the situation was difficult for her. "My girlfriend wishes I had never become a police officer, even though I don't regret the decision. . . . My uncle and brother are both police. . . . I know that the overtime is too much, especially for people with families. But we don't have enough officers to meet the demands of responding to calls. Some are too tired to do a good job. It can be very dangerous. . . . Anyway, they don't pay us enough for all the work we have to do."

Officers in station after station shared similar stories. Low pay, dangerous working conditions, and too few officers available at each station to send out on patrol or to respond to calls were the norm at every site where I conducted research. These interviews further revealed two types of resource constraints: those resulting from insufficient funds and those created by allocation decisions. For Chinese police, resources are limited first and foremost by a lack of money, which can affect frontline police by preventing them from getting many of the basic tools and the support they need to do their jobs. Insufficient funding makes it difficult for stations to cover basic operating costs like overtime pay or patrol-related equipment, although the ministry has tried in recent years to infuse stations with resources for the latter. Funding limitations also translate into lower salaries for officers, which can leave them feeling demoralized and affect productivity. Finally, funding deficiencies and central government restrictions make it hard for stations to hire, train, and retain qualified officers. As a result, many stations are relying on untrained or poorly trained auxiliary officers to make up for the labor shortfall, which can reduce the quality of service that stations are able to provide to the public.

Allocation decisions at the station level also affect ground-level police, and interviews reveal discontent over how stations manage manpower and financial resources. The tendency of senior and well-connected officers to stay in the office rather than go out on patrol, for example, puts stress on a police force that is already stretched thin in terms of absolute numbers. Moreover, when resources are disproportionately funneled into handling certain types of criminal activity, such as mass incidents, other types of crime get short shrift in terms of police response. The funding issues of the 1990s and early 2000s have not vanished with the recent influx of so-called *weiwen* (stability maintenance) money.[2] Observations from the front lines highlight issues that arise from allocation decisions, but they also give insight into why police leaders have a hard time addressing these concerns. Sometimes the bureaucracy's long-standing institutional culture blocks redirection of resources, while at other times local leaders are constrained by the priorities of central government leaders. Going beyond the budget figures from the previous chapter, accounts from the front lines demonstrate in greater detail how ground-level police experience resource limitations and how these shortfalls affect their ability to respond to crime in Chinese cities.

Resource Limitations and Basic Operations

If you spend enough time with local police, you will soon hear talk about the inability of stations to cover basic operating costs. These complaints—whether they are about salaries, overtime pay, or equipment—highlight the resource limitations that affect local police the most. Resource constraints related to basic operation costs are perhaps the most demoralizing for officers and are equally detrimental for response capabilities. This may explain why the most recent round of police reforms during Xi Jinping's tenure aims to rectify the problem of local station funding. As reports from the front lines suggest, however, a full amelioration of these problems may prove difficult.

Salaries

Low pay is perhaps the number one complaint from the front lines. Police salaries are set by a national standard that applies system-wide, meaning that all officers, from patrol cops in the most remote county in Gansu to those in the high-toned districts of Shanghai, should expect to receive the same pay every month for the same job. Ministry officials say that any variation in income depends strictly on local governments, which may pay a higher salary and/or supplement officer income with subsidies like housing allowances or gift cards for everyday items such as mobile phone services. According to one ministry official, other nonmonetary benefits include equipment, clothing, weapons, electronics, lunchtime meals, and other gifts, particularly around the lunar new year. Such benefits come directly from the city or county levels, never from above, and help supplement low salaries, since many have real monetary value.[3] Far too often, however, officers say their local governments fall short when it comes to compensation.

Consider the financial situation of a policeman I'll call Officer Wang. One hot summer day, Officer Wang and I were stuck in traffic when a small, bright-blue Ford cut in front of us. "That's the car I want," he said, "but I'll never be able to afford it."[4] This was somewhat surprising. The car was imported, but it certainly did not resemble one of the luxury items coveted by some young people in China. Wang explained that the car he was driving was not his; he had borrowed it from a colleague. "I'm not from [this city]; I'm from the village, and my family is poor.

This is a good job for me; the test to become an officer is even more difficult than the college entrance examination [*gaokao*], but the pay is so low. I don't even make [RMB] 2,000 a month.[5] That car is over 100,000 [US$16,000)]. How could I ever [afford to] buy it?"

Officer Wang is not alone. In China, the societal expectation is that young, unmarried men should be able to bring big-ticket items like a car and an apartment into a marriage. But with a salary of RMB 2,000 a month (US$294), it is impossible for someone like Officer Wang to pay for such items on his own. In response, families across multiple generations often pool resources to purchase these items, just so their sons or grandsons will be viewed as eligible suitors; but not every family can muster so much cash. Wang's colleague went on to explain the effect of the low salaries on their lives: "We are all dissatisfied with our jobs because we don't make much money. Anyway, there is nothing we can do about it. I became a police officer because I thought police officers were very cool and the job was stable. . . . But we will never be able to afford a car or house [on this salary]."[6]

While some officers live in underdeveloped areas where take-home pay is enough to cover basic needs, others like Officer Wang and his colleague say the costs of living in the city leave them struggling to afford even smaller items like nice meals out with friends or colleagues. With restaurants in third-tier cities charging a few hundred RMB for relatively modest group meals, and KTV (karaoke television) clubs commanding about the same for a night out with drinks, a monthly salary of RMB 1,500 or even 2,500 means that certain cornerstones of Chinese social life and upward mobility are difficult to reach for those who lack family money or other sources of income. For the lowest paid, take-home pay may even drop below a living wage. If, like Officer Wang, they do not have family money or other resources to fall back on, they may have no choice but to look elsewhere for assistance.[7] For example, when stations do not offer housing benefits, some officers must take on second jobs just to keep a roof over their heads and food on the table. While none of my interviewees reported that they themselves were in such a situation, some freely told stories of colleagues who were compelled to seek out private security gigs or embark on small business ventures to pay for basic living expenses.[8] When asked why stations do not increase salaries to help such officers make ends meet, one respondent summed it up simply: "No money!"[9]

What of the national standard that is supposed to ensure a baseline salary for everyone? In practice, this standard is hard to implement, because local governments provide all funds for salaries and overtime. That discrepancies result from such a system is widely acknowledged, but the ministry would prefer to hide or downplay the specifics. One recent crowd-sourcing survey provides insight into salary differences across provinces.[10] Although the survey reveals little about its methodology and should be treated with caution, the numbers are in line with what we should expect to see in 2017, the year it was published online. Across the board, county officers make the least on average, with police in Shanxi and Hubei Provinces earning about RMB 2,500 (US$368) per month, and those in Shanghai making approximately RMB 8,000 (US$1,177) per month. Shanghai police are the outliers, however, since the average nationwide salary according to this data is RMB 3,822 (US$563) a month. City officers make slightly more, averaging RMB 4,419 (US$651) a month, with officers in the lowest-paid provinces (Sichuan and Guanxi) pulling in about RMB 3,500 (US$515) a month, and Shanghai municipal police drawing RMB 8,000. Such numbers demonstrate wide disparities and lend credibility to officer complaints about salaries. Although all the reported averages are above minimum wage, they are also several thousand RMB below available figures for white-collar workers, and less than other civil servants at the same level.[11]

Overtime

Compounding the issue of low salaries is the inability (and occasional unwillingness) of stations to pay officers for overtime work, although how often this happens can vary across locale. In some areas, such as in one field site that was roughly average in terms of per capita GDP, officers are usually paid on time for additional work.[12] But in other cities, overtime is paid only when funds are available, and officers say they can go for long stretches without compensation for the extra hours they work.[13] In less densely populated counties in another province where I conducted research, overtime is rarely paid, but this does not mean an area's size or degree of economic development always indicates whether officers will be compensated for extra work.[14] In one large metropolitan city where I expected to observe frequent overtime pay if not complete compliance, a junior officer put it bluntly: "We never get paid [overtime]."[15]

By all accounts, overtime work is exhausting and commonplace for police in China. With human resources stretched thin at stations across the country, overtime is especially common for patrol cops (*xunjing*) and workers in small county and district stations. These officers are instructed to answer and respond to calls from residents at all times, even in the middle of the night. Sometimes officers are told about the extra hours in advance, but often the work is not scheduled. This means street-level police officers are on call, seemingly at all times, and on more than one occasion during fieldwork, officers were suddenly summoned back to the station or to a site of interest in the middle of an interview, regardless of the time or day of the week. One policing scholar calls such overtime "routine" (*jiachangbianfan*), citing a study that found Chinese police are, on average, working eleven-to-fifteen-hour days with one day off every three weeks (Hu 2009).

Officers say there is little they can do about the lack of overtime pay. Because of the relative hardship such a schedule imposes, I often asked officers if they complained to their boss about not getting paid. Most said no, and some gave me quizzical looks. One officer explained, "What would I say to my boss? He works alongside me, and he also doesn't get paid. It's a big problem, since our salaries are so low, but there is nothing we can do."[16]

Equipment

Modern policing depends on technology to maintain proper records, protect officers, and collect forensic evidence, but Chinese officers say they lack funding for many of the basic tools they need to do their jobs well. Financial constraints at the local level limit equipment purchases such as police cars, computers, and monitoring systems, which can make everyday tasks like responding to calls or recording data more challenging and time consuming. Many police are frustrated by this and compare their situations to that of police elsewhere who are presumably better off. "I wish we had equipment like they do in Hong Kong," explained one mid-level officer.[17] "Even their foot patrol officers have better technology than we do."

Technology resources can vary widely by and within location. While police stations in Beijing proper have stellar resources, many stations in the rest of the country lack the trappings of modern police stations.[18] In my field sites alone, police equipment in two locations was outdated. Police cars were old, the stations had changed little since the 1990s, and what was available in terms of computer equipment was slow and cumbersome to use. In three of the other cities, however, the offerings were more mixed. While the main police stations were modern complexes with new riot vans and other police vehicles, the district stations were in poor condition, and availability of computing technology for patrol was spotty.

The issue of computing technology is an important one, especially for patrol. In this area, station resources often fall short because of a lack of funding for updated machines and software programs. One officer in Hebei explained his station's situation: "Most of the records in the station are computerized, but I don't care about that. Our patrol cars have computers now, but they are too slow. We don't like using them."[19] Officers in Shaanxi also expressed similar complaints about the speed of their police car computers, noting that sometimes they are unusable. A former official compared the situation in China to that of the United States: "They [officers in the US] have a mobile application that gives detailed information about a neighborhood before a patrol goes in. You can see all recent criminal activity and pictures of the perpetrators."[20] He went on to compare that with the situation in China: "Our officers have nothing like this, and I'm not sure when we will be able to develop a similar system."

There is evidence to suggest, however, that the funding situation for equipment has recently improved, thanks to infusions of cash from the central government in the past few years. On returning to the field in 2018 and 2019, I found that cities in two provinces (Hebei and Hunan) that once made do with old police cars and out-of-date computing equipment now have access to new surveillance technologies and body cameras for patrol. Such changes indicate a concerted effort on the part of the central government to provide better funding for local station equipment and overall improvement in terms of station capabilities. Several caveats deserve mention, however. The funds are earmarked specifically for equipment and infrastructure and were not supposed be used to hire more officers or pay salaries, so their utility in addressing frontline concerns remains confined to one area. A ministry official also advised caution on interpreting too much from the funding increases. "Such changes are good," the officer explained. "The technology is very good, but it may not be enough. The criminals also have access to new technology, and it is often much more advanced than what we have. It also takes time to train the officers to use this technology. We might be ten years away from realizing its full potential."[21]

This last point is critical and mentioned often by officers in areas where funding for equipment was sufficient, even prior to the most recent improvements. Just because the equipment exists does not mean there will be enough funds (or will) to train every officer on how to use it. This is particularly an issue for older officers. One officer nearing retirement complained, "A lot of the training in the last three to five years is geared toward learning new technologies. It's only for the young men. If you're over fifty, they don't want to train you. We old guys get left behind."[22] Of course some older officers are perfectly content to leave the new technology to younger officers, but the broader trend of limitations on the number of officers trained to use such technology remains unchanged.[23]

Basic Operations and Police Effectiveness

Officer complaints about salaries, unpaid overtime, and equipment confirm the inadequacy of funding for basic operations, but how do these limitations affect police effectiveness on the ground? For equipment issues, the impact is relatively clear-cut. Outdated computers can make filing reports and inputting information on the go a hair-pulling experience for police, slowing response times and increasing frustration. Older cars can also cause problems for patrol officers, depending on how well they are maintained. Moreover, the number of police cars a station can afford most certainly makes a difference in how quickly stations are able to respond to calls and how much time they are able to spend before moving on to the next case. Because of the room for tangible improvement, it makes sense that the ministry recently began directing financial resources toward equipment and infrastructure purchases; but without more specific station-level data or budget information, it is beyond the scope of this study to make a determination of how widespread these changes are.

The effects of salary and overtime issues on officer satisfaction and performance are nuanced. In interviews, officers report that low and inadequate salary compensation is demoralizing, especially when they compare it to what other government workers make. While one would be hard-pressed to find workers anywhere who do not believe they should be paid more, police officers in China make a pretty good case for themselves, given the low starting salaries, dangers of the job, and the frequency and duration of uncompensated overtime work. According to China's National Bureau for Statistics, recently collected average salaries for police officers are between 60 and 70 percent less than those of other workers in "nonprivate enterprises."[24] But police seldom compare themselves to workers in other occupations. They are instead far more interested in how much police elsewhere are paid, particularly police officers in China, and it is this comparison that officers find most disheartening.[25]

Despite the national standard, it is well known among frontline police that salaries vary widely across the country. When I spoke to officers in Hebei, Hunan, and Shaanxi Provinces in 2012, frontline patrol police and *paichusuo* officers were paid about RMB 2,000 a month (US$296), even though they were doing the same basic work as officers in big cities. Many of these officers compared their salaries to the RMB 10,000 (US$1,477) monthly salary of officers in Guangzhou, a large port city on the Pearl River. In fact, the Guangzhou figure was so high and repeated with such frequency that I began to wonder if it might be an urban legend. It is not; Guangzhou officers earned about RMB 10,000 a month in 2013, nearly five times the salary of the officers where I conducted research.[26]

Such differences in pay leave police dissatisfied, and in a country that still espouses socialist ideals, the topic is taboo. Some leaders even refused to admit that differences in pay existed, and one official in the ministry winced slightly when I asked him about the pay inequality.[27] "It's very sensitive right now," he said. "Officials don't like to discuss it, but of course it isn't the same everywhere."[28] "Chinese people expect that the same jobs should be compensated in the same way," explained one officer before going on to say that local cops see differences in pay as a violation of national policy (*guojia guiding*).[29] Patrol officers in Hebei also say that the differences are unfair (*bu gongping*) before adding there is nothing to be done, a common refrain used by officers in interviews when discussing resources. Such frustration is understandable. Police work across China is tiring and sometimes dangerous, and poorly paid officers say they work just as hard as officers who are better compensated. To make matters worse, moving to an area where police are better compensated is rarely an option for most street-level police.[30]

The low morale that emerges from such comparisons can affect the quality of the work that police do. Few officers I spoke with said that the issue of low salary or lack of overtime had affected their personal willingness or ability to do their job, but nearly all were quick to point out the impact on their colleagues, although none felt comfortable providing specific examples. "My coworkers are lazy," explained an officer who went on to say that there is little incentive to work hard when they are paid so little.[31] "Most only do what they have to"—that is, the bare minimum to keep their jobs. Reports of shirking among officers were common at all field sites, and one patrol captain called dissatisfaction over pay "a big problem" with the men he oversees.[32] This observation of a decrease in police effectiveness when morale is low is backed by research on police elsewhere (Greene 1989).

Beyond effects on morale, salary issues resulting from underfunding can also increase incentives for bribery and other types of corruption that lower the overall quality of policing on the ground. Reliable data is spotty, but reports occasionally surface. On netease, a popular online forum, one local civil servant spoke of his long hours and low pay, explaining that low wages and the hopeless living conditions they induce drive corruption.[33] Moreover, it is commonly known that officers sometimes accept gifts from individuals and companies seeking to curry favor.[34] One recently retired officer listed some of the gifts he received over the course of his thirty-year career, which included everyday household items like rice, oil, milk, cigarettes, alcohol, and the occasional tea set. Such gifts can certainly make life easier for poorly paid police by offsetting low incomes, but they may also harm the reputation of police in the eyes of some members of society or provoke government leaders who are seeking to reduce corruption. For local residents, such greasing of the wheels may improve service or satisfaction for individuals with the ability to pay bribes or give valuable gifts, but it perhaps lowers it for those whose who are unable or unwilling to engage in such behavior.

Resource Limitations and Manpower

Manpower resources are also limited in China.[35] One ministry official explained that this is because current funding levels prevent stations from hiring additional police officers, even though they need more people on the ground, and this claim is further supported by information in Chinese policing journals (H. Huang 2006).[36] Moreover, larger concerns about government bloat have led the central government to place limitations on the number of civil servants that can be hired by each department. Without cash to hire more police officers and bumping up against restrictions on civil servant manpower, many stations have begun using lower-paid auxiliary police to pick up the slack. Such manpower issues and decisions are not without costs. Just as failing to pay police officers overtime wages can cause problems for stations, so too can the reliance on poorly trained part-time workers. Such problems are further compounded by the fact that many official police officers seek to secure office jobs that shield them from the more demanding tasks of frontline work. This reduces the number of officers who deal directly with everyday policing tasks, which in turn undermines police response on the ground for many areas of crime.

A Comparatively Small Police Force

Precise data about the number of police officers in China is not available, but there is evidence to suggest that the force is small. Perhaps because of political sensitivity issues, China has not released manpower figures to international groups since 1997, and the last time the central government directly reported the number in any capacity was in 1999.[37] Vague estimates of the number of police occasionally crop up in state-run media sources and currently hover around two million.[38] This number excludes auxiliary police and the PAP.[39] In a country with a population of around 1.4 billion, a personnel figure of 2 million would put China's per capita police force at 143 per 100,000. If we compare this to data collected by the UN in 2015 on other nations, China's rate is much lower than Russia's 472, Macau's 1,069, and somewhat lower than rates in the United States (198) and Korea (222).[40] Other countries that report a similar per capita rate to China are Myanmar (143), Honduras (130), and Finland (140), although the policing needs in these countries vary widely.[41] Table 2 presents the latest data on police per capita as a further point of comparison. Even if we conceptualize China's security force more broadly by including the paramilitary PAP, China's total internal security force would be approximately 4 million, or 286 per 100,000. This leaves China in the middle, roughly on par with Costa Rica (278), Chile (283), and Andorra (295).

International per capita comparisons are not the only—nor even most significant—evidence to suggest that China's police force is relatively small. In interviews, Chinese police consistently indicate that they need more officers to cover current policing demands. "I don't have enough people to send out on

TABLE 2 Police per 100,000 in international comparison

COUNTRY	2015 RATE	COUNTRY	2015 RATE	COUNTRY	2015 RATE
Madagascar	34.13	Netherlands	351.13	Germany	299.51
Kenya	81.29	Peru	359.72	Czech Republic	375.13
Tanzania	88.35	Spain	363.86	Hungary	380.87
Honduras	130.36	El Salvador	365.11	Colombia	386.11
Finland	140.32	Guyana	474.58	Slovenia	394.54
Myanmar	143.11	Serbia	477.93	Jamaica	408.68
Philippines	158.56	Trinidad and Tobago	482.12	Slovakia	412.09
Singapore	168.29	Croatia	488.71	Lebanon	415.2
Denmark	185.15	Barbados	492.98	Cyprus	423.94
Canada	190.89	Greece	493.14	Algeria	435.91
United States of America	198.14	Malta	498.16	Bosnia and Herzegovina	450.42
Iceland	198.18	Montenegro	640.35	Italy	451.22
Sweden	203.82	Switzerland	218.75	Portugal	451.89
Timor-Leste	299.67	Republic of Korea	222.49	Latvia	455.46
Lithuania	304.06	Liechtenstein	227.03	North Macedonia	465.27
Thailand	319.84	Paraguay	242.68	Russia Federation	471.84
Austria	322.12	Kazakhstan	247.41	Bermuda	643.75
France	324.35	Poland	260.01	Uruguay	680.54
Mexico	333.99	Romania	262.49	Dominica	729.58
Belgium	334.55	Australia	263.91	Argentina	809.67
Luxembourg	334.74	Costa Rica	277.54	Grenada	875.45
Albania	337.01	Chile	283.03	Macau	1,069.44
Bulgaria	337.26	Andorra	294.87	Holy See (Vatican)	14,500.00
Cabo Verde	347.62	Estonia	297.79		

Source: UNODC.org.

patrol," said one captain of a district patrol squad when I asked about police staffing in his jurisdiction.[42] "It is a real problem, but there is nothing I can do about it. We all just have to work more overtime." He is not alone. Officers at all levels of the bureaucracy frequently spoke about staffing shortages, whether in their own districts or elsewhere. Moreover, Chinese policing scholars openly write about the shortages and their negative effects on local police officers (Hu 2009).

Compounding the problem of a small per capita force on the national level is the fact that many areas fall well below the country's average of 143 officers per 100,000. Along the more developed coast and in certain districts of large cities, police force sizes may approach that of the United States or elsewhere; but in less developed areas, force numbers are much lower. One research site in Hebei had only 88 per 100,000, and policing scholar Hu Wannian reported in 2009 that many districts in the countryside have per capita rates of around 80 per 100,000 and sometimes much lower.[43]

Without funding increases, such differences are difficult to correct. The ministry has stressed the importance of developing police manpower to combat rising crime and deal with stability maintenance, but it has yet to develop national standards that address the issue (G. He 2012). One step forward is the requirement that all substations (*paichusuo*) have at least five officers; but five people is usually a mere drop in the bucket, given the population size of most areas.[44] While some urban stations have the monetary means to set force size according to population figures, many others are bound by the financial realities of their geographic location (H. Huang 2006). Even when cities do have sufficient funding, they may nevertheless hit limitations on the number of official police they can hire, since city governments must limit the number of civil servants they employ.[45] As a result, station leaders are turning to other sources to make up for shortfalls in staffing.

Auxiliary Police

More and more cash-strapped stations are hiring unofficial workers because they are plentiful and cheap. These auxiliary or assistant police (*xiejing*) are the adjunct professors of the policing world: a low-paid, overworked, and often unappreciated underclass of security workers. A *xiejing* officer receives no employment benefits and might earn as little as RMB 800 (US$130) a month.[46] Unlike adjuncts, however, *xiejing* are rarely as educated as official police and receive virtually no training. They are primarily hired to do work that might otherwise be handled by official police, and their range of duties can vary widely: *xiejing* have been tasked with everything from watching dissidents to staffing the small, makeshift police kiosks (*gonganting*) that are now commonplace in many Chinese cities.

Because of the temporary nature of the work, *xiejing* are attractively expendable. One police leader said the ability to hire *xiejing* makes it easy for his station to bring in more officers when necessary and concentrate them in the areas where they are needed most.[47] This type of at-will employment is also useful when things go awry. One senior officer explained, "If there is a problem, the station leader can report to local government officials that the person responsible was a temporary worker and has been fired. If they press for further information, the station leader says they can no longer find the individual [*nage ren bujian le*]."[48] This system works well for station leaders in a pinch, adding to the broader appeal of hiring *xiejing*. In Xinjiang, analysis of police recruiting documents suggests that these informal positions may bring other benefits as well (Zenz and Leibold 2019). By offering high salaries with lower barriers to entry than those required for official police positions, stations are able to recruit a wider range of applicants, including ethnic minorities. This strategy enables police to further co-opt Uighur minorities, which may have stability maintenance benefits while simultaneously bolstering their manpower resources.

Despite these seeming advantages, the prevalence of *xiejing* varies by locale. In Hunan, the practice only became common in the last five to seven years, and in many rural counties, *xiejing* are not used at all.[49] At research sites in Hebei and Shaanxi, *xiejing* are commonplace. Big cities like Beijing and Shanghai also use *xiejing*, but their standards are slightly higher. *Xiejing* in Beijing, while still untrained, serve in more limited capacities.[50] One police leader explained the differences: "In Beijing, we have *xiejing*, but they are clearly marked. It's on the sleeve of their uniform. This was unified across all districts two years ago. They all have the same uniform and salary [RMB 2,000], and they are dispatched to help where they are needed. . . . They do not receive formal training. Instead, we limit the range of actions they can take and monitor them closely."[51] The leader went on to provide the rational for using *xiejing*. "We hire *xiejing* because we have limits on how many civil servants can be hired. With *xiejing*, we also don't have to pay for certain other fees in addition to their salary, as we would for police officers." Adding that the auxiliaries were expendable by nature, he concluded, "The *xiejing* can be a big help. We can bring in more when we need them or even concentrate them in certain areas." Despite the leader's seeming ringing endorsement of *xiejing*, problems nevertheless arise from an increased reliance on these temporary, untrained, and typically poorly compensated workers.

Manpower Issues and Police Effectiveness

Manpower issues can impact police effectiveness even more than limitations on basic operations. Officers say understaffing leaves stations struggling to meet increasing demands from the public and ultimately lowers the quality of service they are able to provide. Moreover, added stress on officers and increased reliance on *xiejing* can lead to misunderstandings with the public and abuses of power that sometimes turn violent. These problems are well known throughout the policing world but are difficult to resolve for both financial and institutional reasons.

Respondents across field sites say a shortage of officers makes their job more difficult. In Shaanxi, police complain that a low per capita force means more overtime work and less time to spend responding to calls.[52] In a Hebei Province city that has 88 officers per 100,000 people, the situation is even worse. Officers report heavy strains on patrol officers, such as routine overtime and a lack of personnel to manage call volumes.[53] Moreover, in rural areas facing social unrest, low force numbers can tax local officers to the breaking point. One PAP officer recounted the schedule of his friend, a local officer in an understaffed Xinjiang *paichusuo*, who sometimes works up to forty days straight without going home, even though he lives just twenty kilometers away.[54] "They have the hardest job [*tamen zui xinku*]," he said. Such schedules can have real consequences for the men and women on the front lines. A report on the psychological health of officers in China found that the heavy workloads resulting from "a serious shortage of police" leave officers "physically and mentally exhausted, [with] nervous system disorders, circadian damage, and psychological stress" (Hu 2009, 61).

Unsurprisingly, an overworked, stressed-out police force without enough officers to send out on patrol or manage call volumes does not lead to better policing on the ground. One scholar called the shortage of manpower a "clear and prominent problem" plaguing public security in China (G. He 2012, 78). A young officer in Shaanxi shook his head when I asked about the effects. "We don't serve the people," he said, before going on to explain that officers in his station answer calls as quickly as possible and are often unable to help the callers, leaving all parties dissatisfied. In Hunan another officer explained, "It is very difficult [to manage with a limited force]. Our leaders do the best they can." To assist in the "muddling through" necessitated by low force numbers, stations in Hebei often rely on *xiejing* or partially trained police working under annual contracts to make up for shortfalls in manpower. "It is not the best option, because they lack training," said a patrol captain, "but it is all we can do."[55]

Indeed, problems with using *xiejing* abound. Although Western news sources tend to focus on abuses perpetrated by the *chengguan*, Chinese media outlets routinely report incidents of misconduct by *xiejing*.[56] In one particularly bad stretch at the end of 2015, three *xiejing* groped and attacked a woman outside a Henan KTV club in September, two *xiejing* in Ningxia were fired after a video of them beating a man went viral in November, and in December, *xiejing* in a Shandong SWAT unit were caught on video brutally interrogating a naked couple caught having sex in their car (so-called *chezhen* is usually punished with a fine).[57] These are not isolated incidents: the internet is littered with examples such as one notorious video in Hebei Province of *xiejing* beating suspects and exercising enforcement (*zhifaquan*) not granted to them by the law.[58] Such problems caused by *xiejing* can be a mess for station leaders to clean up, especially in an age of viral videos.[59]

The issues with *xiejing* are well-known in the policing world but difficult to resolve. Regular officers are not surprised by the bad press surrounding *xiejing* and are quick to point out that *xiejing* are not "real police" but instead poor substitutes who often create more troubles than they fix because they lack training and character (*suzhi*). "Most of the problems you hear about on the news come from the *xiejing*," said one senior officer.[60] "These men don't have proper training. Real police rarely act this way."[61] Policing scholars are also well aware of the problems and have called for institutionalized reform and standardization of the *xiejing* (J. Wang 2015). But with barely enough funds to pay assistant police, much less train them, most local stations have few resources and no systems in place to carry out such reforms. Recently, the ministry began the process of addressing some of these problems. In 2015, a meeting on reform led by Public Security Minister Guo Shengkun highlighted the importance of auxiliary personnel for helping maintain public order and admitted that the force had "many problems."[62] Records from the meeting noted that the ministry needs to standardize and streamline the management system, implement safeguard measures, and effectively manage the team. In 2016, calls for reform became more specific when the State Council issued an opinion on regulating the management of auxiliary police that fleshed out some of the measures outlined in the 2015 meeting.[63] The ministry followed up on the issue again in 2018 in a subsequent meeting on police reform that included improvements of the auxiliary police management system in broader efforts to improve supervision.[64] Such developments indicate that the ministry is aware of the problem and interested in implementing improvements but has not yet designated the issue an essential reform objective.[65]

Allocation of Limited Resources

Resource problems within the Public Security Bureau are significant. Limitations on basic operations and manpower force police leaders to make difficult decisions about how to allocate limited resources. These restrictions are further compounded by two additional constraints: the phenomenon of "office officers," and the prioritization of social unrest. Office officers are an semi-institutionalized subclass of police in China that further limits a low per capita force, whereas the prioritization of social unrest directs limited resources away from other everyday policing activities. These two issues affect police in different ways and for different reasons, but both are firmly entrenched.

Office Officers

A strong institutional culture of rewarding senior cops and younger officers who have social connections has created an oversupply of what I call office officers. This deeply rooted yet informal class of men and women is solely dedicated to working in the office and paid about the same or more as officers who go out on patrol or respond to calls. Much of what they do is legitimate work. All stations need workers to handle household registrations (*hukou*), answer phone calls and visits by local residents, or perform other internal (*neibu*) work such as station supervision. These jobs are highly desirable because they lack much of the danger and fatigue brought on by police work performed outside the office. The only problem with these workers is that there are often too many of them in comparison to other officers engaged in more active crime-fighting activities.

Who gets to be an office officer? Those who have family or other exceptional social connections (*guanxi*) may go right into office positions without ever working patrol, or, more commonly, well-connected individuals may assume a cushy office position after working for just a few years. Officers without *guanxi* who prove themselves in the field may also be rewarded with office positions in as few as ten years.[66] Office positions are also commonly held by women. As noted earlier, many stations also hire women with educational training at police high schools or middle schools (*jingxiao*) to work in the office, presumably because stations do not deem it suitable to send women out on patrol—horseback squads notwithstanding.

Finally, police who have achieved seniority, especially those nearing retirement age, are frequently rewarded with office positions. If officers are still working in the field in their fifties, they are typically promoted to the office at age fifty-five, the final age at which such transfers are permitted.[67] Beginning at this age, older officers typically reduce their workloads and come in to the office less frequently. One such officer explained the arrangement:

> We typically work a full day for the first few years, but by fifty-seven or fifty-eight many will stop coming in on most days. Now, I mostly go in just to say hello and get my paycheck. . . . This is because younger officers [even if they are higher ranking] are reluctant to give orders to older officers. They don't feel comfortable. And the older officers probably take advantage of this. We have worked hard for so many years and gone through many hardships. We are close to retirement. It's good that they [the younger officers] respect their elders because we are getting older and no longer need to work so hard.[68]

It is important to note that all officers continue to collect a full paycheck until age sixty, at which point they begin drawing a pension.

If this sounds like a lot of people in the office when stations are complaining about manpower shortages, it is. Precise numbers are hard to come by, but one provincial ministry official explained that many county *paichusuos* may have five official officers working there, but only three of those officers will be charged with doing most of the actual work.[69] This is because, for instance, one of the two remaining officers may be over fifty-five and just collecting a paycheck, while the other might have social connections and a desk job. In the worst-case scenario, a five-person *paichusuo* might have as many as three office officers doing very little work and two officers answering calls and going out on patrol. Such arrangements further strain the effects of a low per capita police force and explain why interviewees with *paichusuo* work experience described twenty-four-hour and thirty-six-hour shifts.

How can stations support so many office officers? The simple answer is they cannot. But leaders often lack the power to correct the issue because of entrenched expectations that office positions are a necessary reward for service, seniority, or *guanxi*. One patrol captain put it bluntly: "It's not fair, but men in the office have connections [*guanxi*] . . . and the leaders cannot force them out of the office."[70] When combined with the high demand for office positions and the unwillingness of police to leave posts once they secure them, it becomes even harder for police leaders to change the system. "Everyone wants to be in the office," said one mid-level supervisor who himself had secured such a position.[71] And even though this particular officer spoke fondly of his days on duty with the people, he confirmed that he had no intention of returning to patrol work because of hardships like the time he was called out in the middle of the night to retrieve a lost cow.

Of course, police everywhere work their connections to attain jobs and promotions when possible. Scholars have identified nepotism and favoritism as a major problem for police chiefs in Turkey (Mutlu 2000), and similar practices have fueled public criticism of police in Mozambique (Seleti 2010). When such practices are ingrained in societies, they can be difficult if not impossible to dislodge, since there is very little internal will to unseat long-established traditions (Dinnen, McLeod, and Peake 2006). What makes the Chinese case interesting is the deep entrenchment of the practice and its far-reaching effects on an already strained force despite efforts on the part of the ministry to disrupt it. Since enacting the 1995 Police Law, the ministry has sought to professionalize the police by implementing an examination process for all entry-level positions, but *guanxi* still matters during the interview stage and makes a big difference in whether someone gets hired and at what level (county or city).[72] Later in the career of an officer, research has shown that the process of promotion depends heavily on how officers network with their leaders and whether or not they give substantial monetary and other gifts at appropriate times (P. Wang 2017). Perhaps most interesting is the widespread prevalence of office officers, which affects nearly everyone at age fifty-five and sometimes much sooner for those who are particularly well connected. *Guanxi* thus permeates the system at every level from start to finish, even as it provides arguably zero benefit to police effectiveness on the ground.

Office Officers and Police Effectiveness

The practice of allowing office officers to hamstring an already limited force hits patrol and call response the hardest. "The problem is very serious," noted a provincial ministry official, "because so many stay in the office and do nothing."[73] A police captain went on to explain the situation at his station: "There are too many men in the station, but not enough where we need them in the field."[74] Officers in other field sites confirmed this assessment, noting that their stations did not have enough officers to send out on patrol, even though the stations were filled with able bodies.[75] With so many people in the office, the practice of office officers reduces police effectiveness by limiting the number of available police to conduct patrols and answer calls.

Moreover, the quality of service that officers on patrol are able to provide may be lower than it would be if more office officers were sent out to the field. Since most of the more experienced officers have been rewarded with positions in the office, patrol cops tend to be younger and greener. These young patrol officers—by virtue of their age and experience level—do not know the territory as well and have fewer long-standing relationships with residents. "Their lack of experience makes it hard for them to do a good job," lamented one assistant station chief.[76]

The institutional culture that binds officers to the office is difficult to break, despite a generally recognized need for restructuring. Change is not, however, impossible. In the middle of my fieldwork, national news of serial killer Zeng Kaigui spread around the country, stoking fears and spurring police stations across south central China to muster all available resources to capture the former PLA soldier.[77] During this time, the public security stations in one of the cities where I was conducting research increased patrol assignments by what was described to me as a "not small" percentage.[78] This necessitated bringing senior and well-connected officers out of the office and onto the streets. To much surprise, the practice continued for many months even after Zeng was apprehended, proving that the ties binding office officers to their posts have limits under the right circumstances. More recently, similar reports emerged during the COVID-19 outbreak. Xinhua reported that one fifty-nine-year-old officer nearing retirement was now on patrol ten hours a day, logging more than twenty thousand steps to conduct inspections and ensure rule compliance with measures to mitigate the spread of the virus.[79] Such developments highlight the ability of police leaders to reverse the entrenched practice of office officers during extraordinary times, but whether these changes can be carried out on a broader scale and for a longer period of time remains to be seen.

Stability Maintenance

On the opposite end of the spectrum is stability preservation. Shoring up funds for *weiwen* is another type of allocation decision, but unlike the issues discussed above, stability maintenance gets the long end of the stick. Performance in the area of stability maintenance is linked to promotion, punishment, and dismissal through the cadre evaluation system, and cadres may be fired if they fail to "maintain public order," regardless of whether they perform well in other areas. In response, government leaders at all levels have made a strong commitment to *weiwen*, which encourages them to ensure that resources such as funding and manpower flow into stability maintenance at a higher rate.[80] It is important to note that funding and attention are concentrated in areas where ethnic and religious tensions drive social unrest such as Xinjiang and Tibet. PAP officers engaged in protest management say the bulk of the central government's *weiwen* resources are devoted to these areas, with support ranging from direct funding for local police stations to the deployment of PAP officers and military units.[81] Reports show that in Xinjiang, domestic security funding has increased dramatically in recent years, doubling in 2010, again in 2014, and spiking in 2017 with the construction of new security-related facilities that include detention camps.[82] Such increases far outpace the rate of growth elsewhere. Moreover, financial support extends beyond the borders of Xinjiang and Tibet. Gangcha County, for example, is located outside of Tibet proper but in a Tibetan Autonomous Prefecture. It spent the equivalent of US$1.3 million on local police in 2012, even though its population was just forty-two thousand.[83] Much of this money must come from the central government directly, as many of these areas are less economically developed.

But Xinjiang and Tibet are the exception, not the norm. Journalists and scholars far too often assume that all or much of China's domestic security budget goes to handling protests, and even more circumspect reports nevertheless give the impression that buckets of money are pouring into the management of dissidents and protest control.[84] Most local officers will tell you this is inaccurate. Police in Hunan say their bureaus rarely see central government funds (*weiwen jingfei*).[85] "That money is for big cities and other places [like Tibet]," explained one officer. "We only get [central government] *weiwen* money for bringing back petitioners who have gone to Changsha [the provincial capital] or Beijing. . . . We get a phone call saying that one of our residents is there and we need to [come get them and] bring them back home. In these cases, the central government 'picks up the check' [*lai maidan*], but it's a lot of trouble for us. Our leaders consider it an embarrassment to our city." A provincial ministry official further explained: "The central government makes sure the funds are used properly. . . . The money cannot be spent on anything else. . . . [This process ensures] a clear record of how the money is spent."[86]

Because protest and dissident management involves a lot more than just capturing petitioners who have skipped levels, however, most police stations depend on local governments to fund stability maintenance.[87] For example, to prevent petitioners from leaving their cities, local governments devote cash and human resources to contain aggrieved individuals and deal with protests before they draw attention from higher-ups. Sometimes this work is carried out by auxiliary police or other hired thugs (Ong 2018), but regular officers are also dispatched to handle these jobs.[88] The work involves rounding up dissidents during sensitive times like the National People's Congress meeting and even longer-term containments. One officer described the case of a seventy-year-old retired teacher who is observed virtually around the clock because he is seeking reparations for abuse he suffered during the Cultural Revolution.[89] Local government officials, fearful of reprisal for too many incidents of unrest in their area, are often eager to fund such *weiwen* activities—though resources are not unlimited. One officer said there is not enough money in the world to subdue the protesters in his city, though most of his peers were more satisfied with their stations' ability to manage *weiwen*.[90]

Stability Maintenance and Police Effectiveness

The funding and prioritization of stability maintenance appear to be working from the standpoint of local police effectiveness on the ground. Across field sites, many of the same officers who bemoaned their low salaries or outdated equipment reported satisfaction with station resources for handling *weiwen*. Officers in Hunan said that they generally knew how to manage protests or dissidents, and one officer there echoed the sentiments of others, calling it "not a big problem."[91] Another officer in Hebei said he enjoys stability maintenance work as a welcome break from the regular routine.[92] He somewhat gleefully described the process of chasing after would-be petitioners:

> From [our city] they are always headed to Beijing to *shangfang* [lodge their complaints]. We have to chase after them. Sometimes we catch them on the highway. We call our friends at the highway toll plazas and

> let them know. When they stop them, they give us a call, and we go get them. The most fun is when we have to chase after them on the train. We get a call that they might have boarded the train to Beijing, so they stop the train before it gets too far to perform an inspection. Once we find [the petitioners/protesters], we bring them back to the station and try to talk to them.

He also described how, during sensitive times, he and other officers detain potential dissidents at motels, offices, or other temporary holding areas. "It's usually the same people every year, so we know them," he explained. "We treat them very nicely [*dui tamen henhao*], buy them food, let them watch movies. Sometimes we'll give them cigarettes or drink with them." In a study of detentions in China between 1998 and 2004, Rory Truex finds that this "catch and release" strategy can be both effective and predictable, resulting in shorter detentions that allow the regime to anticipate and survive politically sensitive events through preemptive repression (Truex 2019). Such predictability helps stations meet stability maintenance targets and appears to be effective in a variety of contexts. Even officers in an area of Shaanxi that tends to see more social unrest were largely satisfied with their ability to handle *weiwen*. "We have to treat minority groups very carefully," said one officer, "but we can hire *xiejing* to help [make up for manpower shortages]."[93]

The key to effectiveness of stability maintenance in the areas where I conducted research is multifold, but from the standpoint of resources, funding from local governments makes a big difference. Central government money for returning dissidents is not insignificant, but money from the local level for detention and auxiliary police helps to streamline frontline response by giving officers the resources they need to respond efficiently and effectively. Moreover, there is evidence to suggest that local stations can boost effectiveness when they increase funding. A *Southern Daily* report on Guangdong's Lianjiang city found that the local government increased spending on stability maintenance by 19 percent (RMB 7 million, or US$1 million) and significantly reduced the number of mass petitions in the city as well as the number of protesters headed to higher levels.[94] Touting this success, local party secretary Xu Shun said that he was "willing to spend money to buy stability." While most cities lack the resources to muster such a response, the case of Lianjiang shows that petitions can be reduced when local governments invest enough money.

Coordination also helps. Because the division of funding is clearly delineated, station leaders receive money for different types of activities and know whom to call for which issue. Spending for returning dissidents to their homes is funded by the central government, whereas spending for local preventive detention comes from the local level. Local governments are more likely to provide funds requested by police departments for stability maintenance than they are for other areas of policing since their leaders have a vested interest in preventing discoverable acts of resistance such as petitioners who make their way to Beijing to lodge complaints. Manpower resources are also better coordinated. When a protest situation attracts too much attention or becomes violent, local governments and police leaders are able to call in the PAP, helping them overcome the manpower shortages that they face for all other tasks. This is not always the first line of defense, since calling in the PAP creates a record that can be used against local government and police leaders under the cadre evaluation system, but it is far preferable to a violent situation getting out of control.

Resource limitations and allocation decisions have consequences for everyday police operations on the ground. Stations' inability to pay for higher salaries, overtime, and increases in manpower imposes burdens on local police effectiveness by driving down officer morale and constraining the amount of time and number of officers available to respond to public demands. Such problems are further compounded by allocation decisions—whether they are driven by institutionalized expectations or central government priorities—imposing further limitations on resources that are already stretched thin. Sometimes, allocation choices make a taxing situation even more difficult, as is the case when an oversupply of office officers forces other frontline police to pick up the slack. At other times, decisions that prioritize one area of policing come at the expense of others, such as when we see local governments funding stability maintenance activities more reliably than other crime-fighting response capabilities.

Recent increases in central government funds for internal security have not created a windfall of cash for most local police stations, nor have they created substantial resources for local stations even in the area of stability maintenance. Most of that money comes from local governments; and while it does appear to be enough to handle social unrest issues in the areas where I conducted research, that may not be true in areas that experience more protest. Moreover, funding from local governments for stability maintenance has limits. The police leaders in my field sites have not been able to parlay those funds to meet needs such as hiring more official police officers or improving station and salary conditions, which would improve response capabilities in other areas. Instead, we see a compartmentalization of resources for *weiwen* that leaves other areas of policing stretched thin.

It is possible, however, that help is on the way. In 2015, central government reforms stipulated an increase in police officer salaries that would bring officer wages more closely in line with compensation for other security system workers so that police are paid "higher than the local level, slightly lower than the military."[95] The reforms also called for improvements to the pension system and the establishment of an insurance program that provides officers with personal accident and other occupational risk protection. These reforms have the potential to address widespread complaints of frontline officers who labor long hours in often dangerous working conditions for low salaries. A source within the Ministry of Public Security says the wage increases are mandatory, but that local governments have asked for more time in implementing them because of the financial burden. In several provinces, the date for compliance was pushed back numerous times, sometimes years past the original deadline.[96] Although the numbers are not yet public, the same source says that officers across the organization have been promised a 40 percent increase in salary. Such an increase, while not extravagant, would be substantial enough to improve the financial situation of official police and may indirectly assist police effectiveness on the ground. "Morale is really low," the officer went on to explain. "The hope is that salary increases will solve some of these problems."

More time and research are required to assess the effects of this change, but a few potential problems are already evident. First, any effect of salary increases on frontline police morale may be short-lived, since the increases only bring salaries to a level where they should have been many years earlier. Second—and more important—salary increases and other benefits are not extended to all employees at the local level and thus do not apply to auxiliary police officers. Even though auxiliary police often do the same jobs as official police, they have long been compensated at half the salary (or less) than official police (Liao 2010). Without concomitant increases for auxiliary officers, the new raises for official police will make differences in salary even greater, which will leave many auxiliary officers more dissatisfied than ever before.[97] Given that stations are relying more and more on the work of lower-paid auxiliary police, this could undercut the benefits of the new salary policy for stations across the country.

3

LIMITATIONS OF POLICE REFORMS

Officers say that life on the front lines is further complicated by police reform. These reports are unsurprising; police displeasure over reform is a story as old as the organization itself. Although few institutions are quick to embrace change, security bureaucracies can be particularly resistant (Talmadge 2015). Police officers labor in demanding and often unpredictable environments, making them all the more prone to resenting policy changes imposed by higher-ups who are far removed from life on the ground. What is interesting, therefore, about Chinese police officers' resistance to reform is not that they are unhappy, but rather what their resistance tells us about the relationship frontline police have with supervising authorities and the specific ways in which even well-intentioned reforms can undermine the ability of officers to perform their jobs, especially since the same is not true for reforms related to stability maintenance.

Stories about the damaging effects of police reform emerged early on in my interviews with frontline cops. Sometimes their tales were painful. Over tea with a patrol leader one evening, I asked what it was like to go out on patrol without a weapon. Gun use for frontline police has been restricted since the mid-1990s when firearms were banned for most police activities in an effort to reduce violent conflict between police and residents. While outright resistance to this rule has long since faded, patrol officers say the restriction continues to put them in harm's way. I knew the patrol leader had extensive experience policing the streets and was likely to have additional insights into the risks officers face.

As soon as I raised the topic, he became quiet. Then he pointed to a long, thick scar on his face.[1] "Do you see this?" he asked. The scar was one of the first things I noticed about the officer when we met several months earlier. He went on to tell the story. "This happened years ago when I was still a *xunjing* [patrol officer]," he explained. "I was on duty one night when we got called to a woman's house. . . . The dispatcher didn't give us much information, but we knew there had been a domestic disturbance. . . . [What] we didn't know [was] the woman who lived there was mentally ill.[2] I went first, walking up to knock on the door, and bam! She opens the door and strikes me in the face with a [cleaver-style] knife. I didn't even have time to react. It was so fast."

As is common with violent confrontations, the patrol officer said he remembers little of what happened that night or the days that followed. Fortunately, he was not alone at the time of the attack. His fellow patrol officers, themselves unarmed, were somehow able to subdue the woman and get him to a hospital as blood rushed from his face. The blade had sliced deep, leaving the officer hospitalized and in critical condition for many days. "I'm just glad I can still see," he said, since the knife had cut close to his eyes.

The patrol officer's wife was sitting beside him as he told the story. At the time, she was working and pregnant with their first child. She jumped in to fill in the remaining details and give her perspective. "I was very pregnant then, and no one would tell me where he was," she said. "He didn't come home for days, and everyone—my family [who were also police officers], his coworkers—they kept telling me he had gone on an important work trip and was too busy to call. I was going crazy. Now I understand why they wouldn't tell me. They didn't want [the shock of seeing him like that] to hurt the baby."

The officer's story, along with its impact on his family, is just one example of the risks police officers face under the firearm restriction and shows the human effects of police reform on the officers serving the state. While the patrol leader freely admitted that a gun probably would not have stopped the initial attack, guns or even tasers would certainly have helped his fellow officers respond to the attacker and get him out of harm's way more quickly. While China is not the only state to restrict patrol officers from carrying firearms, it is one of only a handful of countries to do so.[3] Ministry leaders appear to be increasingly mindful of the risks frontline police face and have recently begun to soften the 1995 reform by allowing a limited number of patrol squads to carry guns. Still, the majority of officers in China continue to go out on patrol unarmed.

Assessing the Effects of Police Reform on Ground-Level Operations

The gun ban is not the only reform that irks police officers in China. While it is fair to say that most officers are not inherently opposed to the general direction of the ministry's reform agenda, it is also true that many take issue with the specifics.[4] Professionalization of the force, for example, is regarded as progress by most officers; but particular regulations, such as those for reporting requirements, are widely denounced as ineffective and worse. Often, it is not the content of reform that causes trouble for street-level police, but the slow and uneven application of change. Many officers wish, for example, that the ministry would do a better job of creating response procedures or improving recruitment practices. But of course not all reforms are received negatively by people on the front lines. On the other end of the spectrum, officers report that some policies work well, particularly in the area of stability maintenance. By talking to street-level police about these issues, we learn more about how police reform in China actually works and how various policies affect day-to-day operations.

The Public Security Bureau has enacted many police reforms in China since the start of the reform era, not all of which directly affect street-level police.[5] If we group reforms aimed at the front lines according to their effects on local police response, three categories emerge: reforms that directly undermine the capabilities of local police, reforms that potentially improve police response but do not succeed at the current level of implementation, and successful reforms. By looking at these policies more closely, we can better understand specific effects like how limitations on gun use achieve broader state goals of limiting frontline police power but increase risks for unarmed officers, or why training programs are filled with information on political ideology but largely neglect to provide officers with practical advice that could help them solve cases or do their jobs more efficiently.

To fully assess police reform in China and understand why the ministry might enact policies that impose challenges for ground-level response, it is important to recall the rationale behind the PSB's reform agenda. Police leaders have molded the police bureaucracy to better serve the party-state and address security problems that arose during China's transition to a market economy. With this in mind, reformers have spent the last thirty years enacting policies that increase central government control, promote rule by law, and enforce stability. More recently, reformers have also begun pursuing changes that attempt to improve service to the public and—hopefully—stave off rising dissent. When we consider these goals, it is easier to see how some reform policies might be at odds with police objectives on the ground.[6]

Assessing the ways in which the ministry's reform agenda shapes policing practices in China shows how various policies diminish or enhance police response from the standpoint of frontline police, revealing broader patterns that help us understand the strength of the ground-level security apparatus in Chinese cities. Importantly, similar problems with reform have been observed elsewhere in China with tax collection (Cui 2015). Just as conversations with frontline police about resource allocation revealed deep dissatisfaction in most areas of frontline crime management, police assessments of ministerial reform policies expose an overall trend in which frontline officers say they are struggling when it comes to everyday tasks like responding to calls or managing everyday cases but achieving a certain degree of success in the area of stability maintenance.

Reforms That Undermine

Some reforms actively undermine police officers' ability to do their jobs well. In recent years, reforms that increase centralization and reduce the degree of individualized power held by local officers and station leaders have provoked resistance from frontline police. Officers often complain about centrally devised reforms that impose restrictions on how and when they can use force, that increase reporting requirements to their superiors, or that dictate further supervision over local station activities. It is in fact rare to have a conversation with police officers about their work without one of these topics surfacing. Reform-related police grievances reveal more than just feelings of powerlessness or irritation at being told what to do by higher-ups. Their objections expose a disconnect between central ministry goals and policing needs on the front lines, especially when reform is applied unilaterally and with little heed to local context or officer input. For issues like reporting requirements, reforms can make the act of doing the job more cumbersome, while other policies—such as those that aim to reduce the use of force—arguably make the work more dangerous. For all reforms in this category, frontline police say new policies shift the rules of the game and leave them struggling, often indefinitely, since policy changes are seldom accompanied by additional resources to help them adapt.

Limitations on the Use of Force

How and when police use force is complicated and controversial. A major goal of police reform in China is to curb the power of officers by limiting the frequency with which they are likely to use violent means. Whether this is achieved by restricting firearms or limiting self-defense, the idea is to decrease conflict between police and society, especially in situations where officers might be perceived as abusing their power or causing undue harm. But restrictions of this nature are inherently fraught, because the very act of policing is a violent pursuit. Police are positioned at the front lines to enforce the state's Weberian monopoly on the legitimate use of force, and violence is often a necessary part of their job. This reality is why some scholars call the notion of democratic policing an oxymoron (Brogden and Nijhar 2013, 233), as there is little opportunity for democratic participation in a vocation whose essential goal is forcing some people to do things they do not otherwise wish to do.[7] In China, debates about use of force and the role of police in society are also playing out in real time, as the ministry tweaks restrictions and officers cope with the aftermath.

All regular officers in China carried guns as a matter of course until 1995 when the central government reversed the policy with Article 10 of the Police Law.[8] Firearms were rounded up and placed in county and city armories that required two keys held by two different people to open the door. A senior officer explained that the actual disarming of officers took several years, partly because it was a major undertaking and partly because some officers had their "own ideas" (*ziji de xiangfa*) about the restrictions.[9] By around 1996 or 1997, all local police stopped carrying handguns. After the change, office officers never touched a gun again, but patrol officers and criminal investigation police (*xingjing*) still had access to firearms when leaders deemed it necessary for particular missions. One more-senior detective said he would often receive permission to carry a handgun when working on murder cases, especially in the early years following reform, but many of the younger officers I spoke with had not fired a gun since their initial training period. Even the 2014 policy easing firearm restrictions for patrol squads has done little for the vast majority of frontline forces that operate outside the largest cities.[10] Perhaps because of the inherent risks involved and the burdens of training officers to use the firearms properly, the rollout has been slow, although some provincial traffic police began carrying guns in late 2018.[11]

The impact of the gun rule on frontline police can vary. Many new officers enter the force excited about the prospect of firing a gun in the line of duty, only to have their hopes dashed. This disappointment can quickly turn to dismay if and when they find themselves in a dangerous situation unarmed. While few officers have experienced the kind of violent confrontation that befell the patrol leader from Hebei, many interviewees on the front lines expressed concern about their ability to defend themselves without firearms.[12] Nevertheless, not all police are bothered by the fact that they are unable to carry guns. Some say that their areas are relatively safe, so they don't worry.[13] One officer nearing retirement said it made no difference to him.[14] Another officer in the same age group said he cared little about the restriction and thought it was probably a good idea to keep close control of the guns in circulation. Of course, both these officers were already firmly entrenched office officers who no longer went out on patrol or responded to calls. Infrequent access and lack of proper training also complicate matters for those who are allowed to carry guns. One officer explained, "Because our work is more dangerous [in this district] we sometimes get permission to carry guns, but I've never fired mine. . . . Most officers around here are afraid to fire their guns and won't use them, even if they have them. They will only use it in the worst situations. . . . It's because we don't have enough experience with [firing the guns]."[15]

Reporting Requirements

Reporting requirements are another category of reform that street-level police say can undermine their work. Police reports are a time-honored part of police work around the globe, and China is no exception. Local *paichusuo* have long maintained comprehensive records of murders, thefts, and other crimes, in addition to keeping archives of residential information under the household registration system. In the early days of the reform era, officers hand-wrote detailed crime reports that logged events and statements of involved parties, but changes in technology and concerns over idiosyncratic reporting styles helped drive a push toward computerization and standardization.[16] Since the 1990s, stations have increased the level of detail provided in reports, and digitization has made it much easier to transfer that information to the higher levels. But in order to understand the content and nature of reporting requirements, we must look beyond the major police reforms such as the Police Law, which typically include only vague language about the necessity of reporting.[17]

More details about the specific nature of reporting requirements can be gleaned from talking to officers and reading police handbooks. These sources reveal that the ministry has devised an extensive reporting system designed to keep the upper levels apprised of how crimes are handled by the local level. Under current practices, officers say all visits and calls to the station must record detailed information about the nature of the call or request, the attending officers, and the eventual resolution.[18] The ministry also requires semiannual summary reports that log station activities.[19] For politically sensitive issues, such as terrorism or dissident tracking, reporting requirements are stricter.[20] All these regulations are in addition to the routine collection of crime data, and most of that information is digitized and search enabled.

At face value, there is nothing particularly egregious about reporting requirements designed to keep upper levels apprised of what happens at the station level. Yet interviews with officers in every research site uncovered systematic problems that center on a lack of available time to meet the requirements *and* do the actual work that needs to be done for the station. Officers say they are not opposed to report filing per se, but they resent the current level of time commitment as well as the stipulation that they must file a report for every single call, even if the content of the call has nothing to do with police responsibilities. The higher up an officer moves, the more time he or she is likely to spend filing such reports, but officers at all levels complain that reporting requirements waste valuable time better spent trying to solve cases or talking to residents while out on a call.[21] One local officer was blunt: "We are not helping people. . . . We are just filling out reports."[22] Frontline officers also bemoan the fact that reports have to be filed for all calls to the station, even if the call is outside the scope of traditional police duties. One officer complained that he was often summoned out at all hours to resolve disputes between neighbors when he worked at the county *paichusuo*, and another confirmed that he wasted time responding to calls that had nothing to do with police work, simply because the reporting requirements dictated it so.[23] "It is really funny," he explained. "People call about lost dogs, and we have to go out. . . . One time someone called about a lost QQ number [a social media website], and we had to file a report."

Accuracy of these reports is also an issue. One officer admitted, "Most of what we write is fake."[24] Although other interviewees were not quite so forthcoming in their assessments, several acknowledged that they or their colleagues cut corners and inputted information that was not accurate. One reason for false reporting is that stations and officers face real consequences if they do not meet certain expectations about case resolution or "clearance" rates. During one interview with a district station officer, a mutual contact was present and told a story about calling 110 (China's emergency hotline) to report a break-in at her home.[25] When the local police arrived, she said they offered to replace her lock for free if she would call back and say the original call was made in error (*da cuo le*). The interviewee confirmed that some of his colleagues make deals like this because they do not want to file reports, especially for crimes they are unable to resolve. Such stories are humorous because they evoke images of officers riding around town with a sack of locks in their trunk, but they also demonstrate the lengths some cops will go to in order to get out of filing reports and keep crime statistics low. When we consider the understaffing of stations and the high workloads faced by officers, it is easy to understand how officers are incentivized to falsify reports or find creative ways to avoid filing them in the first place. Such practices help no one and do little to keep the upper levels accurately apprised of ground-level issues.

Supervision

The story of fixing the lock brings up another reform issue that officers say plagues their work life: supervision. As with reporting requirements, bureaucratic supervision is a routine part of policing that plays a major role in China, not least because of the types of stories recounted thus far. But unlike reporting requirements, internal police supervision methods are painstakingly codified at the highest levels and involve more actors than other reforms. Article 6 of the 1995 Police Law outlines supervision over law enforcement, noting that public security officials must establish a supervisory system that ensures implementation of laws at the local level and checks compliance.[26] Subsequent reform regulations presented in documents such as the Public Security Organ Inspection Regulations and the Public Security, Police and Law Enforcement Responsibility and Accountability Provisions provide even greater levels of detail.[27] In *Police Reform in China*, Kam Wong writes that this heavy emphasis on supervision is guided by an overarching expectation that "police should be professional and subject to both internal discipline and external supervision" (Wong 2011, 12). One local police supervisor echoed this sentiment, explaining that his job is only one part of the oversight mechanisms in place at his station.[28] In addition to internal supervision, he explained, local police are also monitored by representatives from the ministry, journalists, and the public.

Within the bureaucracy, checkpoints have been created at all levels. Locally, designated internal supervisors at city stations and many city district stations monitor police behavior and compliance. The supervisor referenced above works at a city district station and went on to explain that his job focuses on supervision implementation (*zhixing jiandu*) by looking at internal practice coherence with laws on the books.[29] Supervision of the local levels is also carried out by higher-ups in the ministry at both the provincial and central levels. The ministry has internal officers conducting this work full time, as well as officers dealing in external affairs who may be sent out on missions to check compliance for particular cases or issues.[30] Provincial-level officials most commonly conduct such missions, but when higher-profile issues are at stake, central government officials are also dispatched to check compliance.[31]

When possible, the ministry will bypass station leaders because ministry officials (perhaps rightly) do not fully trust reports originating at the local level.[32] Sometimes this entails conducting unannounced inspections, and sometimes it means circumventing local actors altogether by establishing direct lines to the people.[33] Returning once again to the story of fixing the lock: The officer on duty was likely spurred to action because the caller had dialed 110, a national hotline that MPS supervisors monitor. Had she called the local station number, the officer would have had more discretion and might not have needed to file a report (or fix the lock). Beyond using 110 as a way to monitor and control what happens on the local level, the ministry has also established hotlines for city and rural residents with complaints about local problems. These hotlines are managed by the MPS and provide an avenue for ministry officials and aggrieved individuals to get around local government agents who might be unwilling to address their grievances. One ministry official praised the hotlines, saying, "Supervision of the lower levels remains a problem, but the hotlines are very helpful. . . . In the past, our main way of getting information from the local level was to send a team down or read the news."[34] Others agree, explaining that hotlines are a step in the right direction for exposing police misconduct that might otherwise go unreported.[35]

In China, local police objections to supervision are many, and they are not alone. Police everywhere are wary of supervision, partly because frontline policing often requires split-second decisions or working in difficult situations under multiple constraints. This is perhaps one reason why police in many societies have adopted a strong culture of "protecting their own," despite the fact that such defenses can kick up public fury.[36] Even body cameras—the closest thing to a firsthand witness, aside from video surveillance footage—receive mixed reviews from officers and have been criticized by police who say they encourage officers to reduce the use of necessary force (Smykla et al. 2016), often fail to increase the accuracy of incident reports, and do not improve job performance or safety for officers (Katz et al. 2014). More generally, police scholars note that officer resistance to police reform is rooted in both rational and emotional responses to change that disrupt officer routines and thus must be implemented with care by supervisors (More and Miller 2015).

In the Chinese case, there are multiple reasons for officers to dislike supervision, although not all of them are relevant to this study. Some officers invariably do not like current practices of supervision because they make shirking or graft more difficult. Others dislike the uneven implementation of supervision. Certain practices may be commonplace in a station but technically out of bounds, for example, and officers are subject to getting burned if inspectors show up unannounced.[37] One officer recounted the story of a colleague who was fired after a surprise inspection from the ministry. The ministry team was on-site for an unrelated matter, but the officer was caught in the office, sleeping off an alcohol-infused lunch such as is commonplace and even expected for police around the country but prohibited under the "Five Prohibitions" campaign that Minister of

Public Security Zhou Yongkang launched in 2003. These are legitimate frontline issues that the ministry would like to control.

But not all supervision is good for ground-level operations. Another officer explained that checks from the ministry can "sometimes make problems worse" because officials enforce strict rule compliance but do not provide additional resources to help local stations cope.[38] Giving the example of raids, the officer explained that, prior to provincial ministry intervention, the police in his city had leaked information about the approximate timing of drug inspections to local establishment owners (usually KTV clubs). This practice kept police from bagging high-level drug suppliers but allowed them to prosecute lower-level users and maintain a working relationship with the KTV proprietors. The provincial ministry, frustrated that local stations were not following the letter of the law, finally began conducting its own inspections, which local police said only served to push the drug users underground where they could no longer be monitored. Such a practice of not listening to local-level needs when carrying out supervisory practices or crafting reforms can have far-reaching effects for law enforcement on the ground.

Consequences for Police Effectiveness

Looking at the practices that have emerged from these three categories of reform, we see how ministerial efforts to centralize and promote rule by law can nominally achieve state objectives but simultaneously make ground-level operations more challenging. In limiting the use of force by removing guns from patrol, ministry officials have likely reduced fatal conflicts between police and society, and, in the words of one senior station leader, taught officers how to speak using the law instead of their gun ("Buneng yong qiang shuohua"—You cannot use a gun to speak).[39] The practice also helped minimize the risk of firearms falling into the wrong hands, a legitimate concern, given the penchant of some officers to drink after (or during) work hours. The wife of one interviewee recalled her relief when the rules on gun use changed, while her husband chuckled in acknowledgment. "He's always getting drunk," she said. "He can barely walk home. I was afraid he would lose his gun or [accidently] hurt himself."[40] Moreover, with the 2014 easing of restrictions have come controversies surrounding police use of the newly acquired guns, indicating that the ministry may be right to approach the rollback of gun restrictions cautiously, especially since there still appears to be a long way to go in terms of adequate training.[41] But grassroots patrol officers I spoke with say the inability to carry a firearm sometimes puts them at risk of physical harm—as the Hebei patrol officer's scarred face can attest—and may reduce the willingness of certain members of the public to follow their orders. Other sources confirm that the restrictions make it more difficult to stop crime (F. Cai 2015, 35).

Reporting requirements and supervisory practices are even more problematic. These reforms similarly achieve ministry goals of centralization by providing access to accounts of local police activities, should higher-ups have both the will and manpower to look at the reports. But because current reporting rules dictate that essentially everything be reported—even calls about trivial matters like lost passwords that frontline police know should be ignored—officers are required to file reports that are of little consequence.[42] This burden is further exacerbated by the fact that frontline resources are stretched thin by limited manpower numbers, forcing police to work quickly as they try to move on to the next case. If the officer who said that much of what he and his colleagues write is false is to be believed—and under the circumstances his account is certainly plausible—then the absurdity of current reporting practices is thrown into relief: stringent requirements are instituted to keep the center apprised of ground-level activities, but the information transmitted is often inaccurate. Moreover, the burden such requirements impose on street-level police only serves to further limit their resources—in this case their time—to respond.

This raises issues of unintended consequences and the limitations of reform, themes that run deep in this subcategory of reforms that undermine. The effects are particularly apparent with regard to supervision. One ministry official freely acknowledged this, explaining that supervision at the top levels was well developed, but messy at the lower levels (*youdianer luan*).[43] In the case of the emergency hotline 110, local police have come up with methods to circumvent reporting requirements that are far less complicated than fixing locks for individual callers. Visitors to China may have noticed signs on the street like the one in figure 10. These are not just friendly reminders about public safety; they also carry important information about the local station's phone number. When residents call this number instead of 110, calls are answered more quickly and the station is not held to the same reporting standards.[44] This can be very useful to officers who are looking to lighten their workload and/or station leaders who are hoping to keep clearance rates high by allowing them to ignore certain calls without having to create a record.[45] Interestingly, the practice has been widely adopted across the country, demonstrating the need for a work-around solution to the ministry's reporting policies. Even the direct hotlines to the ministry for complaints have their own limitations. The same officials who touted the benefits of the hotlines were also quick to point out the flaws. Aggrieved individuals may not know about the hotlines or avoid them for other reasons, such as the belief that a phone call will do little to resolve their problem.[46]

FIGURE 10. Public security notice in Beijing featuring local station phone numbers. Author's photo, 2012.

Reforms That Fall Short

Local officers also raise grievances about reforms they say do not go far enough in helping police manage ground-level problems. Unlike reforms that undermine, policies in this category are seen by street-level cops mostly as steps in the right direction, but many police are dissatisfied with current levels of implementation by the ministry. At the heart of these issues are complaints about training. Nearly all the officers I spoke with said current training programs are woefully disconnected from the reality of their lives on the ground, even though the ministry has been quite active in increasing training requirements. Relatedly, changes in recruiting—a cornerstone of Chinese police reform—remain an issue that local police and leaders say needs attention in order to improve frontline police effectiveness. Additionally, some officers say a lack of detail in procedural rules can leave the front lines struggling and encourage shirking, although where an officer stands on this issue largely depends on personal preference. All three reform categories stem from broader ministry objectives to promote rule by law and professionalization of the force, but the unevenness of their implementation demonstrates both the limitations to the ministry's capabilities and the stickiness of institutional change and cultural norms.

Training

Training has always been a key part of policing in the reform era, but the ministry's move toward rule by law in the latter half of the reform period has placed even greater emphasis on police training. Article 28 of the Police Law states that police must be trained in police schools or academies and pass related examinations.[47] The law also dictates education and training in political ideology, the legal system, and police work (*jingcha yewu*) and highlights the importance of building facilities for training. With regard to training infrastructure, some programs are carried out centrally in Beijing, but most training occurs at the local police schools scattered throughout the provinces. These institutions operate at the university, high school, and even middle school levels and vary in quality.

While the topic of problematic training rarely surfaces in policing journals, most officers I spoke with were dissatisfied with current training programs, and many spoke about the issue in great detail. It is easy to see why tensions emerge when one considers the order in which the Police Law presents the three emphases (political ideology, the legal system, and police work). From the standpoint of the Communist Party and the Ministry of Public Security, it makes sense to prioritize ideology and adherence to law, but for officers on the ground, this ordering has little practical value.[48] One particularly "well-trained" interviewee attended the police academy in his provincial capital, participates in annual training programs, and spent two years in Beijing at the People's Public Security University, a rare opportunity for most frontline officers.[49] But he said that none of this training was useful. "You don't learn anything," he explained. "Ninety-five percent is just political thinking . . . not really any practical examples you can use." Another officer described the (mostly political) training that he has to go through every year as a chance to rest (*xiuxi*) and catch up on sleep.[50]

So much emphasis on ideology leaves little room for practical instruction, and even when it is offered, the training that officers receive may not be consistent or available to everyone in the station. As one younger district station officer explained, "We are supposed to have training twice a year, but I haven't been in two or three years. Sometimes [during training] we just leave to go eat lunch, and they tell us to study on our own. . . . It's a complete waste of time."[51] Training can also be restricted to certain types of officers, as it was for the older policeman quoted in chapter 2 who complained that most of his station's training programs are reserved for younger officers and focus on how to use new technologies.[52] Given these trends, it is easy to see why officers say training does little to improve police response on the ground.

Recruitment Standards

Another category of reform related to professionalization that police officers say does not go far enough or in quite the right direction is the implementation of recruitment standards. Here again, the real ground-level problems with recruitment standards are not often raised in policing journals because they run counter to ministerial goals by highlighting the persistence of *guanxi*; it is therefore essential to talk to frontline officers to see how the implementation of new standards plays out on the ground. The ministry began the professionalization process by introducing new rules for recruitment in the 1990s. Once again, the 1995 Police Law was the first major codification of this agenda, and subsequent reforms honed these measures, with even the most recent 2015 reform agenda calling for improvements to recruitment and training mechanisms.[53] Changes in recruitment have gradually overhauled police force demographics by replacing the old guard of officers who have military experience but little or no formal education with younger, more educated officers. Using entrance exams, educational requirements, and a formal interview process, these efforts follow the logic that policing problems on the ground such as corruption and poor law enforcement can be improved by bringing in smarter and better-educated officers, though this line of thinking has long been questioned by criminologists (Smith 1978; Carlan 1999).

Despite higher standards and the hardships of life on the front lines, the recruiting of officers is not a major problem in China. As with many other professions, officers join the police force for a variety of reasons, many of which have little to do with quality of life. Potential recruits may seek a spot on the force because their father, uncle, brother, or another influential figure in their life was an officer. Others say they joined because they admired police officers when they were children, wanted to wear a uniform, or hoped to shoot a gun.[54] Many see it as an entry point into the Chinese civil service and a chance to secure their "iron rice bowl."[55] Competition to join the force is perhaps fiercer than ever before, and even a degree from a local police school no longer guarantees a spot on the force. Many officers labor for years in far-flung county stations, often under contracts that must be renewed annually, while they wait to secure coveted city station positions.[56]

Yet no one seems happy about the quality of existing officers or the new recruits. A common complaint about police officers *among* police officers is that too many have poor "quality" (*suzhi*).[57] Frontline officers also voice this concern about their colleagues.[58] The assistant station chief quoted earlier said that the new standards have simply replaced old employment problems with new ones, noting that the officers born after the 1980s may be more educated but are difficult to manage because they have been coddled, "lack experience . . . [and] are not willing to do many types of work" that they see as beneath them.[59]

There are different ideas regarding what should be done to improve recruitment. One strategy employed by station leaders is to attract more applicants, and some well-heeled stations have gone so far as to create movie-style posters in order to drum up interest.[60] But interviews with frontline officers indicate changes also need to target institutionally entrenched hiring practices. In one area of Hebei, for example, potential recruits are still expected to pay money in order to secure a coveted slot at one of the district city stations. "Passing the exam is not enough," said one officer who was hoping to land just such a position.[61] "You have to pay money." Further complicating matters, the officer went on to explain that amounts are not fixed; positions are awarded to whoever pays the most, and even having a family member on the force does not exempt one from making a payment, though it might mean the applicant can get away with paying less. Research on stations in Central China also found that officers were unofficially required to buy promotions (P. Wang 2017). Other interviewees also voiced concerns about the continued importance of social connections (*guanxi*). *Guanxi* is particularly useful during the interview process, and well-connected persons are more likely to be hired. Such preferential practices are problematic because the most qualified individuals may not be getting hired. Moreover, it is highly likely that *guanxi* hiring increases the number of office officers in stations, which further impairs frontline response.

Procedural Rules

Finally, some officers argue that ground-level procedural rules need more attention from reformers.[62] In China, specific rules and regulations develop out of laws set by the National People's Congress or from policy statements made by top government officials. Because these laws and policy statements are usually quite general, ministry officials use them as the basis for creating more specific procedural rules that frontline police then follow.[63] For example, legal articles in the Criminal Procedure Law dictate general ground-level policing practices that the ministry then uses to develop detailed handbooks that hammer out procedures for practical implementation.[64] One such handbook based on the new Criminal Procedure Law is 693 pages long (Sun and Li 2012).

But some say these procedures do not provide enough detail about how to actually manage the real-life criminal activities street-level police encounter on a daily basis. "Officer Xiao" described the extent of the problem over hot pot one night.[65] "There are not enough rules for how to respond in many situations," he said. "It isn't well developed like it is in America." When I asked him to explain, he told a story about going to bust up a local hair salon / brothel: "The boss starts running out of the door as soon as I pulled up, so I went running after him," he said. "I ran for a long time until I finally caught up with him. And when I got him back to the station, my coworkers just laughed at me because I was so sweaty and could barely breathe. . . . It was also summer, and I'm a little overweight. . . . They would have just let the boss go because there isn't any rule about what to do when suspects run." Xiao told the story to make everyone at the table laugh, but he went on to explain that the lack of specific procedures causes real problems for public order:

> Officers in our city won't go after underground blood traders, even though it's a big problem for public health and order. There are many of them in the city, working out in the open, and we ought to be doing something about it. . . . But there is no protocol for this, so the police just ignore it. . . . They also ignore it because they can't get the people to admit that they're doing anything wrong. In China, this is what makes an easy case. If [the perpetrators] don't admit guilt, then the officers have to go out and collect evidence. . . . Most police officers have no idea how to do that and very little desire to figure it out. Without more specific protocols, it's easier just to leave these things alone.

Such complaints about lack of protocols shed additional light on the case of Xiao Hu from the introduction. Even after the incident blew up on social media, the officers returned to work and never faced disciplinary action. A follow-up investigation found that the two police officers were "not involved in the incident" and had broken no rules, which is—given the state of procedural development—technically true.[66] In yet another striking case, four people beat a man to death over a traffic dispute immediately outside a police office in Jiangsu. Upon investigation, the officers inside the office said it occurred outside the partition of their waiting area, and they were thus unaware of the event, even though there was video footage, along with eyewitness reports of bystanders attempting to contact the officers inside to stop the attack.[67] Such cases of police inaction, while extreme, are exactly the kinds of incidents that officers who call for better procedural rules and more training say could be prevented by more carefully devised and implemented reforms.

Consequences for Police Effectiveness

As accounts of police inaction in the face of real crime indicate, police effectiveness is compromised when policies fall short and officers do not know how to respond. With reforms in this category, officers would like to see more action on the part of the ministry to develop existing policies, but because of conflicting ministerial priorities or simply a lack of capacity, ground-level needs are not being met. Training is one area in which the ministry ought to be able to make a difference. Yet in interview after interview, officers say current training programs mostly waste their time. One ministry official noted that there is not a lot of funding for training, but that fails to explain the prioritization of political ideology in the training programs that do exist.[68] Based on reports from officers, it appears that the ministry's continued emphasis on ideology has rendered training an insignificant part of police life, squandering what could be a potentially invaluable tool to improve the quality of policing on the ground.

The implications for frontline operations stretch far. Without proper training and without the right protocols to guide them, many local police are underprepared to do the job they are called on to do, and some take the easy way out. Another officer echoed the concerns of Officer Xiao above: "We have so much work to do, so there is no time to go out and learn new things. We don't have time for forensics. Even if we do have the opportunity to learn new things, we have little time to apply the knowledge and even less money to pay for it. . . . We do training once a year when new policies come out, but it isn't much." The officer went on to explain how professionalization reforms prioritizing a college degree compound the issue of insufficient training. "It's a big issue now because many of the new police are coming in with different majors from college. They have a college degree, but no police experience. They only participate in a three- or four-month training program, [compared to] people from the police schools [*jingxiao*] who had years of training. It's a big difference. Some overcome it with natural ability, but many don't."[69]

Other issues related to recruitment are similarly problematic. It is difficult to say how prevalent the reliance on *guanxi* and the use of cash payments to buy positions are across the country, but at least one officer at almost every field site reported that such practices occur in the station's area. Moreover, the importance of *guanxi* and the buying of positions are by no means exclusive to the police. Such practices are deeply rooted in the institutional culture of the Chinese bureaucracy. From an outsider's perspective, the ministry appears to have made progress in professionalizing the new recruits, and as older officers continue to retire, it should be easier for the ministry to mold the current force more carefully in its desired image. Properly executed reforms and better supervision could rectify the issues street-level police raise about recruitment, but ultimately, complaints about the character problems of officers may be as much related to the way the institution shapes them after they arrive as to the quality of new recruits.

Successful Reforms

Amid a sea of dissatisfaction about everything from gun usage to poor training are once again the largely positive assessments of stability maintenance policies. Ground-level police, for the most part, do not complain about *weiwen* reform and instead indicate that the ministry is doing several things right. However, it is important to note that the findings about police reform and *weiwen* are restricted to locales that do not see extraordinary levels of social unrest. Local police in areas marred by contention, particularly those in Xinjiang and Tibet, may very well view the ministry's reforms differently, and more research is needed to understand those effects.

Frontline security agents—from local police to PAP officers—conduct much of the stability maintenance work in China, and police reform and procedures reflect that. Though the 1995 Police Law technically covered mass incidents as a matter of course, the issue did not consume the lion's share of attention until around 2006 when the "Resolution on Building a Harmonious Society" was released by the Sixth Plenum of the National Party Congress. Since that time, national laws—such as the 2009 People's Armed Police Law that formally charged the PAP with managing rebellions, riots, and terrorist acts—have been updated to codify the management of social unrest, and handbooks for police and other law enforcement agents have been issued, in addition to updates to criminal code handbooks.[70] Further reflecting the importance of the issue, scholars and practitioners in China are engaged in a robust, high-level discussion of stability maintenance in all the major policing and legal journals. Between 2005 and 2019, these outlets published thousands of articles on the issue of mass incidents, covering topics such as prevention (P. Li 2008), disposal (X. Liu 2005), public relations response (Ye, Xiao, and Liu 2006), and even tips for using police dogs (Qin and Luo 2015), to name a few.

Such attention has benefits. In contrast to the problems detailed in the previous section on procedural rules, protocols for handling social unrest are clearly developed, and police say they know what to do in most cases. Often the first responders for street demonstrations are traffic police, who have been trained to clear the street quickly. "We don't let them block the streets," said one traffic police supervisor.[71] Another officer said that while keeping traffic clear is the top priority, officers from his station may be called out for any public demonstration, large or small.[72] "People often go to public squares because they are unhappy [about land expropriation or medical malpractice]," explained the detective. "They will sit down with a banner and try to get people's attention. Sometimes they have a weapon and threaten to kill themselves. . . . We police have to deal with them because they are dangerous [threats] to public security." By chance, I observed one such event on a side street in Beijing in 2012. A man with what appeared to be a head wound unfurled a white banner and stood outside an apartment complex with a woman for perhaps ten to fifteen minutes. During that time, an individual came out to argue with the man, and a few minutes later a patrol car from the local *paichusuo* pulled up to take the protester away, demonstrating how quickly the police can respond to such issues, especially in a city such as Beijing.

In these situations, protocols have been refined and implemented for many years, even if the details are not made public. One interviewee explained that the most recent set of regulations is very well developed and laid out in a classified handbook that is approximately a thousand pages long.[73] Although I was unable to get a copy of this handbook, interviews reveal a number of practices and priorities. Protesters blocking traffic are high priority, and the goal is to get them off the streets as quickly as possible, as the examples above illustrate. Protesters in public squares are also problematic. Often traffic police or patrol officers are the first responders in situations like these, but once dissidents have been identified, there are multiple procedures in place for handling the various situations that might arise.

Once the protesters have been taken to the station, the process is also well defined. Officers, station leaders, and local officials may be called in to negotiate with protesters, depending on the case.[74] One officer explained that there are two types of protesters—reasonable ones (*heli*) with legitimate complaints, and unreasonable ones (*bu heli*) who just want to cause trouble (*naoshi*)—and they have to deal with both types.[75] When it gets to this point, petitioners are often known to people in the system, making it easier for police to decide which office to call. One policeman explained that public protest is often a last resort: "The people go to courts or other government departments, but they can't get justice, so they turn to *shangfang*, which has a long history in China."[76] Sometimes petitioners go directly to the police station. This happens when protesters have already failed to make contact with the appropriate department because they "do not know where to go . . . the staff of the department did not know how to help them . . . or the guards at the gate [of the appropriate department] won't let them in."[77] In these cases, the standard procedure for police is to help the petitioners make contact with the relevant people at the necessary departments. After that, the case is usually out of their hands.

What of large-scale or violent protests? By outlining the specific procedures for protest management, we see clearly how stability maintenance work is divided. In addition to involvement from local government officials, labor is split among ground-level police agents. There are big differences between the *shangfang* cases that local police handle and the mass incidents that develop into riots or demonstrations and are sometimes designated as terrorist events. The latter two are typically managed by the People's Armed Police, because local police are unarmed and more generally not equipped to handle such incidents. Depending on the city, one PAP officer explained, the PAP may also be brought in for small demonstrations if the protesters "have a conflict with another group . . . have become violent . . . [or if] local police do not have enough people to manage the problem. . . . We help the local police because they don't have any sort of weapons or the proper attire to deal with social unrest."[78] Thanks to this division of labor, it is no wonder that the local police report satisfaction with stability maintenance activities or that the regime is able to manage *weiwen* more effectively than other areas of policing.

How does the PAP operate? When a team is dispatched, the response is typically swift. PAP forces are strategically placed throughout the country and stand on call to manage incidents of unrest. One team leader described the process of recruitment: "We only take the best. The testing process is very difficult. . . . We do a job search every two years, and this year we did a search and received twenty thousand applications, which we narrowed down to five hundred before doing an interview. After the interview, [the recruits] were put through a physical strength test and then a health screening to make sure they had no problems. We also checked their background to make sure they have never had any legal cases. In the end, we only accepted 170 or so new recruits."[79] Once on the force, the officers train for protests. The leader went on to explain that his team spends most of its time preparing for big events, which includes working out, running laps, and participating in training exercises or competing in competitions with teams from other cities. With this level of physical training it is unsurprising that PAP officers also report satisfaction with stability maintenance work.

Procedures for calling in the PAP are clear. Prior to 2009, local government leaders were permitted to call in the PAP directly, but the People's Armed Police Law checked that right, possibly because central leaders were concerned that skittish local governments were too quick to make the call and unnecessarily escalated conflicts with protesters.[80] After 2009, official consent was required at the ministerial level to authorize the deployments. Recent reforms, with Xi Jinping's consolidation of military and paramilitary power (Scoggins 2018), have further changed the command structure of the PAP. Effective as of January 1, 2018, control of the PAP is no longer shared jointly between the military and the MPS, disrupting a long-standing division of power between the two agencies that began in the wake of the Tiananmen Square crisis and was cemented with the 2009 People's Armed Police Law (M. S. Tanner 2014). Local leaders must now call PLA officials to authorize the PAP's deployment, cutting the ministry out of the decision altogether. One provincial ministry official believes the change may streamline the process. "The changes will actually make things less complicated. In the past, local governments were too quick to call in the *wujing* [PAP], and the process was a bit of a mess," the official explained.[81] "Basically, the local government would get in trouble and have to contact the provinces. They could go through the office of the provincial governor or the party chairman in order to have the head of the provincial public security bureau authorize the PAP. Then that office had to call the *wujing* directly. . . . With the new change, they just have to contact the PLA and *wujing* without having to go through the other channels."

Results for Police Effectiveness

Unlike the reforms highlighted in the previous sections that deal with everyday policing, the practices and policies in place to deal with social unrest are largely successful. Frontline police across research sites report that protocols for social unrest are effective because police mostly know what to do and have the proper resources they need to redirect or deal with protesters. Whether frontline police are clearing streets quickly, bringing dissatisfied people to another government department, jailing dissidents, or calling the PAP to handle a situation that has spiraled out of control, there are clear procedures and resources to manage different types of social unrest.

While it might be easy to dismiss the reported success of stability maintenance as a mere product of the fact that protest control is less complicated or more easily contained than the myriad types of everyday crimes with which officers must deal, it is important to remember how much time, effort, and government departments have been devoted to the issue in China and how potentially thorny the issue of social unrest is for the regime. By design, central government directives and incentive structures are highly effective at controlling this explosive problem. Levels of dissent can vary dramatically—from a single protester holding up a handmade banner in a public square to more-organized protest events that attract tens of thousands—and the agents of the state must handle each type with speed and accuracy, knowing what protocol works best for which type of incident and calling in the most repressive forces neither too late nor too soon. Such a process is complicated, and mistakes have certainly been made; but through constant tweaking of procedures, the police bureaucracy has gotten better at response, allowing it—thus far—to prevent the spread of a regime destabilizing social movement.

Impacts and Changes under Xi

Assessments of legal and ministerial reforms reveal dissatisfaction in many areas that affect daily police work. Restrictions on the use of force have increased the vulnerability of officers on the streets, while reporting requirements and related supervisory procedures have decreased the amount of time they have to spend on cases while simultaneously failing to provide the ministry with accurate information about ground-level operations. Complaints of frontline police further reveal the one-sided nature of central-local relations in the police bureaucracy. Their reports suggest that local police and station leaders are treated more as problems to be tamed than partners in law enforcement on the ground. Supervision, for example, gets carried out in ways that aim to control the local police, passing expectations down and transmitting information about performance back up, but it is not a two-way street for frontline police. No local officer with whom I spoke ever dared or bothered to pass suggestions back up the chain of command, with one officer bluntly stating that his leaders "wouldn't want to listen" (*bu yao ting*).[82] Moreover, strict enforcement of procedures like the requirement of unannounced drug raids rightly or wrongly prevents local officers from collaborating with the ministry to find work-around solutions that could preserve some of the benefits of existing practices. One officer remarked that this is just not the way the top-down system works.[83]

Complaints about insufficient reforms also reveal deficiencies in the system. The lack of practical training for frontline officers is truly surprising, given the tangible benefits that such programs could provide to enforcement practices. Here, it appears that a myopic focus on political ideology permeates all types of training programs, even and perhaps especially at the university level.[84] When one considers this lack of training in combination with procedural deficiencies, it is easy to see why some officers say reforms do not go far enough. Moreover, the examples officers give of police choosing not to run after criminals or of looking the other way when they see activities that they do not know how to build cases around are disturbing because they raise questions about the willingness and ability of police to ensure public order. They also stand in stark contrast to frontline police accounts of reforms related to protest.

The positive assessments that local officers give of protest control are equally telling. In this area of police work, the ministry appears to have overcome problems of training and procedural ambiguity to create a system that officers say works fairly well from their standpoint. In some ways this is unsurprising, given the attention that stability maintenance gets from all levels of government. Yet it is interesting because it indicates that effective reform policies can and are being devised and implemented. This begs the question of why the ministry is not developing similar reform policies in other areas of crime management, which are arguably just as important for maintaining public order as protest control and far more likely to affect the average person.

This has not been an exhaustive discussion of police reform in China. Such endeavors fill entire volumes (Wong 2009, 2011) that can be consulted for those who wish to know more about how the organization has changed over time. This chapter instead provides an overview of the reform issues that police officers themselves talk about most often and that matter most for police response on the ground. The stark contrasts in how police rate reforms with regard to everyday policing on the one hand and stability maintenance on the other reveal differences between the two, and frontline officers' stories illustrate the specific ways in which management of everyday crime takes a backseat to the policing of protest.

But what of the more recent reforms enacted under President Xi Jinping? In addition to the changes to PAP control, the ministry announced a series of reform initiatives in February 2015 that included the improvements for officer salaries discussed in chapter 2.[85] These reforms are ambitious—seven primary tasks and more than one hundred measures were rolled out in a stated effort to create a more effective force and win public approval—but the timing, content, and practical execution thus far of the reforms tell us much about the priorities of the Xi administration and its ability to enact meaningful change. With the exception of increases in officer salaries, the reforms largely focus on continued improvements in the area of stability maintenance or on Xi's further consolidation of power.

A major focus of the 2015 reforms is to improve national security work, which includes increases in street surveillance. Such efforts are not new; local and national databases have long given officers and anyone else with access the ability to track hotel stays, train and air travel, internet café usage, and other activities requiring an identification card.[86] But during Xi's tenure, recent advances in surveillance technology have allowed police to improve the national database by linking street surveillance camera footage and facial recognition technologies, giving police in China unprecedented capabilities for tracking dissidents and other persons of interest.[87] While some of this surveillance technology may be dual use by enabling street-level police to use CCTV footage to collect evidence for everyday policing cases, it also increases the amount of time and resources that stations must devote to stability maintenance work. For an overworked and understaffed force that often laments the lack of practical training, such capabilities are likely to make the job of frontline police even more difficult.

Other reforms introduced in 2015 indicate that policing under Xi will become increasingly politicized. Given Xi's previous reputation for being tough on corruption, it is perhaps unsurprising that anticorruption campaigns in the public security bureau have been a priority. Yet sources in the ministry say the real efforts have been focused almost exclusively at the higher levels and call for no concrete efforts to stamp out local police misconduct.[88] Soon after taking office, Xi removed Politburo Standing Committee member and former head of the MPS Zhou Yongkang, expelling him from the party and arresting him on charges of corruption. Xi then proceeded to take down Zhou's former associates at the MPS, including committee member and vice minister of public security Li Dongsheng. It has even been said that Meng Hongwei, the former president of Interpol, was removed because of ties to Zhou, although Meng's family disputes this claim.[89] As Zhou's associates were removed from the MPS, Xi also began stacking the organization with long-term political allies, including promoting Deng Weiping, an old associate from Xi's days in Fujian Province, to anti-graft chief.[90] It thus appears that the anticorruption efforts, despite official rhetoric, have less to do with improving the organization than amassing political power.

The changes to the PAP's command structure may have similar motivations. As chairman of the Central Military Commission, Xi has supreme command over all the armed forces, including the PAP. "Moving the PAP limits the power of the provinces," explained one official.[91] "Take Chongqing as an example. Under the old structure, the head of Chongqing would have access to an armed force without any higher-level approval. This [change] helps consolidate central government power." Such a change by Xi in advance of his February announcement on the elimination of term limits was thus smart planning, because it diminished the power of the provinces as well as Li Keqiang's State Council, which controls the MPS. From the standpoint of the police bureaucracy, the move also indicates a political focus on reforms going forward—especially when viewed in coordination with the anticorruption efforts—rather than detailed attention to alleviation of the type of frontline issues and concerns that currently plague the bureaucracy.

4
CONTROLLING THE LOCAL POLICE

As the issues with oversight and reform suggest, China's Ministry of Public Security faces challenges to controlling frontline police. Many aspects of the Chinese police bureaucracy are centralized, and the MPS is charged with setting all police policies and overseeing ground-level implementation.[1] Ostensibly, this means the ministry has a firm command over all frontline policing practices, but in reality, control over the ground level is complicated. In many areas of policing, the everyday activities of the local police are ignored by the ministry, but at other times, local governments get involved. One officer assessed the tensions in this way: "The center wants to manage the local police, but this is very difficult. . . . The truth is that we police must also follow the local government."[2] When exercised, the influence of those government forces can be powerful. So powerful, in fact, that street-level police say they have "two bosses" (*liangge laoban*) who sometimes disagree. How and when upper-level officials exert control affects ground-level response and can tell us much about how coercive capacity in China operates. Ground-level accounts are thus critical for understanding how the ministry and other government entities influence local policing and what that means for differences in response to protest and other types of crime. Interviews reveal variation in the way the ministry controls different types of crime, which in turn shapes the nature of response on the ground in systematic ways. The result is that dissident control and coercive response to some types of crimes, such as protest, end up being very strong, while response to other, everyday crimes is weak.

Variation in levels of control is visible only when we look at a variety of policing functions on the ground. This chapter assesses police reports about capacity to respond to different types of crime, and in the process invokes a broader definition of coercive capacity than we typically see in the literature on authoritarian states (Bellin 2004; Way and Levitsky 2006; Levitsky and Way 2012). Discussions of coercive capacity typically focus on protest control and political policing, primarily because preventing regime-destabilizing protests is essential for state survival. But protests are relatively rare events, and frontline police actually spend most of their time trying to manage and prevent ordinary criminal activity; thinking more broadly about coercive capacity allows us to see issues with the state that we might otherwise miss if we were myopically focused on protest response or political policing. In the case of China, it reveals a wealth of deficiencies in everyday crime response, even as it uncovers differences in how the ministry and local governments exercise power over the local police.

Since official crime statistics are highly unreliable, it is difficult to quantify and compare police response capacity across different areas of crime. I therefore asked officers to describe their own satisfaction with the way their station managed crime, using their responses as a proxy for coercive capacity to control different types of crime.[3] While police officers' self-assessments are not infallible, and the control of crime is sometimes influenced by other state agents in addition to the police, self-assessments from police officers remain one of the best currently accessible measures. The results show a clear pattern: ministry control over protest is highly centralized and strong in terms of capacity, but control over many other types of crime is decentralized and weak. Moreover, control over a few types of crime, such as the trade of illicit substances, is complicated by local government interests. These control patterns and their outcomes showcase another dimension of policing in China and explain why it is difficult to correct the current state of failure in response to many common types of crime.

By grouping the types of control over frontline operations into three main patterns (decentralized, shared, and centralized), we can better understand why they lead to different outcomes for protest and everyday crimes. Assessing levels of centralization in this context means looking at the central law enforcement agency's—in this case, the MPS's—degree of control over local-level protocols and procedures through rule formation, oversight, and implementation.[4] For most types of crime, local police struggle to respond as best they can, given the resource and reform-related limitations they face. Under this pattern of decentralized control, both the ministry and local governments are barely involved with ground-level response beyond rule formation and superficial oversight, and the results for crime management are typically not good. For other types of cases, the ministry and local governments are more active in implementation and end up sharing control over frontline operations. When the two lock horns, local police get caught in the middle, and crime response suffers, although reports from frontline officers indicate that results of shared control are not always negative. When the interests of the two bosses align, however, a third pattern emerges. Under centralized control, rule formation, oversight, and implementation are strong, and local police can focus their energy on meeting goals set forth by the ministry because local government leaders reiterate ministry targets rather than compete with them. Conflict between local governments and the ministry eases, enabling stronger coercive capacity on the ground.

Differences in how the ministry and local governments exercise control reveal deep-seated structural issues within the Chinese bureaucracy that have emerged over time. Reports that Public Security Bureau officials share power with local forces in China will come as no surprise to scholars of the Chinese state. The reality of shared power formed the foundation of the fragmented authoritarian literature in the 1990s and much that has followed since, even as the government tries to limit the administrative powers of local governments.[5] The persistence, however, of shared control in the PSB is interesting because police bureaucracies in authoritarian regimes are typically more tightly managed (Bayley 1985, 64–66). The results presented here thus extend the findings of other studies on fragmentation in the Chinese bureaucracy, which traditionally focus on non-security-related entities.[6] Most interesting, however, is the degree to which control over ground-level policing in China has been ceded to the local level. This de facto decentralization in which the ministry exercises only a superficial degree of control over policing in most areas of crime management brings dire consequences for frontline response, and yet a continued focus on stability maintenance means that very little is being done about the fragmentation of control, even with the latest reform push under Xi Jinping.

Decentralized Control

Most of the day-to-day work of local officers attracts little attention from higher-ups. Handling a theft case, catching a drunk driver, responding to a traffic accident, breaking up a fight: such activities make up the bulk of the daily work for frontline police. These and other issues, from the mundane to the most serious, including violent crimes and murder—and collectively referred to here as everyday crimes—seldom attract attention from the ministry or local government officials. Instead, response to everyday crime is largely left up to local stations. While street-level police must file reports about cases and abide by the ministry's laws and procedures, oversight is limited, and the specifics, like how to deal with threats to public order not covered in the handbook, or the nitty-gritty of when to pursue certain types of investigations, are all decisions left to local police and station leaders. Upper-level control over frontline police with regard to these issues is thus superficial, because ministry and government officials are, for the most part, focused on other matters. This pattern of control is essentially a form of de facto decentralization, and it brings surprisingly few benefits to police on the ground. But unlike with full decentralization, the ministry continues to exercise control in a superficial manner, and officers say that this method of control only adds to existing pressures, further complicating their ability to do their work.

When one considers the scale of policing efforts in China, the ministry's decentralized control makes sense. The task of managing policing in China is monumental. The MPS is large in comparison to many of the other ministries, and the bureaucracy's thirty-six departments are tasked with a wide range of operational and oversight functions, many of which have little to do with frontline police forces. In interviews, police bureaucracy insiders say they lack the manpower and financial resources to influence ground-level operations to the extent they might like. "We don't have the ability to get to the grassroots," explained one provincial ministry official when asked how his office manages the lower levels.[7] "If we get to the city level, this is already not bad [*yijing bucuo*]. . . . We simply don't have the resources to go any deeper. . . . There are too many stations to monitor." This—in addition to the inability of the ministry to fund local police operations beyond infrastructure projects—is why Fu Hualing wrote that "China does not have a national police force; there is no centralised political leadership over the police" (Fu 2005, 246).

Consider the figures: The provincial Public Security Bureau in Hunan had a total staff of around two thousand in 2012 and is not exceptional (the Hubei PSB also has around two thousand total employees). Of those two thousand employees, many work in internal affairs (*neibu*) and have little to no contact with the local stations. The rest may go out to supervise local police operations.[8] To put those numbers in perspective, there are 14 prefecture-level cities and 122 county-level cities, districts, counties, and autonomous counties in Hunan. All of these have public security stations (*gonganju*) and district stations (*fenju*). Beyond those jurisdictions, the province's 1,098 towns, 1,158 townships, 98 ethnic townships, and 225 sub-districts all have local stations (*paichusuo*), making for a total of 2,715 jurisdictions under the purview of the provincial bureau. Given the limited manpower of the provincial ministry and the number of stations available for supervision, it is little surprise that management and oversight of daily operations are difficult.

Ministry officials nevertheless attempt to exercise a certain degree of control over the local levels. The ministry sets regulations and uses police reform to devise methods that will help overcome the provincial level's manpower issues, including requiring reports and managing supervisory procedures. As the last chapter demonstrated, however, the effectiveness of these methods is limited, and the quality of information that gets transmitted up is suspect. In interviews, some ministry officials recognize these limitations but say there is little to be done. One provincial ministry official said that the local police are very closed and will not tell ministry officials the truth of what happens on the ground, no matter what.[9] Another central official explained the ministry's limitations: "The most effective way [to bring local stations in line] is to send a team down from the ministry.... When that happens, the result is very good. But we don't do this often because we don't have enough men or money."[10] Thus, the ministry maintains only a semblance of centralization.

Local governments are equally unlikely to get involved in everyday police operations. Unsurprisingly, officials want to keep crime and, more importantly, crime statistics low, but it is not their job to manage frontline police response.[11] While local governments may involve themselves in certain cases, the details of frontline operations for the majority of police work are left to officers and station leaders.[12] Moreover, the ruse of low crime rates further institutionalizes the distanced relationship between police and local government officials. Police officers and stations leaders are eager to keep crime rates low and clearance rates high by underreporting, suppressing, and manipulating crime data in their areas. The police have obvious professional advancement incentives to do so, but higher levels are also in on the game. Local government leaders have strong incentives to demonstrate improvements in public safety and put pressure on police to make sure the crime rates line up. Xu Jianhua's research on crime statistics has uncovered this relationship in detail, and he quotes one officer who explains the ratcheting up of expectations: "We are under great pressure. Our upper-level department needs to see the decline of crimes and the increase of clearance rates year by year" (J. Xu 2018, 165). Xu argues that even the central government is a willing accomplice, since legitimacy for the regime is pegged on performance measures such as economic development and crime control (156). Thus, so long as the official numbers look good, there are few incentives or resources for the ministry and local governments to get involved with everyday crime control.

Sometimes, however, a particular criminal activity gets out of hand and cannot be ignored, such as a rash of bag snatchings or a spike in drug use. In such cases, local governments and the ministry may step in and temporarily break the pattern of decentralized control, although this was not a frequent occurrence in the areas where I conducted research. In such cases, the local police may be called on to enact anticrime campaigns that address a certain type of crime, or pursue other political goals.[13] Sometimes the campaign is a national one, like the "strike hard" campaigns (*yanda*) that involve multiple government agencies; but smaller campaigns are also used to address local issues, such as the motorcycle bans in Guangzhou aimed at reducing a spate of snatch and theft robberies (J. Xu 2011).[14] Such moves are an exception to the decentralized pattern of control, but they are usually short-lived and of little utility.

Effects of Decentralized Control

The largely hands-off approach adopted by the ministry and local governments in this pattern of decentralized control could, theoretically, yield big benefits for policing on the front lines in China. Autonomy of this nature is the breeding ground for the flexible sort of discretion that allows street-level bureaucrats to provide better service and assistance to citizens (Maynard-Moody and Musheno 2006). Unfortunately, officers report that this is not how frontline policing in China works. In interview after interview, police say they have neither the time nor the desire to make use of discretionary power, and they are not interested in thinking up new techniques or methods for dealing with cases. Instead of exercising street-level bureaucrat-style discretionary power, frontline police are so pressed for time and under-resourced that they are primarily just looking for ways to avoid filing reports, or trying to get an all-important confession statement from a suspect. Innovation is even more of a nonstarter. Out of over one hundred total interviews, only one officer—a provincial ministry official, no less—could recall a single method that local police had devised to help them do their jobs better.[15] In the day-to-day reality of life on the ground, it appears there is little room for such matters. One local officer explained, "We don't have time for that [new methods]. . . . We have a lot of work to do. . . . The same is true for [old and young officers]."[16]

Moreover, the techniques used by ministry officials to exercise decentralized control over the local levels can impose further burdens that ultimately hinder crime response. Prior chapters revealed frontline concerns about the time it takes to follow through on every single call to the station or file reports that local police believe have little practical value. These issues demonstrate the problems that arise out of the ministry's attempts to monitor the local level, but police say they also face difficulties in dealing with new laws that do not take into account local needs. "Police face many pressures," said local officer "Liu."[17] "We get a lot of pressure from new laws set by the central ministry... but there are big differences between the law and the local situation."

Officers also face scrutiny from a partially informed public. Officer Liu went on to explain that people often use the law or policies to pressure police over everyday crime issues.[18] "The pressure on police comes from two sides ... sometimes more. . . . First, it comes from the law. There are many new rules to deal with. Second, it comes from the people. There are many more cases than before, and the people have some knowledge of the law, but they twist it to serve whatever purpose they want. . . . This makes the pressure on police very great because we have to take care of the city or the *paichusuo* twenty-four hours a day, seven days a week. We have to answer all the calls." An assistant station chief in another city echoed these concerns, citing the rise of rights consciousness among residents in his jurisdiction. He explained, "In the 1990s no one knew they had rights. Now everyone knows, and they are quick to talk about rights if they think we are not doing something properly. . . . The demands [*yaoqiu*] from the public are very high... but they often don't know what they're talking about. . . . Now we have to manage them while we are trying to do our work at the same time."[19] With little meaningful communication between the ministry and the local levels, officers have no way to address concerns about how to apply laws and are instead left to deal with public expectations and do their jobs as best they can.

With no room to innovate and with decentralized control from the ministry only adding to the burdens local police face, results for crime management are not good. One officer who complained about reporting requirements had this to say about his station's response to everyday crimes: "We aren't solving cases. . . . This is why Chinese people don't like the police."[20] "Our goal is to serve the people," said another, "but there are many problems we can't solve. We have a lot of cases and problems to deal with."[21] Crunched for time, police instead focus on "easy cases" in which they can get the person or persons involved to admit guilt, and meanwhile try to ignore everything else.[22] Some officers say good leadership at the station level can reverse these effects, but this requires a steady supply of dedicated leaders that is clearly not available at every station, especially since many local police chiefs are political appointees from the local government with no prior policing experience.[23] To make matters worse, officer workloads are only increasing, as everyday crimes continue to rise in frequency.

Is it possible that officers in China are just lazy? Undoubtedly, some lack a good work ethic, but most of the officers interviewed—particularly the younger officers—expressed frustration at the failings on the part of their stations and the system. This was not what they were expecting when they got into this line of work, and many said they wished the ministry would give them more guidance and do something to address the issues of time-consuming reports and poorly directed manpower resources that eat up their ability to respond to everyday crimes. Failures at the local level may also be amplified in an age of technology, especially when problems compound, tensions rise, and violence—justified or not—is involved. Recently, public furor erupted after a video clip spread of a heated argument over a parking ticket that ended with a traffic cop pushing a woman holding an infant to the ground.[24] Ministry officials are no doubt concerned that an age of cell phone cameras and social media connectivity will further expose the bureaucracy to criticism, but thus far, little has been done to provide meaningful supervision over the lower levels.

Shared Control

Control over local-level operations is not always exercised superficially. When certain situations dictate, the ministry and local governments may get more directly involved in day-to-day policing activities for higher-priority issues that pose special challenges to public order or attract the attention of higher-ups for other reasons. Crimes that fall under this category include drug-related offenses, human trafficking of Chinese nationals, and corruption, although depending on the time and place there may be others. For the sake of simplicity, I refer to this group as "priority crimes." Because both the ministry and local governments are interested in these crimes, problems can arise if the two have different objectives. Moreover, when the priorities of the two bosses collide, ground-level police can face competing instructions about how to manage crime, putting them—and ground-level response—in a difficult position.

Even though priority crimes are not elevated to the same level of interest as social unrest, the ministry treats these issues with more care than everyday crimes.[25] This is partly because central government officials vocally stress attention to priority crimes like corruption, but it is also because these issues may be of concern to the Communist Party or more generally deal with greater perceived threats to public or political order. One official described the rationale behind how the ministry approaches one type of priority crime. "Take human trafficking in Fujian province as an example," the official explained.[26] "This problem is really only present in Fujian and surrounding areas, but it is a priority for the ministry to keep it controlled there and not allow it to spread any farther. . . . Human trafficking is rare, but it receives a lot of attention from the higher levels because it is something of extreme concern to people. . . . It makes people very afraid, even if it doesn't happen very often, so we must pay close attention to it." Corruption is also a widely perceived threat to public (and political) order, especially now that the Xi Jinping administration has made fighting both "tigers" and "flies" a priority. Moreover, drug use is seen as both a public health and a public order issue that needs monitoring.

Overall, the ministry's concern for priority crimes is fairly pragmatic, and undergirding this attention is a concern for public perceptions. When a priority crime in a city or region gets out of hand or is made public, cases can make headlines and shame the people involved as well as the supervising authorities; ministry officials therefore have an incentive to increase attention to local response regarding these issues. Moreover, ministry officials may give more attention to certain priority crimes because they feel they can maximize the return on their effort. The same ministry official who talked about the public's fear of human trafficking went on to explain that trafficking is also a priority because the ministry can expend fewer resources for greater benefit, since the phenomenon is relatively rare. He likened spending in this area to giving poor persons something small and inexpensive that could make them very happy and improve their life, which is preferable to giving rich persons something very beautiful and expensive that would only make them somewhat happy. "The ministry is trying to focus on doing the things that will make people the most happy and can be accomplished, not necessarily the things that will make the rich people a little happier," he concluded.

We may assume that local government officials get involved with priority issues for similar reasons. They too follow the political winds of the central government and are concerned with addressing corruption, or at the very least appearing to address corruption. It is also in the best interest of local officials to avoid getting caught up in higher-level sweeps and to do everything in their power to ensure that their city or county stays out of the headlines. If problems with priority crimes arise during an official's watch, it could permanently damage his or her political career, even if that official is not directly responsible; therefore, local government officials have real incentives to be more involved with priority crimes. But fear of embarrassment and retribution is not the only reason local government leaders take an interest in priority cases. Priority cases can and do touch on local official misconduct, and this relationship sets up a very different incentive structure that can create conflicts of interest.

Issues for local police arise when they get caught between competing expectations and demands from local government officials and the ministry. Sometimes this happens because local officials are looking to protect their own financial interests or those of friends or other social and political connections. Reliable data for corruption links to priority crimes is scarce, but a police officer in one Hunanese city said it was possible (*you keneng*) that certain drug dealers in his city have such connections.[27] The firing of one local drug squad leader in another Hunanese city after a publicly successful drug raid also suggests that corruption of this nature is a problem with deep roots.[28] Moreover, Peng Wang, in his investigation into police corruption in China, found that police in Chongqing were ordered by their leader not to investigate illegal clubs routinely and act only if they received public tip-offs or obtained evidence (P. Wang 2017, 58). But local government leaders may exert control for less nefarious reasons that nevertheless run counter to ministry objectives. They might, for example, be seeking to conceal the full extent of a priority crime for fear that it will damage their political careers. In contrast, ministerial officials are primarily concerned with local-level compliance with the law, and it is this difference in priorities that sets the MPS up for conflict with local officials.[29]

Once local governments decide to get involved in frontline police operations, their influence can be difficult for ministry officials to curb. The MPS can send teams down to the city or county level, but the close proximity of local government leaders is something the ministry is mostly unable to replicate. The only exception is situations in which the provincial bureaus are able to appoint their own officials to local station leadership positions or temporarily send officers from the province to work alongside officers at the grass roots; but such arrangements are rare and scattered, given manpower restrictions.[30] Local government officials have also amassed considerable power (Fu 2005) because they ultimately hold control over funding for local police operating costs and wield influence over station leadership appointments (Xie 2013, 82). In fact, despite stepped-up efforts by the ministry to manage the station leadership hiring process, local officers report that many station leaders were installed by local leaders and were chosen for political loyalties, not because they have any experience in law enforcement.[31] If the provincial ministry wants to intervene in a decision, it is often a fight. One local station officer described the conflict over choosing a station leader in his city: "The local government selected a new chief after the bureau appointed the old chief to another position, but the bureau won't approve the new chief. . . . I don't know the reason . . . but we don't have a station chief right now."[32] The officer went on to say that the provincial government would probably have to step in to adjudicate the issue. Such leadership battles are important to both sides. By controlling the local police through their leaders, local officials can exert influence over investigations and protect themselves or their associates against claims of criminal wrongdoing, if and when they so desire.

Effects of Shared Control

What happens to priority cases when local governments and ministry officials share control? Because human trafficking cases are relatively rare and corruption cases are politically sensitive, my data only speaks with authority to the impact of shared control on drug response. Nevertheless, the results for crime management in this area are telling as an example of how police response can be affected when there is conflict between the expectations of local government officials and the demands of the ministry. As previously noted, shared control can leave local police in an awkward position as they attempt to manage competing demands and a lack of resources. In the specific case of drug response, the ministry has made inroads into breaking firmly entrenched local corruption ties, but the results for crime management are decidedly mixed. This is partly because the ministry's strategy toward drug control works against rather than with local practices and partly because of capacity limitations at both the ministerial and local levels.

Shared control makes crime response difficult in several ways. First and foremost, it pushes police in two different directions. Returning to the example of drug raids raised in the previous chapter, police in Hunan were tripped up by a ministry seeking to sever the symbiotic relationship between proprietors of establishments where illegal activities take place and local power holders (in government or on the police force) who may or may not have a vested interest in supporting the continuation of prearranged drug raids.[33] In Hunan, local police leaders were well aware of the ministry's requirement for unannounced raids and the risks they might face if they continued to defy orders. Nevertheless, they persisted in staging coordinated checks right up until the day provincial teams directly intervened by conducting the inspections themselves.[34] Even then, the practice did not entirely stop. One provincial ministry official noted, "One year after we started conducting checks, local police still [make coordinated inspections], but it is less prevalent than before."[35] On the surface, the ministry's intervention looks like a success. After the implementation of unannounced raids, drug use in cities is less visible, and more users have been put in jail. But local police and even some ministry officials say the change has only pushed users further underground to cheap hotels and residences where they are harder for police to find and monitor.[36] This reduces the quality of information police have about drug sales and use and also increases the risks associated with conducting inspections or raids in unfamiliar locales.

If the ministry and local governments were just duking it out over who wins the shared-control battle, the impact on crime response might not be so bad. Unfortunately, there are other characteristics of shared control that negatively impact crime response. Recall that shared control arises because the ministry's power to manage the local levels is weak owing to fiscal arrangements and manpower limitations—issues that also plague decentralized control. This means the ministry is only able to fight certain battles when it comes to managing priority crimes. With regard to drug control, local police say the ministry has not provided them with additional resources such as drug dogs, new surveillance technology, or increases in manpower that would help them develop a new response system for managing drug crimes that does not run afoul of ministry guidelines.[37] With a broken old system and drug users underground, the local police need such resources now more than ever, yet it not clear when or if this assistance will materialize.

A final characteristic of shared control that hinders police response is lackluster coordination between agencies and levels. Though the ministry devotes certain resources to actively managing drug crime response, as evidenced by the interactions between provincial ministry officials and local police, central ministry interactions in this area are rare. No local police interviewees could recall a single central ministry-led, drug-related mission in their area. Furthermore, there is little to no coordination between security agents at the border and police at either the local or provincial level.[38] This means drug trafficking is a big problem for local police, who have few resources to stop the movement of illegal substances into their cities and no regularized means of communicating with border police to know when a new influx might be hitting their jurisdiction.[39] There is some hope for the expansion of local roadside, train station, and airport inspection stations, but police say funds remain limited. Even drug dogs are few or nonexistent and used primarily during high-level raids. Ultimately, both local police and provincial ministry officials in Hunan report that the ministry has failed to create a coordinated response to drug control at the national level, though the situation appears to be better coordinated on the issue of human trafficking.

These problems notwithstanding, outcomes for priority crimes are not always negative. In the areas where police do not experience a high number of priority crimes, officers had fewer complaints about problems arising from shared control. For example, drug crimes are present but not rampant in two Hebei cities and one other city in central China where I conducted research, and officers in these areas reported that response to drug crimes does not elicit the type of conflict arising out of shared control that officers in Hunan report. One officer said that the raids were mostly prearranged, just as they are in Hunan, yet the practice had not (yet?) attracted the attention of provincial ministry officials.[40]

Centralized Control

Standing in stark contrast to patterns of decentralized and shared control is the highly centralized power that ministry officials exert over police response to national priority issues. Centralized control[41] is difficult to achieve because everyone has to be on the same page. As such, centralization requires coordination between frontline police, local governments, provincial and central ministry officials, and Communist Party leaders at all levels. Because city and county governments hold command over financial resources and often appoint local police station leaders, it is not easy for the ministry to overcome local resistance, as the pattern of shared control demonstrates. Yet MPS officials have nevertheless proved able to unify control over *weiwen*, demonstrating the strength of the Chinese state in accomplishing goals it considers essential.[42] The results for (certain types of) policing on the ground are palpable. According to frontline reports, crime management works much better under centralized control because frontline officers receive more attention from the ministry in the form of training and resources. Efforts between local forces are also better coordinated, and clear protocols are in place for what to do when various types of protest events or dissident action occur.

The PSB has many incentives to centralize control over local police response to stability maintenance. Regime-destabilizing events are a concern given the country's history of protests, and the central leadership has charged the ministry with assisting the Communist Party in prioritizing stability maintenance and preventing the emergence and growth of social movements that might pose a threat to the party-state. Proper police management of these events is critical for the CCP and the MPS. Protests and riots must be handled swiftly and with some consideration for public perception. Long, drawn-out events such as the five-month standoff between protesters and police in Wukan village attract unwanted attention from both the press and social media users, in addition to being difficult to suppress.[43] To prevent the spread of such events, the national priority of stability maintenance thus takes precedence over other policing problems, especially since the number of protests has not abated. But even though the priorities are clear and ministry officials know what they have to do, the decentralized nature of policing in China makes unifying control difficult.

In order for the ministry to centralize power over police operations, it must by definition bring local power holders in line. Such coordination works better when the priorities of local government leaders and the ministry lack conflict, but overcoming local resistance in the absence of naturally aligned interests is not impossible. In the case of *weiwen* management, the ministry receives a major boost from central government policies through the cadre evaluation system, and direct accountability for cadres has led local government leaders to divert more resources to controlling social unrest, since central government funds are insufficient to cover all needs in this area. This process is not perfect, however, and local governments have many incentives to hide the extent of unrest in their areas from higher-ups. Small-time dissidents are easier to monitor and control, as are small demonstrations, but larger events or dissidents who are interested and able to establish networks with other like-minded individuals are much harder to hide. In the case of mass incidents, local governments are particularly limited by the capacity of their local police forces. Even though the armories can be opened, most stations lack the proper riot control equipment and training to put down a large event on their own, forcing the local governments to turn to higher levels for support.

The ministry must also coordinate efforts between security forces. Police reforms have been instrumental in this regard by beefing up response protocols and dictating when and under what conditions the PAP is called in to handle stability maintenance work. As a result, police efforts to control protest are well coordinated and exhibit little variation in areas outside of troubled minority regions.[44] In fact, police officers in all research sites were engaged in very similar practices with regard to handling *weiwen*, although officers in Hebei and Shaanxi report being more involved in managing potential protesters during times of political sensitivity such as national meetings or anniversaries of important political events. In contrast, officers in Hunan said their stations were more likely to hire auxiliary officers or other temporary workers to detain potential protesters.[45] Overall, however, descriptions of protest control were similar across research sites.

All this coordination takes effort, and central ministry officials are often involved in overseeing local compliance. They are, for example, far more likely to conduct inspections and provide assistance to local police in the management of social unrest than they are to intervene in other types of crime response.[46] Moreover, areas that experience unusual amounts of protest receive even more attention from the ministry. Protest control efforts take on a distinct character in the turbulent areas of Xinjiang and Tibet. In these provinces, there is far more police presence and coordination between different levels of police, particularly local police, SWAT police, and officials from the ministry. Police also work closely with informants from ethnic minority groups to gather information about past and potential attacks. In politically sensitive areas such as Xinjiang, the ministry will often dispatch teams to monitor the situation on the ground and respond to threats.[47] One SWAT team leader described his experience on such trips, which he noted were far more difficult and prone to violent confrontation than missions in Tibet.[48] "We go to help the local police," he said. "We work side by side with them and become like local police ourselves." Such close contact with higher-level police groups does not end once missions are over. The SWAT leader also described how frontline officers from Xinjiang sometimes take business trips to Beijing despite their tight work schedules back home. Such opportunities to visit the capital for work were not available to most *paichusuo* officers I spoke with, demonstrating the heavy degree of coordination in critical areas.

It is interesting to note that centralized control over social unrest in China is highly standardized but not entirely rigid. On the whole, the MPS engages in far fewer experimental pilot projects (*shidian*) than bureaucracies like the Ministry of Finance, but it nevertheless conducts pilots. One central official explained, "The public security bureau does not conduct as many pilots as other bureaus . . . partly because we don't have the resources. . . . But we are very interested in new pilots that will promote stability."[49] Accordingly, some officers and stations have been allowed space to experiment with lower-cost solutions to manage dissent. In Shaanxi, for example, officers are using social media to collect information about protesters. In 2012, I observed interviewees posting photos on Weibo of protesters engaged in unlawful destruction of property that were accompanied by requests for help in identifying the perpetrators, mimicking the vigilante-style justice techniques used by Chinese netizens who seek out personal details and other identifying information about persons of interest in so-called human flesh searches (*renrou sousuo*).[50] Other solutions include the use of live video petitioning, which is reportedly employed by understaffed stations in Liaoning to reach petitioners more easily.[51] While the central ministry may or may not be actively promoting these methods of crime response as official pilot projects, the pattern of centralized control at the very least does not preclude their existence.

Effects of Centralized Control

The response to social unrest has become highly centralized over time, with local leaders, ground-level officers, and ministry officials teaming up to better manage uprisings and prevent dissidents from organizing and escalating their claims. Centralized control brings local forces in line by creating an incentive structure that has all parties working toward the same goals: providing nationally standardized and enforced practices for managing social unrest and responding quickly to protest events. Centralized control also makes possible a high degree of coordination between agencies, dividing the labor and helping officers properly respond to protest and call for help when need be. As such, frontline forces from local police to PAP officers are largely satisfied with their capabilities in these areas. Of the thirty-nine frontline agents interviewed who worked with or had knowledge of stability maintenance activities, only two said that their station or team was not doing a good job managing protests. "It is not a problem," or "we can handle them [the protesters]" were the most common responses from local police.[52] Many officers went on to say that their stations seldom confront the issue, especially in comparison to other types of crime control. But even among those who worked in areas where social unrest was more common, their reported satisfaction with station response capabilities was high across the board. Moreover, PAP officers who manage riots said they were similarly satisfied with response capacities.

One local officer described the process at his station: "Most of the time, we just have to deal with the small-time petitioners [*shangfang*]. We go and get them before they go anywhere to cause trouble during important political times like *lianghui* [China's annual "Two Sessions" party meeting] or certain anniversaries. . . . The cases they have are often very complicated. We don't have the proper resources to help them, but we can keep them quiet during important times. If they go to the province or Beijing, then we have to get help [from the higher levels]. We [also] get help if there is a big incident."[53] Although the officer expressed some dissatisfaction with the fact that petitioners had few or no other recourses for redress, he nevertheless had no complaints about the police side of the process. "It's a big part of what we do. The system is very clear. Of course the leaders hate this problem because if too many of their people go to petition it makes them look bad . . . so the local government gives us money to deal with [the dissidents] . . . and we also get money [to retrieve the dissidents] from the ministry if they make it to the province or Beijing."

PAP officers were similarly satisfied with their capabilities in handling protest. "I became an officer because I wanted to protect *weiwen*," one officer said. "This is my job."[54] "Our main job is to take care of mass incidents," explained another:[55]

> We don't carry a gun every day, but when we go out on a mission, we go out armed and with a lot of men, at least one to two hundred. Sometimes we are just looking after the leaders when they come to visit . . . sort of like security. . . . Sometimes we go in for riots, and sometimes for something much smaller, like when someone has a conflict with another group or individual. We have cooperation with the local police [when they need assistance]. . . . We mainly work in [(redacted) the area], which is pretty safe and stable. We have [(redacted) minority group] but these people do not cause a lot of trouble. We are more concerned about students. The students are difficult because you can't use weapons to hit them. It would be very bad, especially since there might be cameras [around]. We also feel bad about hitting the students. . . . There is no policy on this, but everyone knows not to hit students. . . . We don't feel so bad about using force on workers or other groups, but we still need to be careful. . . . We help the local police because they don't have any sort of weapons or proper attire to deal with the unrest. . . . They handle

> traffic complaints, theft, and the larger complaints if they are detectives. The local police also only have a few people to handle the problem, so they call us. We always go out in a big group so we don't feel like our job is particularly dangerous.

But while police are largely satisfied with stability maintenance response—especially when compared to virtually every other crime that frontline forces must handle—the system of centralized control is still imperfect. Because of the stipulations imposed by the cadre evaluation system, managing social unrest is not seen so much as an opportunity for the local level to work with the ministry but more as something that must be contained at any cost. One officer explained how they deal with troublemaking dissidents in his city. "We know who they are and go get them during sensitive times. . . . We don't want them getting to Beijing. That's a lot of trouble when we have to chase them down."[56] He said that city officials and the station would face consequences if the dissidents made it to the capital to lodge their complaints, so they hold them until enough time has passed. Another officer explained that his station often hires people who are not police officers to help, which is most likely a reference to the "hired thugs" (Ong 2018) and temporary auxiliary police.[57] Such actions are not officially condoned by the ministry but are nevertheless steps local officers say their stations must take to deal with dissidents who try to call attention to their causes, especially during politically sensitive times. Moreover, although the PAP officers I spoke with were largely optimistic, a squad leader was more circumspect, voicing concerns about the state's longer-term ability to stem social unrest and framing his comments in a broader political context. In regard to his own team's ability to manage riots, however, his confidence was unwavering.

Technically, the way frontline forces suppress and hide protest activities is precisely the goal of central officials: stop social unrest at the local level by any means necessary. But the current system creates an extra set of incentives for local governments to underreport protest events—when possible—and conceal the number of dissidents in their area by keeping them under house arrest with local government funds (the use of which may or may not be reported to higher levels). By using house arrest to prevent countable incidents of unrest—either through visible protest or a petition to a higher level—local governments thwart the flow of information to the center about the exact situation on the ground. While the end result (reducing the total number of incidents) is highly desirable for everyone, the path to get there produces the undesired side effect of limiting information. This in turn may hide potential hot spots from officials in the ministry, burying the true extent of discontent and perhaps making it more difficult to prevent or respond appropriately to threatening protests or riots. The pattern of centralized control thus strikes a tenuous balance, despite all the gains it brings to *weiwen* management.

Exceptions

One exception to these patterns of control is the use of strike-hard campaigns (*yanda*). Campaign-style policing was in many ways a natural byproduct of Mao-era calls to strengthen ideological education work in the police bureaucracy, and the near omnipresence of campaign policing in the early communist period (Dutton 2005) virtually ensured its continuation once the reform era began in 1978. While early campaigns were employed for largely political ends, police in the reform era have used the strike-hard campaigns to target criminal activities as well, even though their ability to reduce crime is mixed at best (Bakken 1993; Dutton and Lee 1993; M. S. Tanner 2005a; Liu and Tang 1997). National campaigns in particular require attention from the ministry, breaking usual patterns of decentralized and shared control. When campaigns are waged, we tend to see increased attention from higher-ups, and stations may receive some extra training and resources as they are in turn expected to produce tangible results. Whether addressing street crime, drugs, or corruption, each wave of the national campaigns has brought spikes in arrests, detentions, prosecutions, and harsh penalties such as capital punishment (Trevaskes 2007).

Campaigns are not a panacea, however, for the problems that plague the ground level, nor did they feature prominently in the accounts of officers I interviewed. Campaigns have persisted because—with their specific targets and flexible nature—they can be an expedient solution for a strained force that is short on manpower but charged with addressing a particular issue (M. S. Tanner 2005a). The persistence of campaigns is further predicated on an internal narrative that they effectively reduce crime.[58] But that assumption is based on the perceived success of the first campaign in 1983, which led a generation of public security texts to focus on the ability of campaigns to bring crime in check and provide a sense of security for the public. Because campaigns are so short-lived, however, they typically fail to overcome the problem of resource limitations. Furthermore, the campaigns themselves are costly. Scholars report that campaign policing takes a toll on ground-level officers, since the long hours required by a campaign are physically exhausting and often unpaid (M. S. Tanner 2005a, 179). Focus on campaigns also takes valuable time and resources away from other areas of policing, which may eventually do more harm than good for overall control of social order (Trevaskes 2010; Dutton and Lee 1993). Campaigns are thus a short-term break in the patterns of shared and decentralized control in which the ministry briefly inserts itself into the affairs of the local station. Since these efforts are not accompanied by longer-term resources or coordination such as what we observe with stability maintenance under centralized control, we fail to see significant benefits to frontline police. Instead, efforts are typically hamstrung by familiar factors such as limited manpower, and officers do just what they need to do to meet quotas before returning to business as usual.

Fragmented Patterns of Control

Assessing coercive capacity by talking to officers about policing on the ground and their experiences with the higher levels helps to further explain the gap between protest and everyday crime control. But how did these patterns of control emerge, and why do they persist? Central government priorities of stability maintenance have enabled the ministry to unify control over the local levels with the help of similarly incentivized local governments, but the fragmentation of China's bureaucratic system is too deep to overcome in other areas of policing. Whereas scholars have written extensively about local interests shaping economic or environmental policies in other bureaucracies, analyzing variation between different patterns of control over the police provides insight into how fragmented authoritarianism works in the Ministry of Public Security. Moreover, each pattern delineates the limits of the MPS's power over the local level, while capacity issues, the persistent strength of local forces, and decision making at the top levels of government create the demarcation lines. Taken together, these patterns of control have implications for coercive capacity and show how cracks in the police bureaucracy's centralized system pose challenges to law enforcement officers on the ground, especially with regard to everyday and even some medium-priority crimes.

Outcomes for the majority of crimes that local police have to deal with on a daily basis are not good, leading to weak coercive capacity. Theoretically, the uneven, decentralized control that is the natural byproduct of fragmentation should enhance police efficacy by opening up space for locally tailored responses to crime. This was one of the key insights from studies of street-level bureaucrats elsewhere (Lipsky 1971; Musheno and Maynard-Moody 2003). But China's system is one of de facto decentralization, and the decentralized control exercised by the ministry ends up creating problems on the ground because resources are limited. Room for innovation is blocked by heavy caseloads and by the demands on police time that are imposed by the monitoring requirements of the ministry. Decentralized control thus undermines basic police operations for a wide variety of crimes, and these failures are important. Managing everyday crimes is essential for public safety, yet the bureaucracy is failing its frontline forces and making a difficult job even harder.

Issues under shared control fare little better, although the end results for coercive capacity are mixed and vary by region and issue. With local government officials influencing both the funding and leadership decisions of police stations, it is easy to see why some scholars argue that successful implementation of central policing policies necessarily depends on "the support of, or at least the compliance of, the CCP committees at the local level" (Fu 2005, 244). It is no secret that those officials can undermine ministerial control when it serves their best interest; and when conflict arises, life gets difficult for local police. In the case of response to drug crimes, shared control means police largely lack the coercive capacity to stop the trafficking of drugs into their jurisdictions. In the most affected areas, police are also struggling to manage drug use within their cities when and if the provincial officials attempt to enforce strict rule compliance.

Yet when central officials overpower local government interests and take an active role in asserting power over the local police, results for coercive capacity improve. Under this pattern of centralized control we observe benefits such as the extensive coordination between security forces, local governments, and central ministry officials. This is the primary reason why response to social unrest works so well in China. Incentives under the cadre evaluation system bring local government officials closer in line, but there are also some undesirable side effects. The cadre evaluation system can incentivize suppression of information that conceals the true extent of discontent in cities outside of traditionally troubled regions. While local officials may not be working actively against the ministry—as they sometimes do under shared control—they may nevertheless end up behaving in a way that ultimately undermines central government goals.

Furthermore, the manner in which local governments deal with dissidents may be counterproductive to the longer-term interests of the regime. The current ad hoc response of suppressing malcontents is difficult to sustain because of the high costs of detention and the difficulty local police have in identifying new dissidents. One officer lamented the soaring costs associated with maintaining stability and called *weiwen* the product of a failing system: "What the government needs to do is reform the institutions," he said.[59] "The court system is not independent, and when people can't get justice they turn to petitioning. . . . The money spent on *weiwen* is a waste [*baihua*]." Moreover, since many localities choose to employ non-police agents to watch dissidents at a lower cost, opportunities for abuse are high. Visual proof of unjust detentions occasionally makes its way to the internet, and in the eyes of some individuals, police actions may end up tarnishing the image of the regime. Negative side effects notwithstanding, the centralized pattern of control still produces better outcomes in the eyes of the state for crime response on the ground than the patterns of decentralized and shared control.

Why does the ministry not replicate the relative success of protest policing? The answer lies in the power of the local governments, the top-down system of information exchange, and the continued prioritization of stability maintenance. In the long run, perhaps additional reform and centralization efforts will enable the ministry to unify control over the local levels and improve policy response to everyday and priority crimes, but the prognosis for the immediate future is not promising. Because of funding decentralization for police operations and the ability of local officials to influence police leadership appointments, the power of local governments shows few signs of decline, even if the ministry is able to step in from time to time to address the most egregious cases. It is possible that the ministry will one day wrest control from the local levels over everyday crimes, if it can garner both the resources and political will to do so, but this is also challenging. Despite the obvious benefits to ground-level crime management brought about by centralized control, the process is expensive in terms of both financial and human resources, and the central ministry has a limited supply of both.

The top-down system of information exchange also hurts the transfer of feedback up to the ministerial level. Just as police on the front lines have no time to innovate, they also have few channels to convey concerns or ideas up the chain of command that might assist reform. One central ministry official described in detail how the system works:

> Most of these big problems start in the city, so [city police officials] notify the province. The province decides what to do about the problem; they don't just listen to what the local police have to say. Maybe along the coast the local police will have more ability to say what they think, but the province will do its own research, maybe with the help of the center level. They will then tell the city or county how they should respond by making new rules to deal with the issues. If this is strictly a local issue, that will be the end of it, but if it's something that happens all over China, then they must take it to the center and get a higher level of approval. Local police cannot just act on their own. . . . Higher-level approval is necessary.[60]

Room for developing better responses at the ground level is thus officially blocked by the internal flow of information. This is likely a contributing factor to why frontline police interviewees report that they do not bother making suggestions to higher-ups.

Beyond the continued power of the local governments and the top-down system of information exchange, these patterns of control persist because of the central government's continued focus on stability maintenance. By prioritizing the control of dissidents and social unrest above all else, the central government is making a dedicated commitment to suppressing large-scale events and networks of dissidents that could undermine or even unseat the party. There is nothing inherently wrong with this choice, strategically speaking, but it has come with significant costs for the rest of policing in China. Moreover, there is little reason to believe that this prioritization will change under Xi Jinping's rule. The 2015 police reforms continue to stress the primacy of social unrest, calling into question the ability of the regime to enact meaningful change to other areas of policing and further opening up the police bureaucracy to criticism from the outside (Scoggins, n.d.).

5

POLITICIZATION AND THE BOUNDARIES OF AUTHORITARIAN RESILIENCE

Officers who say they are not helping people or solving cases. Police reports that do not reflect accurate descriptions of events. Practices that push drug users underground. Stations that are strapped for manpower yet unable to send "office officers" out on patrol or to answer calls. It is little wonder that officers looked confused or openly scoffed when I first began this study by asking them about effective frontline response. In China, the world of everyday policing limps along as overworked, underpaid, and poorly trained officers struggle to get through another week. Yet the contrast between these bleak everyday realities and the same officers' appraisal of the policing of stability maintenance is stark. Here, we see clear protocols for getting protesters off the streets or calling in the PAP. Stations also receive local funding to watch dissidents and ministerial funding to bring protesters back when they "skip levels" to the provincial capitals or Beijing. Furthermore, frontline forces facing protesters can depend on a degree of coordination between agencies that is absent with other issues, even with medium-priority problems like drug control. In China, officers around the country are policing in the shadow of protest as stability maintenance trumps all other concerns.

Many of the everyday policing problems that local police describe are unintended consequences. The outcomes described by officers on the ground are certainly not the goal of ministry officials, as evidenced by the central ministry officer quoted earlier who said the ministry would prefer to exercise a higher degree of control over the local levels by sending teams down to check and enforce compliance but are unable to do so because of logistical limitations.

The same official later laid out a variety of issues the ministry must deal with, including political unrest in Tibet, the spread of rumors on social media sites like Weibo, the risks posed by widespread internet communication, and additional problems with immigration, the control of foreigners, and the management of high-profile scandals and abuse of local police power.[1] The plate of the ministry is indeed quite full, but it is the prioritization of stability maintenance above all else that ultimately sets everyday policing up for failure.

The prioritization of stability maintenance siphons resources away from other areas of crime response, as demonstrated by the accounts from frontline officers. When central government directives to focus on protest are imposed on an inherently fragmented and often decentralized police bureaucracy and coupled with limitations on resources and poorly devised or executed police reforms, everyday crime response suffers. The effects of those problems are not just the collective stories of low police officer morale or of disappointed residents who relied on the police to help them and were let down. The problems with everyday policing also raise much larger questions about the politicization of policing in China, regime resilience, police legitimacy, and potential effects for the governance of other institutions in China and beyond.

(Re-)Politicization of Policing

The prioritization of stability maintenance is best understood as the latest incarnation of political policing, which has a long history in China. Shortly after the founding of the People's Republic, the police were rebranded by the Communist Party as agents of the "mass line" and charged with expunging counterrevolutionaries and waging police campaigns to pursue larger political goals. Because these elements were so omnipresent in policing during that period, police use of the campaign and mass line became "not just a means of doing things, but a way of seeing" for public security (Dutton 2005, 142). The use of campaigns continued into the reform era, but the ministry largely scaled back the institution's political focus, having been burned by the Cultural Revolution and facing significant increases in everyday crime from a newly mobile population. Political work did not disappear entirely, however. As the frontline agents of the party's control, the police were still charged with doing the party's dirty work, which typically entails activities such as illegal detentions or the use of police power to enforce unpopular government actions like forced demolitions or the one-child policy. Nevertheless, the police in the 1980s and 1990s were overall engaged in fewer politicized activities than they were during the communist era.

Once the government began ramping up efforts in stability maintenance, however, the winds shifted again. Political policing in China now assumes the form of ensuring regime stability through the clamping down on protest, the stifling of dissent, and the eradication of dissident networks. These efforts have assumed primacy, even though they account for only a small fraction of the work most stations do on a daily basis, and many of the interviewees for this research noted that they themselves were not actively involved in stability maintenance work. The focus that the ministry puts on funding, reform, practices, coordination, and oversight demonstrate the degree to which stability maintenance bleeds into all other aspects of frontline policing by consuming valuable resources and energy.

Political policing is not a neutral phenomenon. The Chinese case shows just how detrimental the prioritization of political elements can be to the frontline issues of everyday policing that matter most to ground-level officers as well as members of the public. When political policing eats up all the best resources, frontline forces are left to make do with what is left, resulting in poor outcomes for crime management, officer morale, and overall police effectiveness. It also ushers in larger threats to the rule of law in Chinese cites. When police say they are not helping people or solving crimes, this is a red flag for the enforcement of law and order. Moreover, when police turn the other way when suspects run or when faced with blatant social problems such as illegal blood trading because they lack specific protocols, public security and health are at risk. The prioritization of political policing detracts from important everyday issues in a variety of ways, revealing a new dimension to what Fu Hualing has flagged as the "irreconcilable conflict between politics and law" (Fu 2005, 248).

Recent police reforms suggest that the politicization of policing will only continue under Xi Jinping. In addition to the previously mentioned reforms in the area of stability maintenance since Xi took power in 2012, the administration's focus on anticorruption—which in itself might improve the enforcement powers and legitimacy of the police—has been combined with and blurred by political tasks. From Xi's early takedowns of former Standing Committee member and public security czar Zhou Yongkang and his associates to the arrest and detention of former Interpol president Meng Hongwei, Xi's efforts in the area of anticorruption more closely resemble old-school political purges than any meaningful effort to stamp out corruption in the PSB. Moreover, of the seven major tasks introduced by the 2015 police reforms, none addresses local-level police corruption directly.[2] Certain measures, such as the call to enhance the law enforcement responsibility system or the pledge to raise the wages of police officers and improve the pension system, may improve detection of corruption and curb the financial need to engage in bribe taking. But the reforms do not call for concrete efforts to stamp out local police misconduct, and ministry officials have implemented no such interpretation of the 2015 reform measures to date.[3]

With the politicized role of the police in China only increasing through efforts to enhance stability maintenance and confine corruption efforts to political purges, the future for reform of everyday policing looks bleak. While the political focus certainly supports the immediate goals of the leadership (consolidating power) and the regime (providing protection against collapse), a heavy emphasis on political policing at the expense of everyday policing opens the party-state to other serious challenges to its authority and longevity.

Authoritarian Resilience

A myopic focus on protest control and political policing at the expense of everyday policing also infringes on the state's institutional capacity to ensure ground-level security and sheds doubt on prior assessments of China's authoritarian resilience. Regimes that are unable to manage security threats and internal strife are vulnerable; thus, state stability depends on having the coercive capacity to prevent and address violence and instability. Here, a broadened definition of coercive capacity is essential to understanding the police bureaucracy's role in regime resilience. Coercive capacity is a core component of regime survival and change (Skocpol 1979), and studies of authoritarian resilience have revealed much about the will and capacity of states to repress (Bellin 2004) and the importance of institutional factors like cohesion and scope of the coercive apparatus for regime resilience (Levitsky and Way 2012; Way and Levitsky 2006). But the institutions of state coercion are also responsible for enforcing security on the ground, and this is where the Chinese case reveals a critical blind spot in current conceptualizations of assessing a regime's authoritarian resilience and coercive capacity. If we only look at protest suppression, the Chinese coercive apparatus looks remarkably capable. But when we think about coercive capacity more broadly by considering all the functions of coercive organizations such as the police, that image of strength falls apart. A state's security apparatus can be strong in some ways and weak in others, and such variation is visible only when we disaggregate the coercive functions to look carefully at ground-level response to a variety of issues.

As outlined in the previous chapter, coercive capacity in China fares better when control over the lower levels is unified, a pattern that others have noted elsewhere.[4] With regard to protest activities, the centralized pattern of control promotes coordination between agencies, brings local government actors in line, and provides frontline forces with the response protocols and resources they need to handle the issue. But positive reports of protest response stand in sharp contrast to other areas of crime where control is less centralized. Problems are most pronounced when decentralization is strongest. With respect to everyday crimes, decentralized control leaves frontline police ill prepared to handle a critical area of public security, and for medium-priority crimes—where we observe a pattern of shared control—officer reports of coercive capacity fare only slightly better. Police say the uneven nature of the ministry's control often makes their job harder. Here a lack of coordination between the provincial ministry and local police is particularly damaging, especially when provincial government expectations for local station practices stand at odds with local government demands or station practices that have worked in the past.

The day-to-day activities of the police—especially their regular interactions with the public—are a critical part of coercive capacity with respect to regime resilience. Responsibilities such as responding to a call when a home is broken into or a fight breaks out may sound pedestrian in comparison to containing a thirty-thousand-person riot, but the institutional capacity to address such issues matters for maintaining the fabric of a society. When governments do not provide ground-level security, we know that there are real consequences for regimes. In Latin America, studies have shown that crime victimization increases political participation and influences individual preferences for regime type (Bateson 2012). Moreover, in fledgling democracies, security failings such as an inability to stem high crime rates are known to be particularly salient for drops in public approval (Bitencourt 2007; Pérez 2003). In China, we are just beginning to understand the larger political consequences of poor everyday policing, but we know that a diminished sense of safety is correlated with lower levels of trust in the police and other state entities (Sun, Hu, and Wu 2013; Wu 2010; Wu and Sun 2009).

It is therefore necessary to use a broader conceptualization of coercive capacity that includes the day-to-day activities of police and takes seriously the harm that happens to ground-level response for everyday crimes when leaders emphasize protest control at the expense of everything else. Reports from the ground level of China's police bureaucracy have clearly delineated the ways in which frontline policing is failing in the areas of everyday crime. This daily work of the police may fly under the radar during normal times, but the failures of everyday policing nevertheless matter for regime stability, especially during times of crisis. By looking at coercive capacity as a way to control dissent *and* ensure public security with regard to everyday crimes, we gain new insight into the day-to-day functioning of the coercive apparatus and reveal deep cracks in the Chinese state's authoritarian system of control. This study thus presents a far more complex view of public security and coercive capacity and provides just cause for overhauling our assessments of China's regime resilience.

The weakness of police capacity in China could spell trouble for long-term regime stability in ways that have been overlooked by scholars. A dearth of studies on ground-level police has made it easy to take at face value the hefty internal security budget figures, official reports of low crime, and impressive track record of putting down violent protests, without thinking more carefully about the potential weaknesses of frontline security. This oversight has enabled the pendulum of the authoritarian resilience literature to swing too far in the direction of state stability, as those studies are undergirded by an implicit belief that the security state is strong and capable in terms of both managing protests and maintaining order on the ground. Recently, some scholars have begun chipping away at the notion of authoritarian resilience (C. Li 2012), and this study continues that work. Taken in the aggregate, problems with ground-level response can weaken regime control by failing to address the security needs of local residents. There is even evidence to suggest that public dissatisfaction with the failures of frontline policing is feeding back into protest. A rare 2012 report from the state-owned *Legal Daily* revealed that 22.2 percent of protests and riots over an unspecified time period were caused by police-society conflict.[5] The report went on to disclose that this percentage was higher than environmental protests and protests by minority groups combined. Clearly, protest response and the policing of other types of crime do not operate in separate vacuums.

These patterns are bad for authoritarian resilience in several ways. The problems under shared and decentralized control weaken the coercive powers of the organization and contribute to an erosion of faith in the ability of the police to do their mandated job. Specifically, the pattern of shared control opens up room for local autocrats to wield influence over police leaders and pursue activities that may be counterproductive for regime stability, especially when corruption is involved. This tendency can hurt police response on the ground and further impede control over public health and order issues such as the drug trade. But the outcomes for decentralized control are even worse, as a detached ministry fails to develop better protocols, provide adequate training, or address resource issues that would bolster local police capacity, even as it insists on maintaining a modicum of control over the lower levels that further limits police officer time and ground-level response. Taken in the aggregate, weak coercive capacity hampers regime resilience by failing to address the security concerns of local residents, which may ultimately exacerbate the recent downward trends in health and life satisfaction that are in part driven by perceptions of a lack of security (Graham,

Zhou, and Zhang 2015). But if the *Legal Daily*'s report is correct and over one-fifth of all protests are caused by police-society conflict, then the ministry may be facing a far bigger problem in which the failures in one area are actually jeopardizing success in the other.

Thus frontline assessments do not only shed light on the importance of everyday policing failures for authoritarian resilience; they also provide new insight into problems facing protest control. For now, the Chinese state has done a good job of putting down protests, thanks to the redirection of resources, focus on stability-maintenance-related security reforms, and centralization of control in ways that mitigate conflict with local governments. Although the state could continue to succeed for a long time, this balance is tenuous. When officers say things like there is not enough money in the world to subdue the number of protesters out there and that the money the central government spends on *weiwen* would be better spent reforming the institutions that are causing discontent rather than suppressing it, we see signs of distress. Equally troubling is the manner in which local governments hide potential protesters and employ non-police agents to watch dissidents in order to save money and preserve scarce human resources. These practices may ultimately be counterproductive to the longer-term interests of the regime because they suppress the flow of information and increase the chance of violent conflict with residents.

Moreover, the money for stability maintenance is not without limits. In addition to officer reports that their cities lack sufficient funds to manage *weiwen* activities, there are signs that some petitioners are stretching limited resources even further by taking advantage of the system. One leader said police in his area call such people "pestering petitioners" (*chanfang*) because they are troublemakers out for personal gain without real grievances.[6] Another source close to police in central China said that officers there compare these petitioners to menstruation (*yuejing shangfang*) because they show up every month to complain until they are paid to go away. Such petitioners, from the state's perspective, are a downside to a more routinized system, and it is possible they could cause trouble for local budgets if their numbers and demands increase.

Assessing frontline police reports of protest control and everyday policing provides valuable insight into the different dimensions of coercive capacity and ultimately the resilience of the state. While more research is needed to understand frontline police assessments in places like crowded, crime-ridden Guangzhou, lower-crime rural counties, or areas heavily affected by social unrest such as Xinjiang, the main takeaway is that the Chinese state is not nearly as resilient in terms of coercive capacity as previously assumed. Ultimately, regime resiliency is not dependent on any one factor, but broadening our investigation of coercive capacity will help scholars develop a deeper understanding of the role played by the local state and the police in regime resilience and the ways in which ignoring everyday crime control leaves the regime vulnerable.

Legitimacy

Weakened authoritarian resilience is not the only broader issue that emerges when states focus on the politicized elements of policing more than everyday crime. It is important to recall that modern authoritarian states like China are still obliged—albeit in somewhat different ways from their democratic counterparts—to provide public service and promote regime legitimacy. China is not now—nor has it ever been—a totalitarian monolith. The legitimacy of the regime and its ground-level agents is thus of real concern for the central government leadership, and adequate provision of government services has become an undeniable issue for government leaders, even if the process is far from perfect in terms of implementation.[7] Promoting a better life for the residents of the state is also one reason the reform-era party-state has zeroed in on economic growth as the cornerstone of regime legitimacy, surpassing even the more traditional elements on which it also depends, such as nationalism, ideology, and culture (Holbig and Gilley 2010). The Chinese state needs to maintain legitimacy in the eyes of the public perhaps now more than ever. Throughout the reform era, central leaders have also employed tactics such as fomenting nationalism (Gries 2004) or suppressing crime statistics (J. Xu 2018) to buoy perceptions of legitimacy. Such efforts make good common sense. Without regime legitimacy, protest control is far more likely to prove futile, and authoritarian regime leaders appear to recognize the risks of ignoring their standing in the eyes of the public and act accordingly.

While public perceptions of the police are certainly not the only component of regime legitimacy, the police are nevertheless some of the most visible street-level bureaucrats in any state, and they are very much in charge of providing the public good of safety. Research in the United States and Australia has shown that citizens are most likely to view the police as legitimate if they believe the police use procedural justice when exercising their authority (Tyler 1990; Hinds and Murphy 2007), and when the community does not view the police as legitimate, its members are far less willing to cooperate with the police to fight crime (Tyler and Fagan 2008). While much of the literature on police legitimacy is focused on Western democracies, there is evidence to suggest that civilians in the rest of the world are also interested in procedural justice but equally concerned with police effectiveness and the ability to fight crime. These opinions about the police have also been shown to spill over into broader public perceptions about the local or even central state. One recent study of police legitimacy in South Africa found that perceptions of police legitimacy were closely associated with opinions about the wider success and trustworthiness of the state (Bradford et al. 2014).

In China, the Ministry of Public Security appears to recognize the need for police legitimacy in the eyes of the public and thus stresses in its official statements the importance of paying attention to the public and public opinion. Police reform documents in particular are filled with language about serving the people and reminders that police leaders and officers be mindful of public opinion. In fact, 46 percent of the reform documents listed on the ministry's website contain some mention or call for the PSB organs to appeal to or work for the people, the public, or the masses (Scoggins, forthcoming). While it might be tempting to dismiss these statements as lip service, such efforts appear with considerable frequency and make good common sense, given larger state goals of regime legitimacy. More tangibly, the ministry and public security stations have increased their efforts to engage the public in recent years by promoting a more reform- and public-service-oriented version of the frontline police through official statements, news reports, television programming, and social media postings.

The question is whether such efforts are sufficient. Even though getting accurate assessments of state-society relations from civilians in authoritarian regimes is difficult, survey research shows that police-community relations in China are strained (Sun et al. 2013), and scholars are just beginning to investigate how the public views police legitimacy. One recent survey of a thousand residents in a coastal Chinese city found that the strongest predictor of perceptions of police legitimacy was individual assessments of police lawfulness, indicating that respondents were most interested in the police becoming "a rule-bounded institution engaged in the pursuit of justice, following the rule of law" (Sun et al. 2018, 289). While assessing civilian opinions about the police is beyond the scope of this project, the evidence presented here points to a compromised state for police legitimacy in China. Although the politicized policing of protest and dissent may be holding the regime together by suppressing specific threats to the regime and its leaders, the legitimacy of a state in the eyes of the people does not depend on how quickly police and paramilitary forces are able to put down a riot. If anything, the opposite may be the case. Moreover, because protests are relatively rare events, members of the public are far more likely to come into contact with the PSB through everyday policing matters and thus be significantly more interested in the ability of police officers to perform according to expectations during these interactions. This means showing up when residents call the 110 emergency number, listening to their concerns, and doing their best to find a resolution to the problem at hand. At present, however, frontline forces report that they are only able to do the first of those tasks with any degree of regularity. Perhaps some residents will take comfort in the fact that the police show up and (usually) file a report—even if no resolution is eventually reached—but others will no doubt be distressed by the inability of officers to do the job that society expects of them. Given that the Chinese public is especially interested in police lawfulness, police-society relations are also further complicated by rising reports of police corruption (P. Wang 2017), particularly high-profile cases such as the arrest and conviction of public security officials like Zhou Yongkang and his associates.

The failures of everyday policing thus open up the organization to a slow erosion of public trust, as officers fail to engage in effective practices or provide procedural justice for the public. This is perhaps the greatest risk for regime legitimacy that this research uncovers. People everywhere care about the ability of their local police to help them when they have fallen victim, whether it is due to a traffic accident, a theft, or some sort of physical harm inflicted by another. When the police are unable to do so, individual levels of trust plummet, and suspicions of the public security organization set in. Of course, it is the collective experience of individuals that matters most for overall assessments of police legitimacy, but individual experiences add up, and word gets around. Moreover, given that the police officers interviewed for this study reported similar problems with everyday policing across research sites in four provinces, the risks are not just confined to a specific geographic area but appear to be widespread throughout China.

Consequences for Other Institutions

The weaknesses in China's police bureaucracy expose an interesting truth: the security institution that Chinese residents are most likely to encounter on a daily basis is not nearly as strong as studies of protest control have led us to believe. This misperception is significant, since security is one area in which the Chinese state is thought to be doing a better than average job. Furthermore, the police bureaucracy is far more powerful in terms of resources and political standing than other law enforcement organs such as the *chengguan* or the courts. Because evidence from the front lines of policing calls into question the party-state's capacity as well as the prudence of its heavy focus on stability maintenance, we must also ask how other frontline agencies are struggling with similar response deficiencies that may be hurting local governance, legitimacy, or regime resilience.

Problems revealed by everyday policing carry heavy significance for the *chengguan*. There is ample evidence to suggest that the *chengguan* bureau is more poorly run than the police, and this could be unwelcome news for the health of the security state. The Urban Administrative Law Enforcement Bureau lacks the funding, respect, and political standing of the public security bureau, but we know little else about how the *chengguan* are specifically affected by the issues facing frontline police such as a lack of resources, poorly designed reform, and decentralization.[8] In the hierarchy of street-level law enforcement, *chengguan* are at the bottom, and in interviews conducted in southern China, police have scoffed at the powers of the *chengguan* (J. Xu 2013). Moreover, *chengguan* are not considered part of the public service, so their compensation is lower than that of local police officers, and they are not typically granted benefits such as housing. *Chengguan* also lack the training schools, colleges, and universities that are available to many police officers.

Although they are officially governed by the Ministry of Housing and Urban-Rural Development (MHURD), power over *chengguan* is likely largely decentralized or local, since the *chengguan* first emerged in individual cities and spread as a way for local governments to regulate street vending, illegal construction, business signage, and parking (Hanser 2016). This means that *chengguan* bureaus are not likely to enjoy the benefits of centralized control that police typically see with regard to the management of social unrest and are instead likely left coping with many of the same problems of decentralized or local government control. Given what we know about the police and their capabilities in regard to everyday crime, this arrangement is troubling for the *chengguan*, especially in light of their resource limitations. Moreover, the *chengguan* are sometimes expected to operate as "muscle" for their local government officials (Ong 2018), creating opportunities for conflict with the public and abuse of power. While it is difficult to quantify just how unpopular the *chengguan* are, they are generally known across China for their thuggish reputation, willingness to take bribes, and frequent clashes with the public.[9] Because these officers are likely to have an even harder time than police in carrying out their duties, grievances originating with them may be further exacerbating the contentious relationship between Chinese residents and local security forces, especially since the *chengguan*'s uniforms make it difficult to tell them apart from the police. More research is needed to understand how failures of the *chengguan* matter for local state security strength, legitimacy, and the enforcement of law and order.

Questions raised by the *chengguan* invite further inquiry into the job performance of other street-level bureaucrats in China and beyond. Because decentralized control over everyday crime in China leads not to innovation but to further strains on frontline response, the pattern of decentralized control may be creating enforcement problems for other government workers such as grassroots tax collectors, family planning workers, or industry and commerce administration agents.[10] These street-level bureaucrats are all engaged in daily work that may not be attracting the attention and assistance of higher authorities unless something goes seriously wrong. If they are also struggling with problems like severe resource shortages, a lack of training, or reforms that tie their hands, then looking at patterns of decentralized control gives us a better way of understanding both the effects of unfinished decentralization and the deficiencies in local state service provision. With regard to tax collection, we know that administrative decentralization has increased communication costs and undermined tax administration reform in China (Cui 2015). It is also possible that decentralized control over that bureaucracy is undermining other frontline work. Research in these areas would give more insight into the dynamics of bureaucratic control and improve our understanding of the local Chinese state.

More broadly, the undesirable results for ground-level policing observed under the pattern of decentralized control defy our expectations about how decentralization should work for street-level bureaucrats in other countries. Here, the literature typically touts the benefits of decentralization for these agents, since it enables discretion to respond selectively and even with empathy to local actors (Lipsky 1980; Scholz, Twonbly, and Headrick 1991). Moreover, discretionary powers can enable frontline agents to attach meaning to the work they do and improve their overall willingness to do a good job (Tummers and Bekkers 2014). While it takes time to develop such skills, and outcomes are certainly not always positive for every official or every issue, decentralization nevertheless gives street-level bureaucrats autonomy to do a better job than they would if they were required to perform a blanket enforcement of formal rules that were not locally devised.

But the literature on street-level bureaucrats and discretion is not all positive. In a review of the field conducted in 2007, Marcia Meyers and Susan Vorsanger found that more recent studies on the problems of discretionary behavior provide crucial insight into the complexity of frontline work. For this branch of the literature, the case of the Chinese police gives insight into the perils of unrealistic oversight and resource constraints. There is no room for the finesse of discretion when resources are stretched too thin and onerous compliance reports are required. While decentralization and discretion can be wonderful tools for local state governance, unrealistic oversight requirements combined with low manpower can cripple police effectiveness and result in worse outcomes overall. This finding complements concerns raised by other studies in democratic contexts that show the limitations of new policies when existing monitoring systems and incentives were not modified accordingly (Meyers and Dillon 1999) or the ways in which scarce institutional resources limit the bounds of discretionary decision making (Brodkin 1997). But the outcomes for police in the Chinese case are far more extreme, demonstrating the unique problems of decentralized control in a single-party system characterized by hierarchical control that allows little room for feedback. The toxic mix of time constraints and lack of voice on the front lines to change daily work constraints combines with the inherent difficulties of conducting police work and thereby limits any benefits that decentralization might have brought to the organization.

Caveats and Corrections

The findings of this book highlight weaknesses in frontline response and their effects on the larger legitimacy, security, and resiliency of the regime, but the study is also chasing a moving target. The evidence was collected over a nearly ten-year period, with the bulk of the interviews taking place during 2011 and 2012. During this time, there were changes to policing practices and the police bureaucracy itself, changes that were primarily precipitated by the rise of Xi Jinping and his efforts to further consolidate power.[11] Many of these reforms have focused on the policing of protest and dissent, as the new security developments in Xinjiang Province highlight. The Ministry of Public Security has also enacted very specific changes to how police conduct investigations into terrorist activities, monitor dissidents, and distribute manpower in cities by expanding the use of the grid management system.[12] Unfortunately for the state of everyday crime control, however, changes with regard to everyday policing have not kept pace (Scoggins, n.d.). Here the benefits to the changes—the most important of which are the 40 percent increases in salary and station funding changes highlighted in chapter 2—are more diffuse. By limiting compensation changes to official police officers, the MPS may be inadvertently undercutting benefits it could gain in boosting officer morale, because the move fails to address auxiliary officer concerns. Moreover, even the benefits to morale for official officers may be short-lived, since a 40 percent increase, while substantial, remains relatively conservative when the salaries of police are compared to those of other civil servants.[13]

The study also unearths a few positive signs that scholars interested in the internal security state should pay attention to in the future. There is evidence to suggest, for example, that the MPS is becoming more responsive and adept at gathering information in ways that might help officials address problems at the ground level. As is the case in local police stations, the ministry's old guard is gradually retiring, and this makes room for better-educated, younger officers to assume positions of authority. At least two ministry officials with whom I spoke believe the change in command will increase the ministry's overall flexibility. One young ministry official noted, "There has been a change in the attitude of supervisors in just the last five years. . . . My supervisor will sometimes ask for the opinion of lower-ranking officers and actually listen to their suggestions. This never happened before."[14] Another provincial ministry official praised his supervisor's interest in new computing capabilities and willingness to work side by side with him to solve problems.[15] He said that this type of behavior was a break from prior expectations about hierarchal interactions in which supervisors paid little attention to the ideas of lower-ranking officials.

The retiring of the old guard could also make a difference at the lower levels if future research finds that older supervisors are being replaced by men and women who are more dedicated to improving law enforcement on the ground. We know from the policing literature in the United States and the United Kingdom that effective supervisors can make a difference for job performance and officer satisfaction (Brewer, Wilson, and Beck 1994), and the same is likely true in China. At least one lower-ranking interviewee indicated that his district station was operating more efficiently than others in his city because of better leadership. He explained, "If the leader is strict, then the officers won't be lazy. The leader will tell them what to do in various situations so they know how to respond, and they'll do it. But if the leader isn't strict, the officers are going to find ways [to get out of doing work]."[16] While the hands of mid-level supervisors are often tied, more research on station supervisors could show that an influx of younger, more responsive leaders can alter the landscape of policing in ways that trend toward more effective everyday policing (Scoggins and O'Brien 2016). But it remains to be seen whether these developments will be enough to overcome the resource limitations, reform failures, and other structural limitations of the bureaucracy.

The system of grassroots rotation (*jiceng duanlian*) was also recently expanded for ministry officials in ways that may improve the exchange of information between levels. Cadre rotation was always designed to increase upper-level knowledge and control by requiring that young officials who wished to move up in the ranks spend time working at the lower levels (Y. Huang 2002). Prior to changes implemented in 2014, however, rotation was a very selective process at the MPS and available only to those men and women who were being groomed for leadership roles. The new changes have increased the number of ministry employees who are eligible to complete rotation, and this puts more officials in frontline positions than ever before. One benefit of the new system is that it places physical eyes and ears of the provincial ministry on the ground to check compliance and record local problems. Another benefit is that it forces those same officials into the shoes of local officers and provides them with an opportunity to learn about problems with practices, funding, and reform. Rotation work is not, however, a cure for all that ails the system.

First, there is evidence to suggest that the benefits of the old cadre rotation system in other ministries are limited. One study of local leaders in Shanxi, Hunan, and Shandong found that the short time frames and frequent turnover rates associated with cadre rotations led to quick, less-effective implementation of environmental policies in those areas (Eaton and Kostka 2014). Similar issues may be true for the Ministry of Public Security, since the majority of its rotations are far shorter than the three to four years described in the study for local leaders. Second, interviewees in the police bureaucracy who had completed or were in the process of completing rotation work were largely pessimistic in their assessments of what they gained from the experience beyond the ability to meet a core requirement for advancement. One recent college graduate working at the 110 call center remarked, "I don't like this work. I've been here for six months and haven't learned anything. I'm exhausted and cannot wait until I move to another office. If my examination scores were higher, I could have been at another [provincial bureau besides Public Security]."[17] Others who were further removed from their work on the front lines were similarly pessimistic. One provincial official said, "I worked at the *paichusuo* for two years. Life was very difficult. . . . I'm not sure what I learned. . . . I just know I never want to go back."[18]

Although my sample size is small, only one provincial bureau employee with whom I spoke expressed optimism about the system. This particular official was pleased to have been recently assigned to one of the more difficult stations in the city and explained, "I'm very interested in learning about the life of the grassroots police officers. I want to know more about the psychological pressures they face so that our department can better help them."[19] I later followed up to see how the work had gone. The officer offered some reservations:

> It was a good experience for me. The program is for promotion and understanding of the lower levels. . . . But many of my colleagues see it as a stepping-stone more than a learning opportunity and often use it as a chance to rest or even focus on their families. They are also having a hard time getting to know the real situation at the ground level because the local station officers see us as outsiders and don't entirely trust us not to report back some negative things about the station or their own conduct. It is not a perfect system [because it has these problems].[20]

Beyond changes to the old guard and potential benefits arising from a more robust grassroots rotation system, there is the potential that problems with everyday policing will be at least partially alleviated by advancements in new technology, although the jury for this is still out. In particular, the MPS's recent focus on big data and information systems analysis could help local agents do a better job of solving regular crimes. The country's expanding network of cameras and facial recognition software for the purposes of social surveillance can be easily employed for a multitude of other purposes, such as identifying perpetrators and recording details of crimes. Moreover, the national database that is largely used to monitor dissidents can be used to track the activities of other criminal suspects. As the focus on social unrest pushes the police bureaucracy to modernize its surveillance capabilities, the same tools, programs, and training serve a dual purpose by helping to compensate for manpower shortages and protocol issues with regard to everyday crime.

One recent interview with a provincial ministry official provides more insight into the complexity of these changes and calls attention to the ongoing issues with everyday crime response as well as the problems the police bureaucracy may face in the future:[21]

> The funding situation has improved in our province as well [as other provinces]. The stations use the funding to buy new equipment, but maybe the training and other things have not caught up yet. Better funding doesn't mean that officers will get more overtime or higher salaries. There are also issues with the equipment. Our officers may not know how to use the full capabilities of the new technology or even how to use the technology properly so as to make it really helpful to their daily work. This is an investment that may take time to realize the full potential [of the technology]. . . . Part of it has to do with the age and experience level of the officers. Older officers are not suited to this new style of policing, and there are a lot of older officers still employed at the local stations. . . . At one station where I worked, the average age was fifty-two. . . . Age can be very useful in dealing with the public, because these officers have prestige (*weixin*). . . . But they don't use the technology in the same way and can't learn how to use these new things.

The official went on to cast doubt on the ability of new technology to solve ground-level issues from a human perspective. "[Another] problem with the technology is that it is almost trying to make police officers into machines. There is less focus on contact with the people, and this may make it more difficult for us to manage the public, which is the real job of the police . . . not to be like a computer. Our officers may wonder why they need people for this task if maybe they can just use a robot."

The official also provided additional insight into the capabilities of the new artificial intelligence (AI) technology itself:

> The AI technology is now quite good and working very well in cities like Hangzhou. It's not perfect yet, but it is very good. The big issue is that not every province has the best technology. There are many different providers, and each province gets to decide which one they pick. *Guanxi* probably plays a role, so some places are stuck with subpar technology that can't do the job. . . . Even with the best technology, AI is not going to solve all the problems of the police. As the police gain the technology, the criminals are also getting access to the same technology and often have even better capabilities than we do. This can create new categories of crime that increase the workloads of our officers and may be even more difficult to address.

If the assessments of this official are correct, then the idea of the all-seeing, all-knowing big brother state that is conjured up by cameras at every subway turnstile and on every street corner is still far from reality. The Chinese state does not have a monopoly on the use of new technology, and it never will.

6

POOR POLICING AND STATE-SOCIETY CONFLICT

On Saturday night, June 21, 2008, Li Shufen went out with a few classmates. Hours later, witnesses say they heard a girl's voice crying for help. Li's lifeless body was found early the next morning, floating in the Ximen River. Described as a "quiet and nice child" by the aunt who helped pull her from the water, Li was only sixteen years old—a student from the countryside who lived with relatives so she could attend Weng'an No. 3 High School in Guizhou Province.

Within days, Li's death launched a firestorm, embroiling the local police in a political fight that made international news. Residents were furious with the way officers in Weng'an handled the investigation and how they treated the five hundred middle school students who showed up at the police station to protest the official claim that Li's death was a suicide. What followed was one of the largest and best-documented riots against police in China.[1] Before it was all said and done, nearly thirty thousand people would take to the street, burning out the local station, setting squad cars on fire, and spurring the deployment of hundreds of PAP officers who used tear gas and physical force to disperse the angry crowd of men, women, and children, some as young as twelve.[2]

It is hard to know exactly what happened to Li Shufen. Her family says the two young men she met up with that evening had family connections to local police leaders. They believe the boys raped and murdered their daughter, threw her body into the river, and then turned to the police and local officials to cover up the crime. Police say Li's death was a suicide. Officers initially detained three individuals of interest, including at least one of the boys she was with that evening.

But eight hours later, all suspects were released, and the local police station declared that Li had taken her own life. Later, a forensic investigation reported no sign of sexual assault, and the local government released a statement saying Li was "unhappy with life because her parents favored her elder brother."[3]

Angry at the official account, Li's family and community fought back. Her uncle—a middle school teacher—went to the police station to complain and was attacked by six plainclothes security guards. Li's father told reporters that the men who brutalized his brother "weren't police, but they might have something to do with police."[4] An aunt was also beaten. By the end of the week, students from as many as four middle schools went to a local government building carrying banners demanding justice. When they received no response, they marched to the local police station, and things got ugly. Witnesses say officers met the students with electric prods, and the angry crowd retaliated by setting fire to police cars and the station, which was eventually engulfed in flames. Videos capturing the scope and intensity of the scene are still available online.[5]

Overpowered, the local police and government officials called in the PAP to suppress the crowd, regain control of the station, and extinguish the fires. Authorities from the central and provincial public security bureaus then spent the next days and weeks sorting through the aftermath. Security forces rounded up 317 rioters for questioning and detention and launched a counter-campaign to fight the rumor mill on social media.[6] They also conducted follow-up investigations into the case but ultimately stood behind the Weng'an station, upholding the original finding that Li's death was a suicide and bringing no public sanctions against the police involved.

While Weng'an is not the first place we might expect to see an outpouring of anger against the Chinese police, it is also not the last. The county sits smack in the middle of Guizhou Province in one of China's poorest regions. It is also a designated autonomous minority prefecture because of its high concentration of Miao and Buyi ethnic minorities. Importantly, Weng'an County had seen a recent surge of social conflict fueled by anger over natural resource extraction and allegations of government-connected gang activity (Fewsmith 2008). But aside from the riot's size and scope, what makes the Weng'an case interesting is that the conflict it highlights has become increasingly visible.

Rising Tide of Police-Society Conflict

Reports of citizen attacks against the Chinese police have been on the rise for over a decade, and 2008—the year of the Weng'an incident—was a banner year. The riot over Li Shufen's death came just weeks before the Beijing Olympic Games were set to open, which meant it was a sensitive time for Chinese leaders hoping to stage a grand and politically uneventful Olympics. Tibetan monks put a dent in those dreams in March by clashing with police in Lhasa to protest Beijing's rule, and separatists in Xinjiang followed up with a series of unrelated incidents targeting the police.[7] That violence came to a crescendo a few days before the opening ceremony of the Olympics when one group drove a truck into a police station, killing sixteen officers.[8] If anything, the politically oriented Uighurs and Tibetans were expected to stir up trouble at a time when all eyes of the international community were set on Beijing. But they were not the only ones targeting the police that summer.

In mid-July—just a few weeks after Li Shufen was pulled from the river—hundreds of angry migrant workers attacked a police station in Kanmen, Zhejiang, a small city south of Shanghai along China's populous coast.[9] Much like the residents of Weng'an, these workers had no larger political grievances in mind. According to reports, they mobilized because the police had detained one of their own when he complained that a security guard had beaten him for trying to obtain a temporary residence permit. The migrant workers rioted for three days, surrounding the police station, smashing cars and motorbikes, and stoning police officers and their vehicles.

Other large-scale attacks on police have since occurred all over the country. In the span of one week in 2009, state media sources reported that one thousand protesters attacked traffic police in north-central Gansu Province because of an altercation between a cyclist and four officers. Then, reports spread that a farmer in the southern province of Guangdong died in police custody, prompting three hundred tea farmers to assault local police with stones, bricks, and hoes and set police cars and motorbikes on fire.[10] The Shishou riot in south-central Hubei also occurred in 2009. That protest began after police claimed to find a suicide note for a twenty-four-year-old chef that family members believed was a fake.[11] In 2011, a thousand workers in the southern city of Guangzhou blocked traffic and fought officers after city police pushed a pregnant street vender to the ground.[12] In 2015, hundreds of villagers in the south-central province of Hunan attacked a police station after officers declared that a woman died of accidental pesticide poisoning, even though her family said she was murdered.[13] In 2018, thousands of People's Liberation Army veterans gathered in Shandong Province to protest the beating of a group of elderly veterans by a deputy police chief in Pingdu City, and a group of protesters in Yunan beat up a police officer and smashed police cars after a man died under uncertain circumstances during a debate over forced demolition.[14]

These are just the highlights of a few well-known cases that made international news. The internet is also filled with evidence of "everyday violence" between police and civilians that gets recorded by local news sources or on video sharing sites like iqiyi.com. Accounts of these conflicts are typically short on details but often include video evidence of the events. Local news outlets periodically publish stories of police brutality in this way. In one such incident in 2016, multiple outlets reported that local police in Gansu Province severely beat two students who were caught filming police officers, and several of the accounts included pixilated photos of the students' bruised and torn backsides.[15] In another incident in Sichuan Province in 2012, local news recorded the story of a traffic police officer who repeatedly beat a motorist in the head with a baton until he begged for mercy after daring to question a fine; and police in Dongguan, Guangdong, were caught helping a factory owner deal with a labor dispute by beating up unpaid workers who were trying to negotiate for fair wages.[16] While such news stories are typically confined to local and smaller outlets, they nevertheless dot the internet landscape and spread on social media.

Individuals also upload videos that document police-society conflict. One such video showed a violent fight that broke out between police and two different groups of workers in Henan Province in 2012.[17] Another individual video from 2016 shows officers in Hebei Province brutally beating four individuals said to be local gang members. Sometimes, the conflicts result in serious injury, as they did for three police officers in Shandong Province in 2016 who were injured after intervening in a fight. At other times, they may result in the death of civilians or officers, as did one altercation between police and a twenty-two-year-old college student in Heilongjiang Province in 2008, and another between traffic police and a motorist in 2015.[18] Some of these events result in acts of protest that may or may not qualify as mass incidents, but many are more contained acts of police brutality or abuses of power that get recorded on video and persist on various internet sites until censors or users take them down.

Beyond mass incidents and everyday violence, police scandals—whether they result in physical acts of protest or not—also provide insight into police-society conflict. The biggest police brutality scandal in recent years is the Lei Yang case. Lei was a young environmental researcher and new father who died in May 2016 in the custody of Beijing city police. He was reportedly on his way to the airport to pick up relatives who were coming to town to see his new baby when he had a run-in with local police outside a brothel. Family members say police unfairly entrapped Lei and later lied about the circumstances surrounding his death. The incident went viral on Chinese social media, where netizens railed against the official account and what many saw as the unchecked authority of local police. Lei's status as a regular person who was believed to have been in the wrong place at the wrong time caused some commentators to ask whether they themselves could become the next Lei Yang.[19] The case garnered so much attention that even President Xi Jinping weighed in on the matter by releasing a statement that admonished local police to adhere to the law.[20] Although the officers involved were ultimately not found guilty of misconduct, we know that major scandals can and do drive police reform in China (Fu 2005).

Feeding Back into Conflict

The mass incidents, conflicts, and scandals described above demonstrate yet another way in which the mishandling of everyday crime affects Chinese society by feeding back into a loop of protest and dissent. Put simply: bad things happen when the police are underfunded, poorly trained, overworked, underprepared, and subject to the variant whims of local leaders. Some of this anger and strife is of course related to the inherent conflict built into the very practice of policing the public. As the principal agents of ground-level state enforcement, police should be expected to encounter resistance on a fairly regular basis. Moreover, because the police are authorized—and in some cases required—to use force, certain interactions are all but predestined to turn violent. Additionally, corruption and the mere perception of corruption are undoubtedly fueling some of these conflicts in the Chinese case. Even under the best of circumstances, no one expects the relationship between police and society to be conflict free. That is simply not the nature of police work. Yet because central government leaders have elected to prioritize social control—even at the expense of managing everyday crime—the case of the Chinese police takes natural inclinations toward conflict to the next level by exacerbating the existing tensions.

Just how bad is police-society conflict? Although we lack adequate research on absolute numbers, we know that the number of reports in the news has increased in recent years, and there is evidence to suggest that the government is concerned. In the *Legal Daily* article that revealed 22.2 percent of protests were caused by police-society conflict, the authors noted that police should be the defenders of social order but are now often the initiators of "social contradictions," explaining that "improper behavior, perceived injustice, and bad attitudes of officers" are the primary causes of the conflict between police and society that we are now observing.[21] Moreover, the authors explained that police-society conflict is generally caused by unexpected situations in which the police suddenly become targets of public frustration. This causal description echoes many elements of the officers' stories presented in this book. Police who are systematically dissatisfied with their capability to manage everyday crime and fundamentally underprepared to do their jobs do not make for good public servants. When tensions rise, interactions with the public can spiral out of control.

But what of the stability maintenance regime under Xi that has harnessed technology and used brute-force detention methods to stifle dissent? Repression in China has become more preventive in recent years (Truex 2019; Greitens 2016), but social unrest has not ground to a halt. A new database of more than ten thousand news events on mass protests between 2000 and 2015 shows that the percentage of police responses to such protests that use force has steadily increased (C. J. Chen 2017). Moreover, the capabilities of the state are not uniform, and in particular, they are concentrated in areas most likely to experience unrest. The securitization of policing in Xinjiang has reached unprecedented levels, destroying Uighur culture along with the potential social networks that might be able to muster a credible uprising. But the same is not true in other parts of China. As the quote from the ministry official in the last chapter illustrated, technology capabilities vary greatly from province to province, and even if a province has the right equipment, police forces there may not have the personnel resources to harness that technology effectively. Moreover, the police-society conflicts highlighted here are less predictable—as noted in the *Legal Daily* article—and thereby pose a type of threat different from that in Xinjiang or Tibet because they are harder to predict and prevent. This is not to say that regime collapse is coming at the hands of police-society conflict. But any assessment of the strength of the Chinese security apparatus should take a broader view of coercive capacity and look closely at these ground-level interactions. Doing so in China shows us that the security apparatus is more vulnerable and prone to provoking conflict than high-level assessments of protest repression have led us to believe.

The incidents of police-society conflict also highlight another problem faced by frontline officers: unrealistic performance requirements by the government and the ministry. The same *Legal Daily* report went on to explain that the answer to solving police-society conflict is to eliminate triggers such as bad attitudes and require that police officers further regulate their behavior, be polite, and adhere to strict law enforcement. Such goals are difficult to achieve for any police organization and in the Chinese case would require heavy investment in training and psychological support. Even if proper benchmarks could be set, it is possible stations might find a way to meet them on a superficial level without making meaningful progress on the underlying issues. To give one example, in 2004 the ministry launched an anti-murder campaign in which all local public security authorities were required to reduce murders and raise "clearance" rates—the rate at which officers are able to resolve or "clear" a case. Murder rates plunged accordingly, and clearance rates in many cities were reported at 100 percent. Such results continue into the present day and strain credulity—especially since few additional resources were allotted to help local stations meet the new targets. The number of murder cases has since gradually decreased to levels not seen since the early 1980s.[22]

Significantly, unrealistic targets to reduce murders may be driving some of the police-society conflict highlighted by the *Legal Daily*'s report. Recall that the Weng'an riot started when police declared Li Shufen's death a suicide even through her family believed she was murdered. This was also the case with the twenty-four-year-old Hubei chef whose death set off the Shishou incident in 2009. While it is difficult to track these cases systematically, other cases have also surfaced. The family of a female college student in Jinan raised similar claims about the circumstances surrounding their daughter's death, and the protests in Hunan in 2015 erupted over concerns that the police had misclassified a woman's murder as an accidental pesticide poisoning.[23] Were these cases of corruption? Were the police determinations accurate? Were the local stations just trying to get out of logging a murder case? It is hard to go back and investigate these particular claims, but we know that the intentional mischaracterization of murders is not unique to China, although suspicions are usually only confirmed when the evidence is particularly egregious, as it was in Chicago a few years ago.[24] In the Chinese case, the dramatic decline in murder rates alone is enough to raise concern, especially when coupled with anecdotal reports from families of victims.

When we consider the increase in reports of police-society conflict, the folly of subordinating everyday crime to the control of social unrest is thrown into high relief. Suddenly, it is not just about dissatisfied officers, declining police legitimacy, or even compromised regime resilience. We see that by cutting off resources for everyday crime fighting and exacerbating an inherently tense relationship between the police and the public, the preferential treatment given to protest control and its politicized components is likely feeding back into a loop of protest. This in turn creates even more problems for the Communist Party. If it is true that over one-fifth of mass incidents in China are caused by conflict with the police, then the failures of policing everyday crime are responsible for some proportion of this conflict, if not the lion's share. While it is possible that the regime's concentration on protest control at the expense of everything else is a smart strategy that helps bolster the regime, it is difficult to know how long such a strategy will hold. Even within the police bureaucracy, there are signs of concern for the future. The team leader of the People's Armed Police referenced earlier explained, "China needs to be controlled, and it must move at a slow pace to do so. . . . My team can handle anything, but our job may become more difficult [in the years to come]."[25]

This may explain why the Ministry of Public Security has begun engaging in more sophisticated public outreach strategies, turning to social media and high-quality television programming to rehabilitate and shape its public image (Scoggins, forthcoming). But these efforts may be too little, too late for an institution that just embarked on a new reform agenda that improves protest response capabilities but does very little for other types of ground-level policing. Perhaps the party-state is banking that it can continue to manage dissent through these new social control measures. This strategy has certainly worked in the past. Or perhaps police leaders are just doing the best they can, given limited ministerial resources and formidable local challenges. Regardless of the higher-level reasons, the protest loop indicates that this strategy is risky at best.

Policing in the shadow of protest may be a short-term, stopgap solution for authoritarian regimes such as China, or it may be the ticket to China's long-term, coercive success. It is impossible to predict the future. But the problems with everyday policing raise a host of concerns for the public security bureaucracy, the public, and our scholarly conceptualizations of authoritarian resilience and state legitimacy. Talking to police officers on the front lines opens up a new world of disorder and inefficiency that we cannot observe if we only read the news, look at official reports, or stand on street corners. Officer accounts of how policing on the ground actually works strongly suggest that our prior beliefs about state stability in China—created by impressions of a well-funded and highly responsive public security bureaucracy that is capable of putting down protests at every turn—are misplaced. By looking at how police handle resource constraints, experience ministerial reform, and interact with the bureaucracy on the issue of everyday crimes, we see striking weaknesses in what from the outside looks like a well-oiled and highly capable machine. While this does not necessarily apply to tightly controlled cities like Beijing or contested areas such as Tibet or Xinjiang, we nevertheless are presented an image of precarious frontline policing that exhibits a high degree of continuity across geographic distance and city size. The resulting portrait of an underperforming internal security state is difficult to ignore.

The current stability maintenance priorities of the party-state do not encourage better police behavior. Police dissatisfaction was a common thread among nearly all the officers I spoke with during the research for this project. Complaints were so detailed and so universal that the very first paper I wrote upon returning from fieldwork was simply titled "China's Unhappy Police" (Scoggins and O'Brien 2016). But the police are not just unhappy; they are overwhelmed. Every day, many officers wake up to face a wall of impossible expectations and tasks. It is not just that being a police officer in China is difficult; it is that the job is made systematically harder by stations that are staffed with office officers who do not pull their weight, by training programs that do not train officers to manage crime, by reporting requirements that do not report the truth but nevertheless take up valuable time, and by the insistence that every call to 110 or the station be answered and followed up on. This latter issue is particularly burdensome. In a recent interview, one official explained that the government conducted an internal study and found that a staggering 80 percent of the calls to 110 should be answered by other departments, yet police leaders have yet to reform the system or ease the requirements.[26] This is not good policing.

The current practice of prioritizing stability maintenance over everyday crime also does a poor job of fostering community relations. Here we have much to learn about what the Chinese public really thinks about the police. Unsurprisingly, mainland publications have reported relatively high levels of trust in the police, but some studies outside of China have reached similar conclusions as well.[27] One comparative study even found that the public's confidence in the police ranked eighth highest out of forty-nine countries, putting China roughly on par with Switzerland (Jang, Lee, and Gibbs 2015). If these numbers seem suspiciously high, that is because they may be related to an unwillingness of survey respondents to speak openly about their feelings toward the police. While the jury on public perceptions is still out, the research is getting better. Another comparative study reached an opposite conclusion, and finer-grained analyses provide a better understanding of the potential dynamics at play behind positive assessments of the police.[28] For example, a study of college students found that while students indicated an overall satisfaction with police, the majority of respondents had "substantially less positive views of police fairness, effectiveness, and integrity . . . did not consider their local police as honest, upright, or ethical . . . [and] had doubts regarding the police's ability to effectively respond to crime, solve crime, prevent crime, or handle crime victims" (Wu and Sun 2010, 106). Other studies have found potentially valuable variation, such as lower degrees of trust in police held by urban residents (Wu, Sun, and Hu 2016).[29] More research is needed to get a better understanding of public perceptions about state capacity to address specific security and public safety threats.[30]

Solving this piece of the puzzle will also enable a more informed conversation about China's regime resilience. For too long, studies of coercive capacity and regime durability have focused narrowly on protest control and political policing. But these assessments look only at the final act of a long play. We must also consider the lead-up to those protests, not just count the number of armed forces or look at the track record of squashing networks of dissidents and putting down riots. One of the main reasons why riots suddenly spin out of control in previously conflict-free environments is that dissatisfaction often lies dormant and unvoiced until an opportunity appears. Joining a cause with many participants significantly lowers the costs of participation, and if enough people are aggrieved and see the original complaint as just, they will see enough benefit to take to the streets, even if all participants were seemingly peaceful the day before (Lorentzen and Scoggins 2015). This is what happened in East Germany in 1989 when a small demonstration eventually led to the regime's collapse, and it is almost what happened that same year on Tiananmen Square and in other cities across China. Understanding the full range of state capacity and how the public interacts with the state's coercive agents will help scholars make better assessments about how these processes work.

Opening up the definition of coercive capacity to include evaluations of everyday policing goes a long way toward achieving that goal. As recent works on the preventative functions of coercion reveal, coercive capacity is not just about the ability of the state to put down a protest (Truex 2019, Greitens 2016, Ritter and Conrad 2016). The day-to-day interactions also matter, and when we talk to officers on the ground, we see the functions of the police go far beyond protests or political policing. When officers would rather bribe a victim than investigate a crime, we see one indicator that state capacity is low. But more importantly, when police officers on the front lines report that they are unable to do their jobs for systematic reasons, this raises much larger questions about the enforcement capabilities of the police system as a whole. Given the numbers on police-society conflict and the likelihood that problems with everyday policing are feeding back into a loop of protest, it becomes clear that we cannot continue to look narrowly at protest control when assessing regime resilience or state power.

Relatedly, failures in everyday policing raise serious concerns about police legitimacy that may bleed into perceptions of larger state legitimacy. It is hard to have faith in the state when you see the police as corrupt, lazy, brutish, or ineffective, and it is hard for police officers and leaders to turn those negative perceptions around when they face so much pressure to improve stability maintenance work, leaving them with little energy and few resources or incentives to improve responses to everyday crime. As the agents of the local state with whom members of the public are likely to come into contact at some point, police officers must have the ability to do the job the government has charged them with, if for nothing but to shape larger perceptions of both the PSB and the local state more generally. This is perhaps why the central ministry mandated that local stations respond to every single call and provide a detailed report for every case. But without concomitant improvements in other areas that matter for everyday policing—namely training, protocols, manpower, and financial resources—these efforts are woefully inadequate for protecting residents and ensuring public perceptions of police and local state legitimacy.

What can the party-state do to correct these problems? What would better policing even look like? It is likely that further centralization efforts could reduce these issues, since the centralization of protest control in China has brought local forces into line and eliminated many of the difficulties faced in other frontline police matters. But proper training will take time, and the current funding issues will remain—at least for the foreseeable future—as will the preferences of local government leaders to exert control over their police stations with regard to medium-priority crimes. Further increases in budget allocations at the lower levels could also alleviate some of the resource limitations for everyday operations. Where that money would come from remains to be seen, but local government budget increases could allow stations to hire more officers, although those new recruits would likely need to be properly trained official officers—not auxiliary police. In many cities, such hiring would also necessitate that the MPS muster sufficient political resources to bypass staffing restrictions that have been enacted across bureaucracies to trim the size of the government. Those two caveats in and of themselves are a tall order, but budget and personnel increases would additionally need to be accompanied by a dedicated commitment to changing the institutional culture of local stations and the bureaucracy itself. Though professionalization attempts have made headway in dislodging the influence of *guanxi* in hiring practices, reports across research sites demonstrate that *guanxi* still influences the hiring process. Even more challenging to displace, however, is the culture of office officers, especially since the people who hold these positions—officers with seniority or social connections—are some of the most powerful people in individual stations. Finally, shifts in the ideological focus at the highest levels would be necessary in order to retool police training programs that are presently dominated by impractical classes in political ideology.

Changes in priorities from the leadership that extend all the way up to the central government could also make a difference. Such a revision would necessitate either a shift away from the focus on stability maintenance, or the elevation of everyday crime management to a level on par with *weiwen* and anticorruption efforts. Neither seems likely, given the nature of the 2015 reforms, but even if such a shift did occur, it is not clear that the ministry would have the capacity to enact meaningful change. Ministry officials would need to tackle the contested space of shared control with local governments and develop a presence on the ground that is currently out of reach, given the staffing levels of the provincial security bureaus. It would also necessitate an overhaul of crime reporting, since the practice of underreporting crime appears to be widespread. Finally, the ministry would have to overcome any resistance at the local station level to ministerial reforms.

The latter issue can be quite thorny, and an example given by one central ministry official demonstrates the length that some stations will go to in order to resist changes from above.[31]

> Many reforms are implemented at the grassroots level first, which can create a lot of problems. This has been true with recent personnel cuts [throughout the different branches of government], and we've had reports that some police stations are only pretending to comply with the new rules. . . . For example, a station might receive an order to cut their force from fifty to thirty, so they cut twenty. But those twenty just go to a different office and do the same work that they were doing before. The middle levels either don't know or don't care that this is happening, and we can't stop it right now.

When I asked him where the money came from to pay their salaries and electricity, his answer was simple: "corruption." While an increased focus on everyday crime management might not provoke the same level of resistance among local police, the official's example also demonstrates the ways in which issues can lie outside the scope of the ministry's capacity, problems that do not bode well for the future of everyday crime management or the Chinese public.

The public relations efforts in recent years are a seeming acknowledgment of these ground-level challenges. The ministry is sponsoring television programs that aim to "restore the image of the People's Police" by showing them in real combat, creating entertainment troupes to spread the message of police service and approachability, and encouraging the widespread use of social media accounts on Weibo and Weixin by local stations to communicate directly with members of the public.[32] But although the ministry may wish to present the Chinese police as a paragon of power and justice, serving the people's needs with a smile, it is difficult to reconcile these efforts with the actual situation on the ground. One ministry official explained the inherent tensions between what the ministry wants the police to do, what the public expects, and what the police themselves think:

> The issue is that the people and the police have a very different understanding of "public service." The people may think of it more like the service in a restaurant: how was the officer's attitude? Was he polite and helpful? That's not what public service means to the police. Their job is about reducing crime and protecting public security. . . . It's a difficult situation because officer morale is quite low right now. We hope the salary increases will help. . . . But police don't have a lot of options if they leave the force. It is hard for them to find a better job or a job in another

> area. The only real way to use their skills is to work in private security, but these jobs are mostly not well paid. They may not be any better off outside the police force, but the low morale is still a common problem. This is a real challenge that we are facing right now because it affects so many aspects of police work.[33]

Such statements from ministry officials demonstrate the depth of their knowledge about the ground-level situation and the problems facing the police bureaucracy, and they also reveal the thorniness of these problems and the uphill battle that reformers at the MPS will face as they try to address the issues that impact everyday crime control and frontline response. Yet because the reform agenda under Xi Jinping has been so focused on stability maintenance capabilities and further politicizing the bureaucracy's work through high-level anticorruption campaigns, it remains to be seen if reformers will ever get the chance to tackle the everyday crime problems facing the organization. For the foreseeable future, it looks as though the Chinese police will continue to toil in the shadow of protest control, making do on the front lines as best they can, given operating constraints, a lack of support from above, and an increasingly contentious relationship with the public.

Notes

INTRODUCTION

1. Chinanews.com, "Two Policemen in Anhui Witness but Do Not Stop Murder of Girl. Police: Not Afraid of Death" (in Chinese), *People's Daily Online*, 22 August 2013, http://www.chinanews.com/fz/2013/08-22/5192751.shtml; "Two Anhui Policemen Witness Girl Being Stabbed with a Knife Ten Times and Do Not Stop It" (in Chinese), People's Daily Online, 21 August 2013, http://new.qq.com/cmsn/20130822/20130822001939.

2. Comment.news.163.com, "Topic: Two Policemen in Anhui Witnessed Girl Being Killed and Did Not Stop It. Police Say They Were Not Afraid of Death" (in Chinese), 2013, no longer available online.

3. Ran Zhou and Guoshui Chang, "Two Policemen in Anhui Witness Girl Being Killed and Do Not Stop It. The Police Deny That They Were Afraid of Death" (in Chinese), People's Daily Online, 22 August 2013, http://politics.people.com.cn/n/2013/0822/c1001-22652003.html.

4. See Comment.news.163.com, 2013.

5. See Te-Ping Chen, "Chinese Police Suppress Wukan Protests in Violent Clashes," *Wall Street Journal*, 13 September 2016, https://www.wsj.com/articles/chinese-police-arrest-13-people-in-wukan-to-suppress-demonstrations-1473753790; Tom Phillips, "In China's Far West the 'Perfect Police State' Is Emerging," *Guardian*, 22 June 2017, https://www.theguardian.com/world/2017/jun/23/in-chinas-far-west-experts-fear-a-ticking-timebomb-religious, and Paul Mozur, "Inside China's Dystopian Dreams: A.I., Shame and Lots of Cameras," *New York Times*, 8 July 2018, https://www.nytimes.com/2018/07/08/business/china-surveillance-technology.html. Chinese officials in Guiyang even allowed BBC reporter John Sudworth to "test drive" the technology, using the city's extensive network of cameras to locate the journalist in just seven minutes. Joyce Liu, "In Your Face: China's All-Seeing State," BBC News, 10 December 2017, https://www.bbc.com/news/av/world-asia-china-42248056/in-your-face-china-s-all-seeing-state.

6. In these early interviews I used a number of tactics to explore the development and use of ground-level innovation and effective practices. This included asking about station-specific response practices and giving simple examples of police innovation or experimentation that I had come across in my research on policing in China and the United States.

7. In the context of policing in China, a "dissident" is any individual who formally or publicly lodges a complaint against the government or agents of the state by commenting in a public forum, lodging a petition at a government office, or engaging in public displays of protest.

8. Interviews with retired county and city-level officers, Hebei, 2010. (All interviews conducted by the author.)

9. Hu Jintao, "On Building a Socialist Harmonious Society" (in Chinese), 19 February 2005, http://www.china.com.cn/chinese/news/899546.htm.

10. For a discussion on how *weiwen* is assessed under the cadre evaluation system see the work of Xie Yue (2012, 20–21).

11. The original report for the figures is unavailable, but one official reprint is on the Communist Party News Network. See Lixing Wang, "Mass Incidents: Fragmentation and Construction" (in Chinese), 1 September 2009, http://theory.people.com.cn/GB/49154/49155/9963074.html.

12. "Why Protests Are So Common in China," *Economist*, 4 October 2018, https://www.economist.com/china/2018/10/04/why-protests-are-so-common-in-china.

13. *Legal Daily*, "2012 Mass Incident Report" (in Chinese), 27 December 2012, not currently available online.

14. There are many such examples in the popular press. Well-publicized protests include the Wukan village riots that began in 2011 and the anti-Japanese protests that swept the major cities in 2012.

15. Interview, district station officer, Shaanxi, 2012.

16. Overtime work for frontline police is both common and problematic (Hu 2009).

17. The government releases, for example, information about homicides and drug seizures to the UNODC, but little else. United Nations Office on Drugs and Crimes UN-CTS Crime and Criminal Justice Statistics, https://data.unodc.org/#state:60. More data is available in *The China Law Yearbook* and in official state news articles.

18. Interview with district station officer, Shaanxi, 2012.

19. Megan Keller, "State Dept. Official: China Holding 800k Muslim Minorities in Internment Camps," the Hill, 5 December 2018, https://thehill.com/homenews/administration/419855-state-dept-official-china-holding-800k-uighurs-others-in-internment.

20. Top-down studies dominate the literature for good reason, since authoritarian states by their very nature engage centralized decision-making structures (Nathan 2003; Geddes 1999; Levitsky and Way 2012; Magaloni 2008; Dimitrov 2009). But the emerging literature on lower-level process fills a crucial gap by drawing attention to how policies and processes are actually implemented (Slater and Fenner 2011; Lee and Zhang 2013).

21. Multiple studies address coercive capacity, both within and outside of China studies (Lee and Zhang 2013; Bellin 2004, 2012; Way and Levitsky 2006).

22. Brian Taylor has found that this hybrid system creates opportunities for greater exercise of power by local police leaders (Taylor 2007, 2011).

23. Notable exceptions in political science include the works of scholars such as Brian Taylor (2011, 2006) or William Muir (1979, 1980). For more work on local police see Lauren McCarthy (2015, 2014).

24. Several studies explore these themes in relation to the police in detail (Lipsky 1970; Muir 1979).

25. Scholars have also faced similar difficulties reaching veterans (O'Brien and Diamant 2015).

26. One recent study collected survey evidence of repressive encounters experienced by scholars doing research in China (Greitens and Truex 2018).

27. Interview with police detective, Hebei, 2009.

28. See, for example, the work of William Muir (1979), or, in the popular press, David Brooks, "The Cop Mind," *New York Times*, 8 December 2014, http://www.nytimes.com/2014/12/09/opinion/the-cop-mind.html?_r=0.

29. Interview, 2014.

30. Villages are overseen by village heads, and county police may be called in as needed. Traditionally, villages in China are unaccustomed to police presence, although this too is changing as urban sprawl creeps into the Chinese countryside.

31. Interview, Hebei, 2010.

32. Power in military and police bureaucracies is consolidated in the top leadership, making those organizations less vulnerable to the influence of bottom-up or outside forces (Wilson 1989).

1. POLICING CHINA

1. Edward Wong, "Clampdown in China Restricts 7,000 Foreign Organizations," *New York Times*, 28 April 2016, http://www.nytimes.com/2016/04/29/world/asia/china-foreign-ngo-law.html?_r=0.

2. Fauna, "Shanghai Traffic Police Officer Dragged to Death," chinaSMACK, 18 March 2015, http://www.chinasmack.com/2015/videos/shanghai-traffic-police-officer-dragged-to-death.html.

3. Moving beyond studies that focus on the front lines, scholars have also written broad historical accounts of Chinese policing (Dutton 2005; Wong 2002, 2009; Sun and Wu 2010) and developed discussions of community policing in the Chinese context (Jiao 1995; Wong 2001a, 2001b; Zhong 2009; Sun and Wu 2010; Wang and Wong 2012). Much has been written about police reform (Ma 1997; Wong 2011) and its relationship to the Communist Party (Fu 1994, 2005; Y. Wang 2014) and police legitimacy (Wong 2004b, 2005). Scholars have also analyzed crime rates and their causes during the reform era (Bakken 2005; J. Liu 2005). Michael Dutton (2000), Susan Trevaskes (2010, 2003), Harold M. Tanner (1999), and Murray Scot Tanner (2000) have written about "hard strike" campaigns and police efforts to fight major crime. Moreover, Murray Scot Tanner has conducted research on policing and protest, looking at internal policing policy debates (2004) and the potential effects of the decentralized public security apparatus in China (2005b). Finally, Sarah Biddulph's study on the legislative control over powers of detention provides an account of the use and abuse of police powers (Biddulph 2007).

4. For a comprehensive review of the literature on policing in China that includes analysis of missing pieces and suggestions for future research see Scoggins 2018.

5. In his book on collective resistance in China, Cai Yongshun (2010, 4) downplays the role of police in protest control by noting that final decisions on collective-action incidents are typically made "by the government or their top leaders and not the police," citing a survey of one thousand police officers in Fujian Province as evidence. While this is indeed true, it ignores the lead-up to final decisions and the necessary back-and-forth discussions that take place between protesters and officers.

6. See, for example, Simon Denyer, "Chinese Riot Police Crush Grasslands Protest over Chemical Pollution," *Washington Post*, 6 April 2015, https://www.washingtonpost.com/world/asia_pacific/chinese-riot-police-crush-grasslands-protest-over-chemical-pollution/2015/04/06/0c4a0cf2-dc6a-11e4-b6d7-b9bc8acf16f7_story.html.

7. Examples of police abuse abound. In one report from Shanxi in 2014, news spread of a female migrant worker who was beaten to death after making a demand for unpaid wages. In a widely circulated photo online, a police officer stood on the worker's hair while she lay unconscious on the street. For details of the story and translated excerpts of Chinese netizens' reactions see Fauna, "Shanxi Chinese Police Beat Woman to Death, Stand on Her Hair," chinaSMACK, 29 December 2014, http://www.chinasmack.com/2014/stories/shanxi-chinese-police-beat-woman-to-death-stand-on-her-hair.html.

8. In early 2016, Guangdong police were ridiculed for being unable to tell the difference between a practical joke and rumor spreading (a criminal charge in the PRC) when they detained a man who created a fake news page and sent it to his friends over WeChat, a social media messaging platform. See Samuel Wade, "Police Criticized over 'Two Wife Policy' Detention," China Digital Times, 25 January 2015, http://chinadigitaltimes.net/2016/01/police-criticized-over-two-wife-policy-detention/. In 2015, news sources reported that an auxiliary police officer in central China accidentally fired an air gun after a night out drinking, killing his companion. Sidney Leng, "Police Officer Detained in Central China after He Fires Airgun by Accident and Kills Civilian," *South China Morning Post*, 14 December 2015, http://www.scmp.com/news/china/society/article/1891120/police-officer-detained-central-china-after-he-fires-airgun.

9. This estimate represents the total number of people's police and ministerial officials. It excludes the People's Armed Police, a paramilitary force governed by the People's Liberation Army and the Central Military Commission, and the *chengguan*, who are governed by the City Urban Administrative Law Enforcement Bureau. It is not clear if the number includes the temporary auxiliary police officers employed by the ministry.

10. Chapter 2 explores the impact of these numbers on Chinese police response in detail.

11. Transfers to office-level positions for civil servants are not permitted after age fifty-five, so many officers transfer at this age. Once in office positions, they typically see a reduction in hours. For more information on transfer regulations see State Administration of Civil Service, "Civil Service Transfer Regulations" (in Chinese), 8 December 2008, http://www.scs.gov.cn/zcfg/201409/t20140902_376.html.

12. In addition to an age requirement of eighteen, the 1995 law required that officers have at least a high school diploma, support the constitution (*yonghu xianfa*), be healthy (*shenti jiankang*), have a good political and professional character (*you lianghao de zhengzhi, yewu sushi he lianghao de pinxing*), and voluntarily work on the force (*ziyuan congshi renmin jingcha gongzuo*). It also stipulated that officers may not have been punished for a crime (*ceng yin fanzui shouguo xingshi chufa de*) or been expelled from office (*zeng bei kaichu gongzhi de*). Finally, Article 27 of the law required prospective recruits to take a public examination that would encourage selection based on merit.

13. Interview, 2012. (All interviews conducted by the author.)

14. China stopped reporting all personnel figures in 1997. At this time, there were 1.2 million police officers in the country, 133,000 of whom were female. United Nations, Sixth United Nations Survey of Crime Trends and Operations of Criminal Justice Systems, covering the period of 1995–1997, http://www.unodc.org/pdf/crime/sixthsurvey/publication_by_country_screen.pdf.

15. Interviews with two former female police office workers in Hebei, 2011 and 2012.

16. Interview with provincial ministry official on rotation at a local station's *hukou* division, 2012.

17. Song Guanghui, "Dalian Police: Female Mounted Police Is Not a 'Vase'" (in Chinese), 28 May 2013, http://zqb.cyol.com/html/2013-05/28/nw.D110000zgqnb_20130528_1-05.htm; People.com, "8 Cities across the Country Establish Women's Mounted Police Teams, Kunming Quietly Terminates Its Team" (in Chinese), 29 May 2013, http://js.people.com.cn/html/2013/05/29/231060.html.

18. Interview in Southern China, 2012.

19. Interview with provincial ministry official, 2019.

20. Matt Schiavenza, "Meet the 'Chengguan': China's Violent, Hated Local Cops," *Atlantic*, 22 July 2013, http://www.theatlantic.com/china/archive/2013/07/meet-the-chengguan-chinas-violent-hated-local-cops/277975/.

21. For insight on how real police officers and *chengguan* officers interact see J. Xu 2013.

22. Other names for *xiejing* include *xie qin yuan*, *lianfang dui yuan*, and *zhi an yuan*, although *xiejing* is the most commonplace and is now the official term for auxiliary police in Beijing. Interview with district station leader, Beijing, 2012, and Liao 2010.

23. For more information on the activities of *xiejing* and *chengguan* as hired thugs see Ong 2018.

24. 2006 China Defense White Paper, http://www.china.org.cn/english/features/book/194480.htm; Fisher 2010, 5, 33.

25. Interview with PAP officer, 2012.

26. Viola Zhou, "Why China's Armed Police Will Now Only Take Orders from Xi and His Generals," *South China Morning Post*, 28 December 2017, http://www.scmp.com/news/china/policies-politics/article/2126039/reason-why-chinas-armed-police-will-now-only-take.

27. In Beijing, *xiejing* uniforms are clearly marked. Interview with district station leader, Beijing, 2013.

28. Interview with district station officer, Shaanxi, 2012.

29. A full list of MPS departments is available on the ministry's website, www.mps.gov.cn.

30. Personal communication with internet monitors, Beijing, 2007.

31. For an in-depth analysis of how the censorship game plays out in China see the work of Rongbin Han (Han 2015a). A broader overview of censorship is also presented in King, Pan, and Roberts (2013, 2014). For information on how pro-government online commentary is encouraged see Han 2015b.

32. Interview with provincial ministry official, Hunan, 2012.

33. Xiao Qiang, "Internal Document of the Domestic Security Department of the Public Security Bureau," 26 January 2010, http://chinadigitaltimes.net/2010/01/internal-document-of-the-domestic-security-department-of-the-public-security-bureau-part-i/.

34. Interview with ministry official, Beijing, 2012.

35. Even policing in democratic countries is political (Brodeur 1983, 2007, 2010). In China, the political functions of the police are overt and articulated by officers at all levels.

36. Yuhua Wang looks at the political empowerment of public security chiefs on the provincial level (Y. Wang 2014). See also Fu (2005, 243).

37. Interview with station officer, Hubei, 2015.

38. Since the police are the frontline agents of the party, they have historically been charged with doing the party's dirty work. Fu Hualing reports that some officers feel betrayed by new campaigns that hold them accountable for activities performed in the service of the party, but recent evidence of give and take on the issue has also emerged. In 2012, for example, local police were officially granted detention powers that had long been used but were formally outlawed (Fu 2005).

39. Neighborhood committees were made up of local cadres and members of the community, often retirees. Aiming to root out local crime, members acted as a bridge between the police and the masses, serving as additional eyes and ears of the organization (Dai and Huang 1993; Chen 2002), but their utility during the reform era was limited. Sarah Biddulph rightly argues that the most detrimental effect to state control was the way in which the mobile population undermined the effectiveness of the household registration system (Biddulph 1993, 340–41). Even with the neighborhood committees, the mobility of the population and concomitant declining utility of the household registration system ensured that officers no longer enjoyed a close level of contact with the communities they served, which undermined preventive crime measures.

40. Ben Blanchard and John Ruwitch, "China Hikes Defense Budget, to Spend More on Internal Security," Reuters, 5 March 2013, http://www.reuters.com/article/us-china-parliament-defence-idUSBRE92403620130305.

41. Chinese officials have repeatedly denied that public security funds are for stability maintenance, and there is no separate budget category for stability maintenance activities. Haiyan Wang, "Stability Maintenance Fees over 700 Billion? Ministry of Finance: One Conceptualization" (in Chinese), *Southern Metropolis Daily*, 7 March 2012, http://gcontent.oeeee.com/1/41/1415db70fe9ddb11/Blog/6da/8d38ae.html?bsh_bid=83321550.

42. Ministry of Finance, "2017 Central and Local Budget Implementation Report and 2018 Central and Local Budget Plan Report," 5 March 2018.

43. Adrian Zenz estimates that the annual budget might be as high as RMB 1,240 billion (Zenz 2018).

44. See also "Ministry of Finance Announced the Central Budget Yesterday, Five-Year Public Security Spending to Grow 7 Times" (in Chinese), *Beijing Youth Daily*, 26 March 2014, http://finance.people.com.cn/n/2014/0326/c1004-24737430.html.

45. The US Bureau of Justice Statistics estimates total "police protection" to be approximately $124 billion based on 2010 Census data: BJS.gov, http://www.bjs.gov/index.cfm?ty=pbdetail&iid=5049.

46. Based on reported police per capita. "Most Heavily Policed: Countries," Bloomberg, 2013, http://www.bloomberg.com/visual-data/best-and-worst/most-heavily-policed-countries.

47. Eugene Written, Maxim Tovkaylo, and Alexei Nikolsky, "Health and Education Want to Add 700 Billion Rubles Annually" (in Russian), *Vedomosti*, 14 February 2012, http://www.vedomosti.ru/politics/news/1502548/proschaj_oruzhie?full#cut. It is possible that the budget is higher than reported here. Lidia Kelly, "Russia's Secret Spending on Rise, Budget Risks Not Properly Assessed: IMF," Reuters, 26 May 2014, http://www.reuters.com/article/2014/05/26/us-russia-policy-imf-idUSBREA4P0A020140526.

48. 2006 data from the Tenth United Nations Survey of Crime Trends and Operations of Criminal Justice Systems (Tenth CTS, 2005–2005), https://www.unodc.org/unodc/en/data-and-analysis/Tenth-CTS-access.html. This number may not include the prefectural police budget.

49. "Crime in India: 2012 Statistics," http://ncrb.nic.in/CD-CII2012/Statistics2012.pdf.

50. Cao.go.jp, "FY2014 Cabinet Office General Account Expenditure Budget with Specifications" (in Japanese), http://www.cao.go.jp/yosan/soshiki/h26/h26naikakufu_tousyo.pdf. This number does not include all prefectural police spending.

51. In the time period in question, Turkey spent US$49 per capita.

52. Ministry of Finance of the People's Republic of China, Yss.mof.gov.cn, "2014 Central Government Public Expenditures Budget Report" (in Chinese), 2014. The 2014 budget is used because it is more detailed than the one for 2015, which omits transfer payment information. Interestingly, the published budget numbers for 2014 do not add up. The first six categories should total RMB 138.9 billion, but they only amount to 126.8 billion. Prior budget reports have included a seventh category of "other public security expenses" that may have been omitted online.

53. In a statement to the press, a Ministry of Finance official said part of the money goes to public works unrelated to stability maintenance, including public health, public transportation, construction safety, and increased supervision of food safety. The official provided neither a detailed account of these activities nor an explanation for why they were not included under the separate budget categories of health care, transportation, and general public service. Haiyan Wang, "Stability Maintenance Fees over 700 Billion? Ministry of Finance: One Interpretation" (in Chinese), *Southern Metropolis Daily*, 7 March 2012. Article no longer available online.

54. Zhang Youyi, "This Year the Central Budget for Public Security Is 128.9 Billion Yuan, Higher Than Spending On: Education; Science and Technology; Culture, Sport and Media; and Health and Family Planning," *Sina News*, 28 March 2013, http://news.sina.com.cn/c/2013-03-28/030526662346.shtml.

55. Based on a random sample of ten prefectural-level cities across China. Many of the cities selected provided no or partial information about the ratio of police to public security budget. This is a preliminary estimate, and more research is needed.

56. Hrbczj.gov.cn, "2013 Harbin Local Public Budget Balance Sheet Arrangements," and Zwgk.harbin.gov.cn, 2013, "Description of the Harbin Municipal Public Security Bureau 2013 Departmental Budget" (in Chinese). Reports no longer available online.

57. "Report on Beijing's 2018 Budget Implementation and 2019 Budget" (in Chinese), *Beijing Daily*, 31 January 2019, http://bjrb.bjd.com.cn/html/2019-01/31/content_3234782.htm.

58. This number may be higher than reported because of a note in the budget line marked "special." "Report on the Implementation of the Budget for Shenzhen in 2017 and

the Draft Budget for 2018" (in Chinese), Shenzhen Finance Committee, 2 February 2018, www.sz.gov.cn/cn/xxgk/zfxxgj/zjxx/szfczyjs/201802/t20180202_10764703.htm.

59. For a discussion of fine levying over time see Fu Hualing (2005, 247).

60. Spending appears to be up in larger cities as well. In Beijing, the 2017 budget figure for internal security of RMB 24.42 billion (US$3.6 billion) is a significant increase from the RMB 3.87 billion (US$630 million) figure reported in 2013. But without more specific details of each budget, any comparisons must be made cautiously. "This Year's Public Security Budget in Beijing Nears 3.3 billion, Details Are Classified" (in Chinese), *Beijing News*, 21 March 2013, http://news.qq.com/a/20130321/000043.htm.

61. Interview, Hunan, 2019.

62. Interview, Beijing, 2013.

63. It is not uncommon for the press to publish stories on police brutality, particularly when the beatings result in death. For a well-known 2016 case of a young environmental researcher's death in Beijing see Didi Kristen Tatlow, "Chinese Man's Death in Custody Prompts Suspicion of Police Brutality," *New York Times*, 12 May 2016, https://www.nytimes.com/2016/05/13/world/asia/china-lei-yang-police-death.html. Although most bribes go unreported, accounts sometimes surface in the press. See "Police Accept 90,000 Yuan in Bribes to Release Suspects, Said the Suspects' Knowledge of Law Is Lacking" (in Chinese), *Southern Metropolis Daily*, 7 September 2013, http://news.sohu.com/20130907/n386087346.shtml. Reports of police acting above the law are sometimes covered by the media and range from hit-and-run incidents to helping offspring gain university admission through improper means. See "Police Car Driver in Liaoning Fumeng County Hit-and-Run Case Detained According to the Law" (in Chinese), *Xinhua*, 17 April 2013, http://news.xinhuanet.com/legal/2013-04/17/c_115428978.htm; and "Hunan Longhui Police Commissioner's Daughter Uses an Imposter to Attend University" (in Chinese), *China Youth Daily*, 5 May 2009, http://news.163.com/09/0505/08/58HMPUF500011229.html.

64. The *chengguan* recently grabbed headlines around the world when *chengguan* officials killed a watermelon seller in Hunan. See Schiavenza, "Meet the 'Chengguan.'"

65. Several in-depth analyses show how the state influences the media (Stern and Hassid 2012; Stockmann and Gallagher 2011). By allowing stories of local police misconduct to surface, the Chinese state is also engaging in information collection. For more on how watchdog journalism can serve the goals of the state see Peter Lorentzen's work (2014).

66. Ian Johnson and Jonathan Ansfield, "Key Figure in Scandal That Felled Bo Xilai Is Charged," *New York Times*, 5 September 2012, http://www.nytimes.com/2012/09/06/world/asia/key-figure-in-bo-xilai-scandal-is-charged.html.

67. Kiki Zhao, "China Clears Police Officer in Death of Unarmed Man, but Controversy Isn't Over," *New York Times Blog*, 15 May 2015, http://sinosphere.blogs.nytimes.com/2015/05/15/china-police-shooting-xu-chunhe/?_r=0. Sophie Beach, "Former Chinese Police Chief Sentenced to Death in Gangland Case," China Digital Times, 14 April 2010, http://chinadigitaltimes.net/2010/04/former-chinese-police-chief-sentenced-to-death-in-gangland-case/.

68. Fauna, "Chinese Police Car Hits Crossing Pedestrian Then Drives Away," ChinaSMACK, 18 April 2013, http://www.chinasmack.com/2013/videos/chinese-police-car-hits-crossing-pedestrian-then-drives-away.html. "Haikou Deals Severely with Beatings during Mass Incident; Youying District Chief Admits Responsibility and Resigns" (in Chinese), *Xinhua*, 2 May 2016, http://news.xinhuanet.com/legal/2016-05/02/c_1118783295.htm.

69. Interview with ministry official, Southern China, 2012.

70. Interview with municipal police leader, Beijing, 2012.

71. Interview, Beijing, 2013.

72. Interview with provincial-level ministry official, 2019.

73. Wu and Sun's study on citizen trust in police found that trust in police declined for individuals who also reported worries about corruption. They cite a study (no longer available online) that found nearly one-quarter of complaints to a national hotline were about police corruption (Wu and Sun 2009, 176–77).

2. UNEVEN RESOURCES AND MANPOWER CONCERNS

1. Interview, Shaanxi, 2012. (All interviews conducted by the author.)
2. Fu 2005 discusses the underfunding of stations.
3. Interview with central ministry official, 2012. This type of compensation is not unique to the police bureaucracy. Extravagant gift giving during special occasions and holiday times is woven into the fabric of Chinese workplaces. Gift giving more generally is deeply ingrained and permeates Chinese society at all levels (Yan 1996).
4. Interview with SWAT officer, 2012.
5. Officer Wang's salary should have increased since we spoke in 2012 as he gained seniority and salaries were adjusted to keep up with inflation. He should also be eligible for recent pay increases mandated by the central government, which should increase his salary by 40 percent (RMB 800 based on a RMB 2,000 salary).
6. Interview with SWAT officer, 2012.
7. In many Chinese cities, bill splitting is uncommon, especially outside the larger cities. Friends are expected to take turns picking up the check, even when groups are quite large or meals expensive.
8. Interview with district station officers, Shaanxi, 2012.
9. Interview with patrol captain, Hebei, 2012.
10. "How Much Is the Police Salary? National Police Payroll Summary" (in Chinese), 19 November 2017, http://news.ifeng.com/a/20171119/53397710_0.shtml?_cpb_remenwz6.
11. Interview with ministry official, 2017; Alexander Chipman Koty and Zhou Qian, "A Complete Guide to 2017 Minimum Wage Levels across China," China Briefing, 15 November 2017, https://www.china-briefing.com/news/complete-guide-2017-minimum-wage-levels-across-china/; "China White Collar Average Salary Went Up in the Third Quarter," Zhaopin Limited, 19 October 2017, https://www.prnewswire.com/news-releases/china-white-collar-average-salary-went-up-in-the-third-quarter-of-2017-1-300539661.html.
12. Interview with patrol captain, Hebei, 2012.
13. Interview with mid-level station supervisor, Hunan, 2012.
14. Interviews with officers, Hunan, 2012, and Hebei, 2012.
15. Interview, Shaanxi, 2012.
16. Interview with district station officer, Shaanxi, 2012.
17. Interview with junior district officer, Shaanxi, 2012.
18. This observation is based on my time spent living in Beijing and observing police on the street, as well as an interview with a Beijing district police station chief in 2012. There is also evidence on the internet and in police journals that confirms the modernity of police station outfitting in the capital. See, for example, records of forensic equipment purchases: "Beijing Police Academy in 2014 Laboratory Equipment Purchase Project," http://www.bgpc.gov.cn/news/news/news_id/4479,2014; or see Zhang Xiaoduo (2006) for an account of equipment demonstrations in Beijing's Changping district.
19. Interview with junior district officer, Shaanxi, 2012.
20. Interview, 2014.
21. Interview, 2019.
22. Interview with two district station officers, Shaanxi, 2012.

23. Interview with a senior district station officer, Shaanxi, 2012.

24. This calculation is based on previously cited crowd-sourced data for county- and city-level station officers and national averages for 2017 published in the *People's Daily*. See News.ifeng.com, "How Much is the Police Salary? National Police Payroll Summary"; and "Average Salary of China's Urban Employees Reaches $11,000 in 2017," People's Daily Online, 16 May 2018, http://en.people.cn/n3/2018/0516/c90000-9460829.html.

25. Officers often asked me how much officers in the United States made, and most were astounded to learn that starting salaries in Oakland, which were then advertised at $67,000 a year when I was conducting fieldwork, were higher than what most American university graduates could hope to make and roughly on par with starting salaries for college professors.

26. Interview with station officer, Shenzhen, 2013.

27. Interview with district police leader, Beijing, 2013.

28. Interview, 2012.

29. Interview with internal supervisor, Hunan, 2012.

30. College graduates working higher up in the ministry may enjoy considerable upward mobility, but the majority of local officers have little hope of going much beyond their initial posting. Entry to municipal-level jobs is extremely competitive and requires a high examination score and the ability to pass an interview that often depends on the strength of one's social connections (interview with municipal station officers, Hebei, 2011). Space is limited, and even capable officers who are well connected find themselves first laboring in far-flung stations out in the county (interview with district station supervisor, Hunan, 2012). The most these officers can do is bide their time and hope for an opening in one of the district stations in the closest cities. Such a move typically means a salary increase, better benefits such as housing, and sometimes a lighter workload, but improvements are incremental at best. Thus, the demoralizing effects of low salaries are an inescapable reality for most.

31. Interview with local station officers, Shaanxi, 2013.

32. Interview, Hebei, 2012. See also Scoggins and O'Brien 2016.

33. "Grassroots Civil Servants Say the Key to Civil Servant Corruption Lies in the Low Wages" (in Chinese), Netease Education Forum, 21 November 2012, http://edu.163.com/12/1121/18/8GRTTMVH00294JA1.html#from=relevant#xwwzy_35_bottom newskwd.

34. The process of giving and receiving gifts is a gray area for policing in China. Companies and individuals alike may provide gifts to the police, both as an annual tradition during holidays as a form of insurance and on an as-needed basis.

35. China's low per capita force problem can puzzle those who have visited major Chinese cities and witnessed what appears to be a strong police presence. But adequate manpower and police presence are not necessarily the same thing. Police leaders in China, whether intentionally or not, have done a good job of manufacturing a police presence that belies manpower limitations in many cities. This topic merits more research, but in short, police presence in China can be enhanced by police signage (J. Xu 2013), strategically parked police cars, and ambiguous uniforms worn by non-police security personnel.

36. Interview with ministry official, Beijing, 2012.

37. China often participates in the UNODC's Surveys on Crime Trends (UN-CTS) but has left many of the questions blank, including those about personnel data, since the Sixth Survey on Crime Trends and the Operations of Criminal Justice Systems (1995–1997). A report from the Ministry of Public Security put the total number of police personnel at 1.57 million (129 officers per 100,000 people) in 1999. See Ministry of Public Security, "Impregnable Shield of the Republic: 50 Years of Policing in the People's Republic of China," 1999. Eight years later, in 2007, a figure released by *Xinhua* was still

just 1.6 million: "China to Unify Police Identity Card from January 1," *Xinhua*, 1 January 2017, http://china.org.cn/english/news/194799.htm.

38. It is unclear if these estimates include part-time workers. See, for example, Kathrin Hille, "China's Police Ill-Equipped to Combat Unrest," *Financial Times*, 5 February 2012, http://www.ft.com/intl/cms/s/0/526b2508-4d49-11e1-8741-00144feabdc0.html; Li Jing and Teddy Ng, "China Approves Police Reform Plan Aimed at Improving Force's Efficiency and Public Image," *South China Morning Post*, 16 February 2015, http://www.scmp.com/news/china/article/1714252/china-approves-police-reform-plan-aimed-improving-forces-efficiency-and.

39. One official in the ministry put the total number of security personnel at four million, but this number likely included the PAP, a now separate force that is also estimated at two million. Interview with ministry official, Beijing, 2012.

40. 2015 data from United Nations Office on Drugs and Crime (UNODC), https://data.unodc.org/. Data for 2016, 2017, and 2018 is also available, but in these years fewer countries reported per-100,000 police personnel figures. Moreover, countries with lower police rates were underrepresented in these years. In 2018, for example, all but one country reported a police-per-100,000 rate that was lower than China's suspected rate.

41. Per capita policing needs in a place like Honduras, which at the time of data collection boasted the highest reported annual homicide rate in the world (84 per 100,000) and recently created an entirely new military police force to manage corruption and violence, are vastly different from those in Finland, which in 2013 recorded just ninety-three homicides (1.7 per 100,000) and six total incidents in which police discharged their firearms. Data from UNODC, https://data.unodc.org/; Sibylla Brodzinsky, "The New 'Police Recruits' in Latin America: Soldiers," *Christian Science Monitor*, 8 February 2014, http://www.csmonitor.com/World/Americas/2014/0208/The-new-police-recruits-in-Latin-America-soldiers; Uutiset, "Finnish Police Fired Guns Only Six Times in 2013," 12 December 2014, https://yle.fi/uutiset/osasto/news/finnish_police_fired_guns_only_six_times_in_2013/7701005.

42. Interview, Hebei, 2011.

43. Hu gives the example of Lanzhou's Yantan district, which has just 18 officers to serve 120,000 residents.

44. Interview with provincial ministry official, Hunan, 2012.

45. Interview with district station leader, Beijing, 2012.

46. Interview with patrol leader, Hebei, 2011. One policing journal confirmed the RMB 800 figure, noting that high school graduate *xiejing* in Chengdu earn RMB 800–1,000, and college graduates might earn as much as RMB 1,500, which is nearly three times less than what an official officer with the same educational background earns in Chengdu (Liao 2010).

47. Interview with detective, Hebei, 2010.

48. Interview with detective, Hebei, 2011.

49. Interview with provincial public security official, Hunan, 2012.

50. Interview with district station leader, Beijing, 2012. Interestingly, Beijing *xiejing* command the same salaries as official police at a similar level, although they do not receive any benefits.

51. Interview with district station leader, Beijing, 2012.

52. Interview with station officers, Shaanxi, 2012.

53. Interview with *xunjing* officers, Hebei, 2011; interview with patrol captain, Hebei, 2012.

54. Interview with SWAT leader, Shaanxi, 2012.

55. Interview, Hebei, 2011.

56. See, for example, Kiki Zhao, "China's Most-Hated Official Is No Surprise," *New York Times Blog*, 29 May 2014, http://sinosphere.blogs.nytimes.com/2014/05/29/chinas-most-hated-official-is-no-surprise/?_r=0.

57. Da Chui, "Henan *Xiejing* Who Beat Person at KTV Captured" (in Chinese), Tengxun, 15 September 2015, http://news.rugao35.com/newsshow-149656.html; "Two *Xiejing* in Ningxia Fired for Beating Man" (in Chinese), *Beijing Times*, 18 November 2015, http://news.sina.com.cn/o/2015-11-18/doc-ifxkwaxv2405328.shtml; "Shandong: Couple Engaged in 'Car Sex' Suffer Cruel Interrogation by Four *Xiejing*" (in Chinese), *China Daily*, 22 December 2015, http://www.chinadaily.com.cn/micro-reading/dzh/2015-12-22/content_14420497_2.html.

58. "Internet Airs Hebei Cangzhou Auxiliary Police Violence Law" (in Chinese), 2014, http://v.youku.com/v_show/id_XNzk2NzA4OTAw.html.

59. When news spread that workers in a Beijing suburb were severely beaten by *xiejing* in the local police station, station leaders had to go to the hospital to visit the victims and call a special meeting with higher-ups to handle the matter and meet with other workers at the construction site: "Baotao Workers in Beijing Suburb Police Station Violently Beaten, *Xiejing* Responsible Detained with Criminal Charges" (in Chinese), Hebei News Network, 30 August 2010, http://hebei.hebnews.cn/2010-08/30/content_619192.htm.

60. Interview, Hebei, 2010.

61. Of course, official police are also known to abuse power and treat suspects violently, but the officer's point that such occurrences are less common with official police is plausible.

62. Ministry of Public Security, "Guo Shengkun Emphasized the 12th Meeting of the Leading Group for Deepening Reform of the Ministry of Public Security" (in Chinese), 13 July 2015, http://www.mps.gov.cn/n2255079/n4876594/n4974590/n4974598/c4975752/content.html.

63. "The General Office of the State Council Issues and Publishes 'Opinions on Regulating the Management of Police Auxiliary Personnel in Public Security Organs'" (in Chinese), *Xinhua*, 29 November 2016, http://www.gov.cn/xinwen/2016-11/29/content_5139897.htm.

64. "Unswervingly Take the Road of Reform and Strengthen the Police to Further Deepen the Reform of Public Security" (in Chinese), *People's Public Security News*, 2 February 2018, http://www.mps.gov.cn/n2255079/n5967516/n5981117/n5981187/c6011163/content.html.

65. For more on police reform objectives under President Xi Jinping see Scoggins, n.d.

66. Interviews with a patrol captain in Hebei, 2011, and a district station supervisor in Hunan, 2012.

67. State Administration of Civil Service, "Civil Service Transfer Regulations" (in Chinese), 8 December 2008, http://www.scs.gov.cn/zcfg/201409/t20140902_376.html.

68. Interview with former district station police officer, Shaanxi, 2012.

69. Interview, Hunan, 2012.

70. Interview with a district station patrol squad leader, Hebei, 2012.

71. Interview with a mid-level supervisor in district station, Hunan, 2012.

72. Interview with patrol officer, Hebei, 2011; interview with city officer, Shaanxi, 2012.

73. Interview with a provincial ministry officer, Hunan, 2012.

74. Interview, Hebei, 2011.

75. Interview with senior and former officers in Shaanxi, 2012; interview with junior district station officer in Shaanxi, 2012; interview with senior detective, 2012, among others.

76. Interview with an assistant station chief, Hunan, 2012.

77. For a media description of Zeng Kaigui and his crimes see "Former Soldier Linked to Earlier Robberies, Murders," *China Daily*, 12 January 2012, http://www.chinadaily.com.cn/cndy/2012-01/12/content_14426375.htm.

78. Interview with a provincial bureau official, Hunan, 2012.

79. Guodong Feng, "Policeman Pi Mingwei: Perseverance and 20,000 Steps" (in Chinese), *Xinhua*, 4 March 2020, http://www.xinhuanet.com/politics/2020-03/04/c_1125659319.htm.

80. For a discussion of how *weiwen* is assessed under the cadre evaluation system see Xie 2012, 20–21.

81. Interview with SWAT leader, Shaanxi, 2012.

82. Cui Jia, "Xinjiang Security Funding Increased by 90 Percent," *China Daily*, 13 January 2010, http://www.chinadaily.com.cn/china/2010-01/13/content_9311035.htm; Andrew Jacobs, "3 Dead in Clash at Police Station in Western China, Report Says," *New York Times*, 23 January 2014, http://www.nytimes.com/2014/01/24/world/asia/3-dead-in-clash-at-police-station-in-western-china-report-says.html; Adrian Zenz, "Xinjiang's Re-education and Securitization Campaign: Evidence from Domestic Security Budgets," China Brief, 5 November 2018, https://jamestown.org/program/xinjiangs-re-education-and-securitization-campaign-evidence-from-domestic-security-budgets/.

83. As a point of reference, Keshan County in western Heilongjiang has over twice the population of Gangcha but spent considerably less (RMB 5.865 million, or US$950,000) on local police in 2014. "Keshan County Police Department's Public Budget" (in Chinese), www.keshan.gov.cn/jone/keshan/fujian/%E5%85%8B%E5%B1%B1%E5%8E%BF%E5%85%AC%E5%AE%89%E5%B1%80%E9%A2%84%E7%AE%97%E5%85%AC%E5%BC%80.doc.

84. Charles Hutzler, "Watching Dissidents Is a Booming Business in China," Associated Press, 27 May 2003, http://bigstory.ap.org/content/watching-dissidents-booming-business-china.

85. Interview with local station supervisor, Hunan, 2013.

86. Interview with ministry official, Hunan, 2012.

87. Interview with ministry official, Hunan, 2012.

88. Interview with district station detective, Hebei, 2011.

89. Interview with district station supervisor, Hunan, 2012.

90. Interview with district station officer, Shaanxi, 2012.

91. Interview with district station supervisor, Hunan, 2012.

92. Interview with district station detective, Hebei, 2011.

93. Interview with district station officer, Shaanxi, 2012.

94. "Guangdong's Lianjiang City Spends over Thirty-One Million in One Year on Comprehensive Stability Maintenance, Says Money Is to Buy Stability" (in Chinese), *Southern Daily*, 25 August 2010, http://news.sohu.com/20100825/n274452880.shtml.

95. "Central Government Passes Comprehensive Public Security Reforms" (in Chinese), Sina, 15 February 2015, http://news.sina.com.cn/c/2015-02-15/120631523829.shtml.

96. Interviews with provincial ministry official, 2018 and 2019.

97. Interview with ministry officer, 2017.

3. LIMITATIONS OF POLICE REFORMS

1. Interview, 2011. (All interviews conducted by the author.)

2. Managing distress calls from individuals with mental illness has long been an issue for frontline police. Evidence from both the United States and Australia indicate that such

encounters are more likely to end in violence and even death, usually for the men and women with mental illness (Fuller et al. 2015; Kesic, Thomas, and Ogloff 2010).

3. Patrol officers in Britain, Ireland, Norway, New Zealand, and Iceland also do not carry firearms.

4. This type of conflict over reform implementation is familiar to Chinese scholars, although it is seldom discussed outside of policing circles. In his book on police reform in China, Kam Wong outlines a number of concerns and reservations held by both reformers and officers in China (Wong 2011, 5).

5. See the work of Kam Wong for extensive overviews of public security reform (Wong 2011, 2002, 2009). For additional information on public security reform see Fu Hualing's scholarship (Fu 2005). Elsewhere, I outline a more recent treatment of police reforms under President Xi Jinping (Scoggins, n.d.).

6. China is not unique in this regard. Police bureaucracies around the world pursue reform for a variety of reasons that often have little or no relation to what ground-level agents would call "effective" in the sense of helping them do their jobs more efficiently. For example, reformers have pursued policies designed to achieve broader goals like increasing democratic development (Bayley 1995; Manning 2010; Sklansky 2008; Stone and Ward 2000), demilitarizing the bureaucratic structure (Herzog 2001), and moving toward centralization (Hale, Heaton, and Uglow 2004) or decentralization (Taylor 2011, 150–54; Eaton 2008). Police leaders and higher-ups may also use reforms to pursue political agendas like repressing political or economic rivals (Taylor 2011, 34). See also Sharon LaFraniere and Jonathan Ansfield, "Crime Crackdown Adds to Scandal Surrounding Former Chinese Official," *New York Times*, 27 March 2012, https://www.nytimes.com/2012/03/27/world/asia/bo-xilais-china-crime-crackdown-adds-to-scandal.html.

7. This is also perhaps one reason why local policing in the United States is arguably just as violent today as it was in 1953 when policing scholar William Westley wrote that the municipal police "conceive of violence as a personal property to be used at discretion" (Westley 1953, 34).

8. The Police Law, 1995 (in Chinese), http://www.mps.gov.cn/n16/n1282/n3493/n3763/n4138/427625.html.

9. Interview with detective, Hebei, 2011.

10. In 2014, a pilot program was launched in Shanghai that allowed one thousand beat-cops to carry revolvers. Participating officers underwent a two-month training period and psychological assessment. Later, the size of the force was increased, and similar programs were rolled out in other major cities like Qingdao, Changsha, Xi'an, and Kunming. While the change is significant, it affects only a small percentage of patrol officers and is concentrated in larger cities. Most patrol officers remain unarmed, and it is unclear when and whether the reforms will be broadened to arm patrol officers in smaller cities or the county stations. For more information see CCTV News Video, "Ministry of Public Security Official Discuss the Arming of People's Police in Shanghai" (in Chinese), Sina, 22 April 2014, http://news.sina.com.cn/c/2014-04-22/093029985238.shtml.

11. "Traffic Police Are Fully Equipped with Guns, But Is It Appropriate?" (in Chinese), Tencent News, 23 August 2018, https://cd.qq.com/news/newsplus/rifle.htm.

12. Interviews with patrol officer, Hebei, 2011; district station officer, Shaanxi, 2012.

13. Interview with city officer, Hunan, 2012.

14. Interview with detective, Hebei, 2012.

15. Interview with station officer, Shaanxi, 2012.

16. For an account see Y. Xu 1996.

17. See, for example, the general language in Article 33 of the Police Law, "City Police Patrol Regulations," which stipulates that patrol officers must file reports on important

cases immediately: Mps.gov, 1995, http://www.mps.gov.cn/n16/n1282/n3493/n3793/n4348/436063.html.

18. Interviews with district station officers, Shaanxi, 2012; district station supervisor, Hunan, 2012; provincial ministry official, 2019.

19. Interview with provincial ministry official, Hunan, 2012.

20. An internal police document from Zhejiang describes a color-coded system in which red warnings are to be issued when local police encounter cases of terrorism or persons fleeing government capture. The deadline for raising a warning level about such cases to the higher level is fifteen minutes during sensitive times, and the deadline for first providing feedback on how the situation was handled is twenty-four hours. Report available at Chinadigitaltimes.net, "Zhejiang Police's Internal Document: Controlling the Movements of Critical Persons," 19 January 2011, http://chinadigitaltimes.net/2011/01/zhejiang-psb-internal-document-controlling-the-movements-of-critical-persons/.

21. Interviews with patrol captain, Hebei, 2011; provincial ministry official, Hunan, 2012. Examples of this type of resistance are found elsewhere as well. Kam Wong discusses resistance to the "three items of education" campaign among police managers and officers to whom "it was more important to engage in police work (e.g., arresting criminals) than to participate in . . . off-site education and filling out reports for the campaign" (Wong 2011, 252).

22. Interview with station level officer, Shaanxi, 2012.

23. Interview with district station supervisor, Hunan, 2012; interview with district station officer, Shaanxi, 2012.

24. Interview with district station officer, Shaanxi, 2012.

25. Interview, Shaanxi, 2012.

26. This chapter of the law is detailed. Under Articles 42–47, local police are formally subjected to oversight by higher police authorities, the people's procuratorates, administrative prosecution authorities, and the public. Higher police authorities are granted the right to annul or alter decisions or other actions taken by local police, and the law further lays out mechanisms for handling conflicts of interest and managing accusations against local police. Mps.gov 1995.

27. The 1997 original and 2011 updates are available (in Chinese) at http://www.gov.cn/zwgk/2011-09/08/content_1943257.htm; "Public Security, Police and Law Enforcement Responsibility and Accountability Provisions," 2016, http://www.mps.gov.cn/n16/n1282/n3493/n4390881/5036606.html.

28. Interview, Hunan, 2012.

29. Interview, Hunan, 2012.

30. Interview with internal provincial ministry official, Hunan, 2012.

31. Interview with provincial ministry official, Hunan, 2012.

32. Interview with provincial ministry official, Hunan, 2012.

33. Interview with central ministry official, Beijing, 2012.

34. Interview with ministry official, Beijing, 2012.

35. Interview with a small group of ministry officials, Beijing, 2012.

36. In the US see, for example, local police response to the deaths of unarmed black men and youths such as Oscar Grant in Oakland, Eric Garner in New York, Alton Sterling in Baton Rouge, and Michael Brown in Ferguson, Missouri, to name a few. These cases received national news attention and helped spark and maintain the Black Lives Matter Movement. For brief overviews of these and other cases see Holly Yan, "'Black Lives Matter' Cases: When Controversial Killings Lead to Change," CNN, 4 May 2017, https://www.cnn.com/2017/05/04/us/black-lives-matter-updates-may-2017/index.html.

37. Interview with internal district supervisor, Hunan, 2012. For background on the Five Prohibitions campaign see "259 Chinese Policemen Fired for Poor Conduct,"

China Daily, 20 November 2003, http://www.chinadaily.com.cn/en/doc/2003-11/20/content_283267.htm.

38. Interview with supervisor, Hunan, 2012.

39. Interview, Beijing, 2012.

40. Interview, Hebei, 2011. A similar scenario was captured in Lu Chuan's 2002 film *The Missing Gun*. In the film, a police officer in rural Guizhou loses his gun after a night of heavy drinking at a wedding, resulting in an increasingly panicked search for the weapon. In the film, the officer ultimately sacrifices his life to get the gun back and dies happily when he succeeds.

41. In the summer of 2015, a petitioner was shot by newly armed police in a Heilongjiang train station. The case attracted attention from law firms in Beijing and figured somewhat prominently in discussions about the national crackdown on rights lawyers in 2015, as attorneys from the firm involved in the case disappeared. For information on the shooting see Luo Yuming, "Man Shot in Heilongjiang Was a Serial Petitioner, Family Awarded Assistance after Death" (in Chinese), *Southern Weekend*, 6 May 2015, http://news.qq.com/a/20150506/014644.htm?ADUIN=519013714&ADSESSION=1430896173&ADTAG=CLIENT.QQ.5389_.0&ADPUBNO=26466. One report from police officers in China notes that most of the patrol cops now being armed have not fired a shot since the five bullets they were required to shoot during their initial training. William Wan and Xu Jing, "Newly Armed Police in China Say They Fear Their Guns as Much as Public," *Washington Post*, 26 September 2014, https://www.washingtonpost.com/news/worldviews/wp/2014/09/26/newly-armed-police-in-china-say-they-fear-their-guns-as-much-as-public/.

42. Interview with district officer, Shaanxi, 2012.

43. Interview with ministry official, Beijing, 2012.

44. Dialing 110 does not immediately connect the caller to the local *paichusuo*. The call usually goes through three tiers of bureaucracy before it finally gets down to the appropriate *paichusuo*. Interview with district station officer, Shaanxi 2012.

45. Interviews with district station officers, Shaanxi, 2012; Hunan, 2012.

46. Such beliefs have merit. The ministry's resources for managing calls are limited, and many issues that surface in the calls cannot be addressed. One official explained, "There is very little we can do if someone calls about a stolen wallet, but if they have a complaint about a fundamental problem with a rule, we can take the issue under review" (interview with ministry official, Beijing, 2012). Whether and how often they do so, however, is not immediately clear, and none of the officials interviewed could provide additional information about the process.

47. The Police Law, 1995 (in Chinese), http://www.mps.gov.cn/n16/n1282/n3493/n3763/n4138/427625.html.

48. Political control of the police is common in communist states (Bayley 1985), and the Chinese police are no exception (Fu 1994).

49. Interview with district station supervisor, Hunan, 2012.

50. Interview with patrol captain, Hebei, 2011.

51. Interview, Shaanxi, 2012.

52. Interview with district station officer, Shaanxi, 2012.

53. "Opinion on the Framework for Comprehensive Deepening of Police Reform and Large Problems" (in Chinese), *Xinhua*, 15 February 2015, http://news.xinhuanet.com/legal/2015-02/15/c_1114379121.htm.

54. Interviews with local district supervisor, Hunan, 2012; local station officer, Hebei, 2011.

55. Interviews with local district station officer, Shaanxi 2012; district officer, Hunan, 2012.

56. Interviews with patrol officer in Hebei, 2011; local district supervisor, Hunan, 2012.

57. Fu Hualing calls this individualistic blame game the "people factor" (Fu 2005, 245).

58. Interviews with patrol officer, Hebei, 2011; district station officer, Shaanxi, 2012; ministry official, Beijing, 2012; Beijing municipal police leader, Beijing, 2013; assistant station chief, Hunan, 2012.

59. Interview with assistant station chief, Hunan, 2012.

60. Lei Zi, "Chengdu Police Recruit Officers with Cool Hong Kong–Style Blockbuster Poster" (in Chinese), Chengdu News Network, 3 July 2014, http://cd.qq.com/a/20140703/011313.htm#p=9.

61. Interview with patrol officer, 2011.

62. Complaints about procedural development were not common. This possibly reflects an unwillingness on the part of the officers interviewed to suggest anything that might create more work for them.

63. Interview with ministry official, Beijing, 2012.

64. People's Republic of China Criminal Procedure Law (in Chinese), 17 March 2012, http://www.gov.cn/flfg/2012-03/17/content_2094354.htm.

65. Interview with district station officer, Shaanxi, 2012.

66. Xiao Hui and Fu Zongheng, "Investigation Finds Two Police Officers Who Witnessed a Young Girl's Murder Will Not Lose Their Jobs" (in Chinese), *Beijing Daily*, 23 August 2013, http://www.bjnews.com.cn/news/2013/08/23/279965.html.

67. "Jiangsu Responds to the Death of a Man Who Was Beaten to Death in Front of a Traffic Police Team," People's Daily Online, 6 August 2013, http://sd.ifeng.com/zbc/detail_2013_08/06/1076774_0.shtml.

68. Interview with central ministry officer, Beijing, 2012.

69. Interview with city officer, Hubei, 2015.

70. For updates to the People's Armed Police Law see People's Armed Police Law (in Chinese), 27 August 2009, http://www.gov.cn/flfg/2009-08/27/content_1403324.htm. For handbooks and updates see People's Daily Press 2009. Sun and Li 2012.

71. Interview, Hunan, 2009.

72. Interview, Hebei, 2009.

73. Interview, Hunan, 2019.

74. Interview, Hebei, 2011.

75. Interview with city station officer, Hebei, 2009.

76. Interview, Shaanxi, 2012.

77. Interview with city station officer, Hebei, 2009.

78. Interview with PAP officer, 2012.

79. Interview with PAP leader, 2012.

80. Wang Yukai, professor at China's National School of Administration, quoted in Michael Wines, "China Approves Law Governing Armed Police Force," *New York Times*, 27 August 2009, http://www.nytimes.com/2009/08/28/world/asia/28china.html?_r=2.

81. Interview, 2018.

82. Interview with district station officer, Shaanxi, 2012.

83. Interview with district station supervisor, Hunan, 2012.

84. This, incidentally, is not the case with the People's Armed Police. One team leader reported that he often participates in high-level, technical training programs in Beijing or with foreign police forces that have helped him gain knowledge to take back to his team (interview, 2012).

85. "The Ministry of Public Security: Comprehensive and Systematic Reform Touches on Principles" (in Chinese), 16 February 2015, http://bj.people.com.cn/n/2015/0216/c82837-23928025.html.

86. The roots of China's surveillance system extend back to 1998, with the MPS's initiation of the "Golden Shield Project" (Walton 2001); and by 2007 the National Citizenship

Information System was in place, linking information from the household registration system with user data from the major telecommunications companies.

87. For one descriptive report of how China uses street cameras and facial recognition technology see Paul Mozur, "Inside China's Dystopian Dreams: A.I., Shame and Lots of Cameras," *New York Times*, 8 July 2018, https://www.nytimes.com/2018/07/08/business/china-surveillance-technology.html.

88. Interview with provincial ministry official, 2018.

89. "Daggers Drawn: Some Clues on Why China Arrested the President of Interpol," *Economist*, 9 October 2018, https://www.economist.com/china/2018/10/09/some-clues-on-why-china-arrested-the-president-of-interpol; Choi Chi-yuk, "Ex-Interpol Chief Meng Hongwei 'Was Never Close' to Former Security Tsar," *South China Morning Post*, 10 October 2018, https://www.scmp.com/news/china/politics/article/2167708/ex-interpol-chief-meng-hongwei-was-never-close-disgraced-former.

90. Angela Meng, "Two of Xi Jinping's Associates Promoted to Key Public Security Ministry Posts," *South China Morning Post*, 29 March 2015, http://www.scmp.com/news/china/article/1749910/two-xi-jinpings-associates-promoted-key-public-security-ministry-posts.

91. Interview, 2018.

4. CONTROLLING THE LOCAL POLICE

1. This is in contrast to decentralized police systems like those of the United States, where station practices and capabilities can vary vastly from city to city. Japan and the United Kingdom also have centralized systems.

2. Interview with city police officer, Hunan, 2012. (All interviews conducted by the author.)

3. In interviews, I asked officers to characterize their station's capacity to manage different types of crime and coded it along a three-point continuum of weak, neutral, and strong. While police officers' self-assessments are not infallible, and the control of crime is sometimes influenced by other state agents in addition to the police, self-assessments from police officers remain one of the best currently accessible measures, since the state purposefully conceals accurate figures on protest, crime, and clearance rates.

4. This conceptualization of centralization and decentralization draws from the fragmented authoritarianism literature that focused on both the "structural allocation of authority and the behavior of officials related to policy process" (Lieberthal and Lampton 1992; Mertha 2005).

5. The literature on fragmented authoritarianism as a framework for understanding the Chinese bureaucracy is vast (Lieberthal and Oksenberg 1988; Lieberthal and Lampton 1992; Mertha 2008, 2009). It is also worth noting that the *tiao-kuai* principle meant to centralize control over the local-level bureaucracies by minimizing the power of local governments was implemented for the legal organs (W. He 2007) yet remains incomplete and at best achieves a "soft centralization" (Mertha 2005). For matters of policing, local government officials can be particularly tenacious in exerting control over areas of interest.

6. In their edited volume on fragmented authoritarianism, Kenneth Lieberthal and David Lampton acknowledged that the framework had primarily focused on the economic bureaucracies. In the book, they were able to broaden the scope somewhat but nevertheless lacked detail on what they termed the "civilian security cluster," which includes the public security system as well as the judicial system, prison and forced labor administration, and intelligence units (Lieberthal and Lampton 1992, 3).

7. Interview with provincial ministry official, Hunan, 2012.

8. Interview with provincial bureau officials in Central China 2012, 2015.

9. Interview in central China, 2015.

10. Interview with central ministry official, Beijing, 2012.

11. See chapter 1 for a discussion of the difference between actual crime and reported crime rates.

12. In all likelihood, local government officials intervene in cases that involve personal friends and contacts, although I do not have evidence for this type of behavior. I would suspect that any such intervention is case specific and not likely to produce changes in the way officials interact with police on similar cases to which they lack a connection.

13. At the national level, anticrime campaigns are usually politically motivated (Dutton 2000; Trevaskes 2007).

14. Criminologists call this type of targeted anticrime campaign "situational crime prevention" (Clarke 1983; Clarke, Gemuseus, and Cornish 1983).

15. Interview, Hunan, 2012. The innovative technique mentioned by the official was the use of personal social media accounts by some officers to solicit information from the public about open investigations. The benefit of this practice is that it provided police needed assistance, when stations were either unable or unwilling to post such requests on official websites or social media accounts.

16. Interview with local station officer, Hubei, 2015.

17. Interview with local station officer, Hubei, 2015.

18. Officers often use the Chinese words for "law" and "policy" interchangeably in interviews. Laws are set by the National People's Congress, and the ministry interprets laws into specific policies or regulations.

19. Interview, Hunan, 2012.

20. Interview with district station officer, Shaanxi, 2012.

21. Interview with city officer, Hubei, 2015.

22. Interview with district station officer, Shaanxi, 2012.

23. Interview with internal supervisor, Hunan, 2012.

24. Chris Buckley, "Video of Police Officer Knocking Down Woman and Child Incenses China," *New York Times*, 2 September 2017, https://www.nytimes.com/2017/09/02/world/asia/china-video-police-woman-and-child.html.

25. Under the leadership of Xi Jinping, corruption could join social unrest as a higher-priority issue.

26. Interview, Beijing, 2012. Fujian Province has historically been an exit point for Chinese nationals seeking to immigrate to other countries through black-market means. Some of the human trafficking rings have also been found guilty of child abduction, which is of particular concern to the ministry.

27. Interviews with city police officers, Hunan, 2012.

28. In 2012, city leaders dismissed the drug squad leader Huang Bailin in Chenzhou City, Hunan, shortly after he successfully oversaw a large drug bust. At least one suspect who was detained as a result was later released, and subsequent official statements indicated that this individual was incorrectly charged. Some speculate that the squad leader was improperly fired because the bust imprisoned individuals with connections to city leaders. See "How One Policeman Got Burned," China Digital Times, 21 May 2012, http://chinadigitaltimes.net/2012/05/how-one-policeman-got-burned/.

29. Interview with central ministry official, Beijing, 2012.

30. Interviews with provincial ministry officials, Hunan, 2012, 2014.

31. Interview with provincial ministry official, Hunan, 2013.

32. Interview, 2012.

33. Interview with provincial ministry officials, Hunan, 2012.

34. Interviews with city police officers, Hunan, 2012; provincial ministry officials, Hunan, 2012.

35. Interview with provincial ministry officials, Hunan, 2012.

36. Interviews with city police officers, provincial ministry officials, Hunan, 2012.

37. Interview with district station supervisor, Hunan, 2012.

38. Interviews with provincial ministry officials, Hunan 2012; interviews with city police officers, Hunan, 2012.

39. Interviews with city police officers, Hunan, 2012.

40. Interview, Hebei, 2011.

41. This pattern of control is also referred to as "unified power" in the federalism literature on policing (Taylor 2007).

42. The Chinese Communist Party has periodically proven adept at implementing cherished central policies with the help of street-level bureaucrats, even when those policies were almost universally disliked at the lower levels. Some examples include the agricultural quotas implemented during the Great Leap Forward and, more recently, the family planning requirements of the "One Child Policy."

43. Ai-Shan Lu, "The Wukan Effect," *Diplomat*, 25 February 2012, https://thediplomat.com/2012/02/the-wukan-effect/.

44. Interview with PAP team leader, 2012.

45. Interviews with city station officer, Hunan, 2012; city station officer, Hebei, 2011; city station officer, Shaanxi, 2012.

46. Interviews with central ministry official, Beijing, 2012, and PAP team leader, 2012.

47. Personal communication with central ministry official, Beijing, 2008.

48. Interview, Shaanxi, 2012.

49. Interview, Beijing, 2012.

50. Observation of social media accounts, 2013.

51. Original link no longer available. For a summary see China Digital Times, "Liaoning Police Take Live Video Petition," 11 December 2008, http://chinadigitaltimes.net/2009/12/liaoning-police-take-live-video-petition/.

52. Interviews with station officer in Hunan, 2012; detective in Hebei, 2011.

53. Interview, Hebei, 2012.

54. Interview with PAP officer, 2012.

55. Interview with PAP officer, 2012.

56. Interview with senior detective, Hebei, 2011.

57. Interview with district station supervisor, Hunan, 2011.

58. The ministry has often endorsed the effectiveness of campaign policing (Jiang and Dai 1990; M. S. Tanner 2005a).

59. Interview with city district station officer, Shaanxi, 2012.

60. Interview, 2011.

5. POLITICIZATION AND THE BOUNDARIES OF AUTHORITARIAN RESILIENCE

1. Interview, 2012. (All interviews conducted by the author.)

2. "Central Government Passes Comprehensive Public Security Reforms" (in Chinese), Sina, 15 February 2015, http://news.sina.com.cn/c/2015-02-15/120631523829.shtml.

3. Interviews with ministry officer, 2017, 2019.

4. In looking at coercive apparatuses in authoritarian states, Sheena Greitens (2016) finds that the optimal bureaucracy type for managing social unrest is unitary and inclusive. Fragmentation, in contrast, hampers the ability of a state to deal with popular unrest by creating intelligence and incentive problems for coercive agents.

5. "Mass Incident Report" (in Chinese), *Legal Daily*, 27 December 2012.

6. Interview, Beijing, 2012.

7. In their study of "mayor mailboxes" Greg Distelhorst and Yue Hou (2017) found that local service institutions in China were comparable to similar institutions in democracies in terms of responsiveness. Service provision is far from perfect, however, especially

when costs are high and/or the population in question lacks social power. Alexsia Chan and Kevin O'Brien's study (2019) of migrant workers in China found that local governments resist and undermine central government requirements at every turn by creating "phantom services" that deflect and deny demands whenever possible.

8. The *chengguan* are even more understudied than the police in China, although a few more-recent works touch on the jurisdiction of *chengguan* and their activities (Sigley 2013; J. Xu 2014; Hanser 2016; Ong 2018).

9. If anything, violent altercations between local residents and the *chengguan* may be worse than those with the police. An attack in Hunan by *chengguan* officials resulted in the death of a watermelon seller and sparked local protests that made headlines around the world. See Chris Luo, "Fury as Hunan Watermelon Seller Is 'Beaten to Death by Chengguan,'" *South China Morning Post*, 28 July 2013, http://www.scmp.com/news/china/article/1285309/watermelon-vendors-death-triggers-overnight-protest-hunan. Later that same year, eighteen *chengguan* officers in Xiamen were severely burned after being doused with sulfuric acid by angry residents. Jeremy Blum, "Eighteen *Chengguan* Officers Hospitalized after Acid Attack," *South China Morning Post*, 13 October 2013, http://www.scmp.com/news/china-insider/article/1334519/eighteen-chengguan-officers-hospitalised-after-acid-attack.

10. Recent relaxation of the one-child police is reshaping the work of the grassroots family-planning offices as the focus shifts from preventing births to encouraging better prenatal care, but the changes are slow, and the offices must still enforce the new family-planning policy. See Wang Xiaodong, "Changes Improve Efficiency of Family Planning Services," *China Daily*, 8 January 2018, http://www.chinadaily.com.cn/a/201801/08/WS5a52afeba31008cf16da5979.html.

11. For example, Xi's removal of the People's Armed Police from the control of the State Council and therefore the Ministry of Public Security.

12. For information on changes to terrorism response see "Anti-Terrorism Act of the Peoples Republic of China" (in Chinese), Xinhuanet, 27 December 2015, http://news.xinhuanet.com/politics/2015-12/27/c_128571798.htm. For one descriptive report of how China uses street cameras and facial recognition technology see Paul Mozur, "Inside China's Dystopian Dreams: A.I., Shame and Lots of Cameras," *New York Times*, 8 July 2018, https://www.nytimes.com/2018/07/08/business/china-surveillance-technology.html. For more information on the grid management system see Wei Liqun, "Realizing a New Leap from Social Management to Social Governance" (in Chinese), *Beijing Daily*, 28 March 2019, http://theory.people.com.cn/n1/2019/0318/c40531-30980546.html.

13. Interview with ministry official, 2017.

14. Interview in southern China, 2012.

15. Interview, Hunan, 2012.

16. Interview, Shaanxi, 2012.

17. Interview, Hunan, 2012.

18. Interview, Hunan, 2012.

19. Interview, 2014.

20. Interview, 2019.

21. Interview, 2019.

6. POOR POLICING AND STATE-SOCIETY CONFLICT

1. This narrative draws from accounts of what is often called the Weng'an Incident. Certain details vary. For example, state news media reported Li's age as seventeen, while other accounts said she was fifteen. Most international news sources reported her age as sixteen. See Jill Drew, "Anger over Rape-Murder Case Sparks Riot in China," *Washington*

Post, 30 June 2008, http://www.washingtonpost.com/wp-dyn/content/article/2008/06/29/AR2008062900805.html; Jim Yardley, "Chinese Riot over Handling of Girl's Killing," *New York Times*, 30 June 2008, http://www.nytimes.com/2008/06/30/world/asia/30riot.html?_r=0; "Up to 30,000 Took Part in Guizhou Mass Action," *China Daily*, 1 July 2008, http://www.chinadaily.com.cn/china/2008-07/01/content_6807540.htm; "Weng'an Riots Follow-Up Report" (in Chinese), News.boxun.com, 29 June 2008, http://news.boxun.com/news/gb/china/2008/06/200806291715.shtml.

2. Early reports had the figure at ten thousand and lower, but *China Daily* later put the number at thirty thousand.

3. Fu Jing, "Guizhou Official: Third Finding on Rape Claim to Be Made Known," *China Daily*, 3 July 2008, http://www.chinadaily.com.cn/china/2008-07/03/content_6814968.htm.

4. Bill Schiller, "Girl's Death Inflames China," *Toronto Star*, 2 July 2008, https://www.thestar.com/news/2008/07/02/girls_death_inflames_china.html.

5. For links see Liu Yong, "Girl's Death Sparks Rioting in China (Updated)," China Digital Times, 28 June 2008, http://chinadigitaltimes.net/2008/06/girls-death-sparks-rioting-in-china/.

6. "Guizhou Weng'an County Court Held a Public Hearing for Criminal Cases during the '6.28' Incident" (in Chinese), News.Xinhua, 26 November 2008, http://news.xinhuanet.com/newscenter/2008-11/06/content_10318180.htm.

7. Jim Yardley, "Violence in Tibet as Monks Clash with Police," *New York Times*, 15 March 2008, http://www.nytimes.com/2008/03/15/world/asia/15tibet.html.

8. Edward Wong and Keith Bradsher, "16 Killed in Attack on Western China Police Station," *New York Times*, 4 August 2008, http://www.nytimes.com/2008/08/04/sports/olympics/05china.html?_r=0.

9. "Migrant Workers Riot in Eastern China," *New York Times*, 14 July 2008, http://www.nytimes.com/2008/07/14/world/asia/14iht-china.1.14477228.html.

10. Wu Gang, "Anti-Police Sentiment Spills," *Global Times*, 22 May 2009, http://www.globaltimes.cn/content/431766.shtml.

11. Sophie Beach, "Video: Riots in Shishou, Central China over Death (Updated)," China Digital Times, 20 June 2009, http://chinadigitaltimes.net/2009/06/video-riots-in-central-china-over-death/.

12. Peter Foster, "Migrant Workers in China Attack Police in Third Day of Riots," *Telegraph*, 13 June 2011, http://www.telegraph.co.uk/news/worldnews/asia/china/8572680/Migrant-workers-in-China-attack-police-in-third-day-of-riots.html.

13. "China Arrests after Hundreds Attack Police in Hunan Province," BBC News, 20 June 2015, http://www.bbc.com/news/world-asia-china-33210165.

14. Wong Siu-san and Lau Siufang, "Thousands of Chinese Army Veterans March over Police Beatings," Radio Free Asia, 8 October 2018, https://www.rfa.org/english/news/china/soldiers-protest-10082018123809.html; "The Zhaotong People Beat a Police Car and Force an Officer to Kneel Down" (in Chinese), Sohu.com, 27 January 2018, http://www.sohu.com/a/219361150_99908438.

15. "The Police Say 'The College Student's Buttocks Wounded Severely by the Police'" (in Chinese), Xinhua News, 18 May 2016, http://china.huanqiu.com/article/2016-05/8943938_2.html.

16. "Chengdu Traffic Police Beat the Owner of the Video" (in Chinese), Wenxue City, 4 September 2012, http://www.wenxuecity.com/news/2012/09/04/1959511.html. Details on the Dongguan factory incident on Wickedonna.blogspot.com, "2015.5.9 Guangdong Dongguan" (in Chinese), 9 May 2015, http://wickedonna.blogspot.com/2015/05/201559.html.

17. The videos and articles referenced are no longer available online at their original links. For additional details please contact the author directly.

18. "A College Student in Harbin Was Killed by the Police" (in Chinese), Radio Free Asia, 13 October 2008, https://www.rfa.org/cantonese/news/police_killer-10132008112040.html; "Luoyang City Intermediate People's Court Held a Public Hearing to Hear the 11.4 Attack Police Case" (in Chinese), *Luoyang Daily*, 14 May 2016, http://news.lyd.com.cn/system/2016/05/14/010617728.shtml.

19. For a selection of social media reactions to the Lei Yang incident see Manya Koetse, "'We Could All Be the Next Lei Yang'—Chinese Netizens on the Lei Yang Case," What's on Weibo, 18 May 2016, https://www.whatsonweibo.com/lei-yang-case/.

20. "Commentary: Don't Exploit Powers in the Name of Law Enforcement; Did You Hear What Xi Said, Police?," People's Daily Online, 21 May 2016, http://en.people.cn/n3/2016/0521/c90000-9061035.html.

21. "Mass Incident Report" (in Chinese), *Legal Daily*, 27 December 2012 (full report no longer available online).

22. "Murder Mysteries: Official Figures Showing a Sharp Drop in China's Murder Rate Are Misleading," *Economist*, 6 April 2013, https://www.economist.com/china/2013/04/06/murder-mysteries.

23. "A Female College Student in Jinan Died of Suicide and Said That She Didn't Want to Go to School" (in Chinese), *China News*, 22 December 2016, http://www.chinanews.com/sh/2016/12-22/8102075.shtml.

24. For a deep dive into similar practices in Chicago see David Bernstein and Noah Isackson, "The Truth about Chicago's Crime Rates," *Chicago Magazine*, 7 April 2014, https://www.chicagomag.com/Chicago-Magazine/May-2014/Chicago-crime-rates/.

25. Interview with PAP team leader, 2012. (All interviews conducted by the author.)

26. Interview, 2019.

27. Wu and Sun 2009 found nearly 75 percent of respondents trusted police. A later study also found urban residents "exhibited a highly favorable opinion of the police," with the caveat that the respondents may be reluctant to acknowledge or simply be ignoring problems with police (Sun, Hu, and Wu 2012, 100).

28. Cao and Hou (2001) found that "confidence" in the police was lower in China than it was in the United States.

29. This finding contrasts with that of an earlier study using a smaller sample by the same group of scholars (Sun, Hu, and Wu 2012).

30. We must be cautious with studies surrounding public perceptions, since potential indicators like fear of crime are deeply rooted in social, cultural, economic, psychological, and geographic considerations, and not a mere reflection of how well the security state is functioning. For an overview of the literature on fear of crime see Pain (2000). Individual vulnerability also matters. For analysis of fear of crime and vulnerability in China see Zhang et al. (2009).

31. Interview, 2012.

32. *Police Training Camp* (video, in Chinese), 2016, http://tv.cctv.com/2016/05/01/VIDEO1LPJDiDMoPbpuBviaSp160501.shtml. The ministry's Grassroots Police Culture Group was formed in 2006 and is known for over-the-top entertainment specials. Similar groups, known as "police officer art troupes" (*jingcha yishu tuan*), have also formed at the provincial and municipal levels and frequently put on performances in their area and beyond.

33. Interview with provincial ministry official, 2019.

Works Cited

Bakken, Børge. 1993. "Crime, Juvenile Delinquency and Deterrence Policy in China." *Australian Journal of Chinese Affairs* 30: 29–58

Bakken, Børge. 2005. *Crime, Punishment, and Policing in China*. Lanham, MD: Rowman & Littlefield.

Bateson, Regina. 2012. "Crime Victimization and Political Participation." *American Political Science Review* 106 (3): 570–87.

Bayley, David H. 1971. "The Police and Political Change in Comparative Perspective." *Law & Society Review* 6 (1): 91–112.

Bayley, David H. 1985. *Patterns of Policing: A Comparative International Analysis*. New Brunswick, NJ: Rutgers University Press.

Bayley, David H. 1995. "A Foreign Policy for Democratic Policing." *Policing and Society: An International Journal* 5 (2): 79–93.

Bellin, Eva. 2004. "The Robustness of Authoritarianism in the Middle East: Exceptionalism in Comparative Perspective." *Comparative Politics* 36 (2): 139–57.

Bellin, Eva. 2012. "Reconsidering the Robustness of Authoritarianism in the Middle East: Lessons from the Arab Spring." *Comparative Politics* 44 (2): 127–49.

Biddulph, Sarah. 1993. "Review of Police Powers of Administrative Detention in the People's Republic of China." *Crime & Delinquency* 39 (3): 337–54.

Biddulph, Sarah. 2007. *Legal Reform and Administrative Detention Powers in China*. Cambridge: Cambridge University Press.

Bitencourt, Luis. 2007. "Crime and Violence: Challenges to Democracy in Brazil." In *Citizenship in Latin America*, edited by J. S. Tulchin and M. Ruthenburg, 171–86. Boulder, CO: Lynne Rienner.

Bo, Jiang, and Dai Yisheng. 1990. "Mobilize All Possible Social Forces to Strengthen Public Security—a Must for Crime Prevention." *Police Studies: International Review of Police Development* 13 (1): 1–9.

Boittin, Margaret L. 2013. "New Perspectives from the Oldest Profession: Abuse and the Legal Consciousness of Sex Workers in China." *Law & Society Review* 47 (2): 245–78.

Bradford, Ben, Aziz Huq, Jonathan Jackson, and Benjamin Roberts. 2014. "What Price Is Fairness When Security Is at Stake? Police Legitimacy in South Africa." *Regulation & Governance* 8 (2): 246–68.

Brewer, Neil, Carlene Wilson, and Karen Beck. 1994. "Supervisory Behaviour and Team Performance amongst Police Patrol Sergeants." *Journal of Occupational and Organizational Psychology* 67 (1): 69–78.

Brodeur, Jean-Paul. 1983. "High Policing and Low Policing: Remarks about the Policing of Political Activities." *Social Problems* 30 (5): 507–20.

Brodeur, Jean-Paul. 2007. "High and Low Policing in Post-9/11 Times." *Policing* 1 (1): 25–37.

Brodeur, Jean-Paul. 2010. *The Policing Web*. New York: Oxford University Press.

Brodkin, Evelyn Z. 1997. "Inside the Welfare Contract: Discretion and Accountability in State Welfare Administration." *Social Service Review* 71 (1): 1–33.

Brogden, Mike, and Preeti Nijhar. 2013. *Community Policing: National and International Models and Approaches*. Cullompton, UK: Willan.

Cai, Fanghua. 2015. "Decisive Shot? A Worthy Conundrum" [Guoduan kaiqiang? Yige jiazhi nanti]. *People's Police* 10:35.

Cai, Yongshun. 2010. *Collective Resistance in China: Why Popular Protests Succeed or Fail.* Stanford, CA: Stanford University Press.

Cao, Liqun, and Charles Hou. 2001. "A Comparison of Confidence in the Police in China and in the United States." *Journal of Criminal Justice* 29 (2): 87–99.

Carlan, Philip E. 1999. "Occupational Outcomes of Criminal Justice Graduates: Is the Master's Degree a Wise Investment?" *Journal of Criminal Justice Education* 10 (1): 39–55.

Caster, Michael. 2017. *The People's Republic of the Disappeared: Stories from Inside China's System for Enforced Disappearances*. Safeguard Defenders.

Chan, Alexsia T., and Kevin J. O'Brien. 2019. "Phantom Services: Deflecting Migrant Workers in China." *China Journal* 81 (1): 103–22.

Chen, Chih-jou Jay. 2017. "Policing Protest in China: Findings from Newspaper Data" [Youxiao zhili de zhigu: Dangdai zhongguo jiti kangzheng yu guojia fanying]. *Taiwanese Sociology* 33 (June): 113–64.

Chen, Xiaoming. 2002. "Community and Policing Strategies: A Chinese Approach to Crime Control." *Policing and Society* 12 (1): 1–13

Chen, Zheng. 2016a. "An Exploratory Study of Police Cynicism in China." *Policing: An International Journal of Police Strategies & Management* 39 (1): 175–89.

Chen, Zheng. 2016b. "Measuring Police Role Orientations in China: An Exploratory Study." *International Journal of Law, Crime and Justice* 44:43–67.

Chen, Zheng. 2016c. *Measuring Police Subcultural Perceptions: A Study of Frontline Police Officers in China*. New York: Springer.

Clarke, Ronald. 1983. "Situational Crime Prevention: Its Theoretical Basis and Practical Scope." *Crime and Justice* 4:225–56.

Clarke, Ronald, Victor Gemuseus, and Derek Blaikie Cornish. 1983. *Crime Control in Britain: A Review of Policy Research*. Albany, NY: SUNY Press.

Cui, Wei. 2015. "Administrative Decentralization and Tax Compliance: A Transactional Cost Perspective." *University of Toronto Law Journal* 65 (3): 186–238.

Cuvelier, Steven Jay, Di Jia, and Cheng Jin. 2015. "Chinese Police Cadets' Attitudes toward Police Roles Revisited." *Policing: An International Journal of Police Strategies & Management* 38 (2): 250–64.

Dai, Yisheng, and Zu-Yuan Huang. 1993. "Organization and Functions of Public Security Agencies of the People's Republic of China." *Eurocriminology* 5:137–43.

Deng, Yanhua, and Kevin J. O'Brien. 2013. "Relational Repression in China: Using Social Ties to Demobilize Protesters." *China Quarterly* 215:533–52.

Dimitrov, Martin. 2009. "Popular Autocrats." *Journal of Democracy* 20 (1): 78–81.

Ding, Tongxing. 2002. "On the Use of Police Firearms" [Tan wo guo jingcha qiangzhi de shiyong]. *Journal of Jiangsu Police Officer College* 17 (2): 159–62.

Dinnen, Sinclair, Abby McLeod, and Gordon Peake. 2006. "Police-Building in Weak States: Australian Approaches in Papua New Guinea and Solomon Islands." *Civil Wars* 8 (2): 87–108.

Distelhorst, Greg, and Yue Hou. 2017. "Constituency Service under Nondemocratic Rule: Evidence from China." *Journal of Politics* 79 (3): 1024–40.

Dutton, Michael. 1995. "Dreaming of Better Times: 'Repetition with a Difference' and Community Policing in China." *Positions* 3 (2): 418–49.

Dutton, Michael. 2000. "Strike Hard! Anti-crime Campaigns and Chinese Criminal Justice, 1979–1985." *China Quarterly* 162:575–77.

Dutton, Michael. 2005. *Policing Chinese Politics: A History*. Durham, NC: Duke University Press.

Dutton, Michael, and Lee Tianfu. 1993. "Missing the Target? Policing Strategies in the Period of Economic Reform." *Crime & Delinquency* 39 (3): 316–36.

Eaton, Kent. 2008. "Paradoxes of Police Reform: Federalism, Parties, and Civil Society in Argentina's Public Security Crisis." *Latin American Research Review* 43 (3): 5–32.

Eaton, Sarah, and Genia Kostka. 2014. "Authoritarian Environmentalism Undermined? Local Leaders' Time Horizons and Environmental Policy Implementation in China." *China Quarterly* 218: 359–80.

Feng, Chongyi. 2013. "Preserving Stability and Rights Protection: Conflict or Coherence?" *Journal of Current Chinese Affairs* 2:21–50.

Fewsmith, Joseph. 2008. "An 'Anger-Venting' Mass Incident Catches the Attention of China's Leadership." *China Leadership Monitor* 26:1–10.

Fisher, Richard, Jr. 2010. *China's Military Modernization: Building for Regional and Global Reach*. Palo Alto, CA: Stanford University Press.

Fu, Hualing. 1990. "Patrol Police: A Recent Development in the People's Republic of China." *Police Studies* 13 (3): 111–17.

Fu, Hualing. 1994. "A Bird in the Cage: Police and Political Leadership in Post Mao China." *Policing and Society: An International Journal* 4 (4): 277–91.

Fu, Hualing. 2005. "Zhou Yongkang and the Recent Police Reform in China." *Australian and New Zealand Journal of Criminology* 38 (2): 241–53.

Fu, Hualing, and D. W. Choy. 2003. "Policing for Profit: Fiscal Crisis and Institutionalized Corruption of China's Police." In *Police Corruption: Paradigms, Models and Concepts—Challenges for Developing Countries*, edited by Stanley Einstein and Amir Menachem, 129–46. Huntsville, TX: OICJ.

Fuller, Doris A., H. Richard Lamb, Michael Biasotti, and John Snook. 2015. "Overlooked in the Undercounted: The Role of Mental Illness in Fatal Law Enforcement Encounters." Treatment Advocacy Center. December.

Geddes, Barbara. 1999. "What Do We Know about Democratization after Twenty Years?" *Annual Review of Political Science* 2 (1): 115–44.

Graham, Carol, Shaojie Zhou, and Junyi Zhang. 2015. "Happiness and Health in China: The Paradox of Progress." Global Economy and Development at Brookings. June.

Greene, Jack R. 1989. "Police Officer Job Satisfaction and Community Perceptions: Implications for Community-Oriented Policing." *Journal of Research in Crime and Delinquency* 26 (2): 168–83.

Gries, Peter Hays. 2004. *China's New Nationalism: Pride, Politics, and Diplomacy.* Berkeley: University of California Press.

Greitens, Sheena Chestnut. 2016. *Dictators and Their Secret Police: Coercive Institutions and State Violence*. Cambridge: Cambridge University Press.

Greitens, Sheena Chestnut. 2017. "Rethinking China's Coercive Capacity: An Examination of PRC Domestic Security Spending, 1992–2012." *China Quarterly* 232:1002–25.

Greitens, Sheena Chestnut. 2019. "Domestic Security in China under Xi Jingping." *China Leadership Monitor* 59 (March).

Greitens, Sheena Chestnut, and Rory Truex. 2020. "Repressive Experiences among China Scholars: New Evidence from Survey Data." *China Quarterly* 242:349–75.

Guo, Yongsheng. 2003. "Prevention of Police Ethical Failures" [Lun jingchazhe bai de daode yufang]. *Journal of Sichuan Police College* 15 (6): 49–53.

Hale, Chris, Rob Heaton, and Steve Uglow. 2004. "Uniform Styles? Aspects of Police Centralization in England and Wales." *Policing & Society* 14 (4): 291–312.

Han, Rongbin. 2015a. "Defending the Authoritarian Regime Online: The "Voluntary Fifty-Cent Army." *China Quarterly* 224:1006–25.
Han, Rongbin. 2015b. "Manufacturing Consent in Cyberspace: China's 'Fifty-Cent Army.'" *Journal of Current Chinese Affairs* 44 (2): 105–34.
Hanser, Amy. 2016. "Street Politics: Street Vendors and Urban Governance in China." *China Quarterly* 226:363–82.
He, Guangying. 2012. "Reflections on Improving the Quality of Police and Police Human Resource Development" [Jingcha shuzhi tigao yu jingcha renli ziyuan fa guanxi sikao]. *Science and Technology of West China* 78:78–80.
He, Weifang. 2007. "The Police and the Rule of Law: Commentary on 'Principals and Secret Agents.'" *China Quarterly* 191:671–74.
Heilmann, Sebastian, and Elizabeth J. Perry. 2011. *Mao's Invisible Hand: The Political Foundations of Adaptive Governance in China*. Cambridge, MA: Harvard University Asia Center.
Herzog, Sergio. 2001. "Militarization and Demilitarization Processes in the Israeli and American Police Forces: Organizational and Social Aspects." *Policing and Society: An International Journal* 11 (2): 181–208.
Hinds, Lyn, and Kristina Murphy. 2007. "Public Satisfaction with Police: Using Procedural Justice to Improve Police Legitimacy." *Australian and New Zealand Journal of Criminology* 40 (1): 27–42.
Holbig, Heike, and Bruce Gilley. 2010. "Reclaiming Legitimacy in China." *Politics & Policy* 38 (3): 395–422.
Hsing, You-Tien. 2010. *The Great Urban Transformation: Politics of Land and Property in China*. New York: Oxford University Press.
Hu, Guanlu, and Ren Keqin. 2006. "Psychological Stress and Mental Health Issues for Police" [Lun jingcha de xinli ying ji yu xinli jiankang]. *Journal of Hubei University of Police* 2 (89): 65–68.
Hu, Wannian 2009. "Causes and Response Policies to Psychological Health Problems among the Police" [Jingcha xinli jiankang wenti de chegyin ji qi yingdui zhice]. *Policing Studies* 3:59–64.
Huang, Hongbo. 2006. "On the Police Human Resources Features, Configuration and Development" [Lue lun jingcha renli ziyuan de tezheng peizhi yu kaifa]. *Journal of Wuhan Public Security Cadres College* 3 (73): 34–36.
Huang, Yasheng. 2002. "Managing Chinese Bureaucrats: An Institutional Economics Perspective." *Political Studies* 50 (1): 61–79.
Jang, Hyunseok, Joongyeup Lee, and Jennifer C. Gibbs. 2015. "The Influence of the National Government on Confidence in the Police: A Focus on Corruption." *International Journal of Law, Crime and Justice* 43 (4): 553–68.
Jiang, Bo, and Dai Yisheng. 1990. "Mobilize All Possible Social Forces to Strengthen Public Security—a Must for Crime Prevention." *Police Studies* 13:1–9.
Jiao, Allan Y. 1995. "Community Policing and Community Mutuality: A Comparative Analysis of American and Chinese Police Reforms." *Police Studies: International Review of Police Development* 18 (3, 4): 69–92.
Katz, Charles M., David E. Choate, Justin R. Ready, and Lidia Nuño. 2014. "Evaluating the Impact of Officer Worn Body Cameras in the Phoenix Police Department." Phoenix: Center for Violence Prevention & Community Safety, Arizona State University.
Kesic, Dragana, Stuart D. M. Thomas, and James R. P. Ogloff. 2010. "Mental Illness among Police Fatalities in Victoria 1982–2007: Case Linkage Study." *Australian and New Zealand Journal of Psychiatry* 44 (5): 463–68.

King, Gary, Jennifer Pan, and Margaret E. Roberts. 2013. "How Censorship in China Allows Government Criticism but Silences Collective Expression." *American Political Science Review* 107 (2): 326–43.

King, Gary, Jennifer Pan, and Margaret E. Roberts. 2014. "Reverse-Engineering Censorship in China: Randomized Experimentation and Participant Observation." *Science* 345 (6199): 1251722-1-10.

Lee, Ching Kwan, and Yonghong Zhang. 2013. "The Power of Instability: Unraveling the Microfoundations of Bargained Authoritarianism in China." *American Journal of Sociology* 118 (6): 1475–508.

Levitsky, Steven R., and Lucan A. Way. 2012. "Beyond Patronage: Violent Struggle, Ruling Party Cohesion, and Authoritarian Durability." *Perspectives on Politics* 10 (4): 869–89.

Li, Cheng. 2012. "The End of the CCP's Resilient Authoritarianism? A Tripartite Assessment of Shifting Power in China." *China Quarterly* 211:595–623.

Li, Pengzhan. 2008. "Role of the Local Police Stations in Preventing and Handling Group Events" [Lun paichusuo zai yufang he chuzhi qunti xing shijian zhong de zuoyong]. *Journal of Jiangxi Public Security College* 2 (119): 60–63.

Liang, Bin. 2005. "Severe Strike Campaign in Transitional China." *Journal of Criminal Justice* 33 (4): 387–99.

Liao, Jianchun. 2010. "On the Enforcement of Auxiliary Police" [Xiejing zhifa wenti yanjiu], *Journal of Guangxi Administrative Cadre Institute of Politics and Law* 25 (2): 58.

Lieberthal, Kenneth, and David M. Lampton. 1992. *Bureaucracy, Politics, and Decision Making in Post-Mao China.* Berkeley: University of California Press.

Lieberthal, Kenneth, and Michel Oksenberg. 1988. *Policy Making in China: Leaders, Structures, and Processes.* Princeton, NJ: Princeton University Press.

Lipsky, Michael. 1970. "Protest in City Politics." *National Civic Review* 59 (6): 342–43.

Lipsky, Michael. 1971. "Street-Level Bureaucracy and the Analysis of Urban Reform." *Urban Affairs Quarterly* 6 (4): 391–409.

Lipsky, Michael. 1980. *Street Level Bureaucracy: Dilemmas of the Individual in Public Services.* New York: Russell Sage Foundation.

Liu, Jianhong. 2005. "Crime Patterns during the Market Transition in China." *British Journal of Criminology* 45 (5): 613–33.

Liu, Jianhong, and Steven F. Messner. 2001. "Modernization and Crime Trends in China's Reform Era." *Contributions in Criminology and Penology* 53:3–22.

Liu, Li-Ming, and Li Heng 2013. "Explorations and Analyses of Police Corruption in Places under Police Supervision and Control" [Gongan jianguan changsuo jingcha fubai wenti tansu]. *Guangxi Police Higher Polytechnic School Journal* 26 (6): 1–4.

Liu, Renwen, and Tang Junqui. 1997. "1996–1997 Chinese Social Order Trends: Analysis and Forecast" [1996–1997 nian zhongguo shehui zhian xingshi de fenxi yu yuce]. *Social Blue Book*, Chinese Academy of Social Sciences.

Liu, Xinghua. 2005. "Reflections on Public Security Disposal of Mass Incidents" [Dui gonganjiguan chuzhi qunti xingshi gongzuo de sikao]. *Journal of Hebei Vocational College of Public Security* 5 (3): 48–50.

Lorentzen, Peter. 2014. "China's Strategic Censorship." *American Journal of Political Science* 58 (2): 402–14.

Lorentzen, Peter. N.d. "Controlled Burn." Book manuscript.

Lorentzen, Peter, and Suzanne Scoggins. 2015. "Understanding China's Rising Rights Consciousness." *China Quarterly* 223:638–57.

Lu, Jun, and Qiao Mei-ling. 2006. "Analysis of Regulation Factors in Police Corruption" [Shi xi jingcha fubai de zhidu yinsu]. *Shanxi Police Officer Higher Polytechnic School Journal* 14 (1): 18–19.

Ma, Yue. 1997. "The Police Law 1995: Organization, Functions, Powers and Accountability of the Chinese Police." *Policing: An International Journal of Police Strategies & Management* 20 (1): 113–35.

Magaloni, Beatriz. 2008. "Credible Power-Sharing and the Longevity of Authoritarian Rule." *Comparative Political Studies* 41 (4–5): 715–41.

Manning, Peter K. 2010. *Policing Contingencies*. Chicago: University of Chicago Press.

Maynard-Moody, Steven, and Michael Musheno. 2006. *Cops, Teachers, Counselors: Stories from the Front Lines of Public Service*. Ann Arbor: University of Michigan Press.

Maynard-Moody, Steven, Michael Musheno, and Dennis Palumbo. 1990. "Street-Wise Social Policy: Resolving the Dilemma of Street-Level Influence and Successful Implementation." *Western Political Quarterly* 43 (4): 833–48.

McCarthy, Lauren A. 2014. "Local-Level Law Enforcement: Muscovites and Their Uchastkovyy." *Post-Soviet Affairs* 30 (2–3): 195–225.

McCarthy, Lauren A. 2015. *Trafficking Justice: How Russian Police Enforce New Laws, from Crime to Courtroom*. Ithaca, NY: Cornell University Press.

Meng, Xiangyu. 2013. "Media Strategies for Grassroots Police Leadership during Crisis Management" [Gongan jiceng lingdao zai weiji guanli zhong de meiti yingdui celue]. *Theoretic Observation* 79 (1): 27–29.

Meng, Weidong. 2006. "Police Enforcement and Self Defense Training" [Jingcha zhifa zhong de ziwei qi xunlian]. *Journal of Jiangxi Public Security College* 103 (3): 109–12.

Mertha, Andrew C. 2005. "China's 'Soft' Centralization: Shifting Tiao/Kuai Authority Relations." *China Quarterly* 184: 791–810.

Mertha, Andrew C. 2008. *China's Water Warriors: Citizen Action and Policy Change*. Ithaca, NY: Cornell University Press.

Mertha, Andrew C. 2009. "'Fragmented Authoritarianism 2.0': Political Pluralization in the Chinese Policy Process." *China Quarterly* 200:995–1012.

Meyers, Marcia K., and Nara Dillon. 1999. "Institutional Paradoxes Why Welfare Workers Cannot Reform Welfare." In *Public Management Reform and Innovation: Research, Theory, and Application*, edited by H. George Frederickson and Jocelyn M. Johnston. Tuscaloosa: University of Alabama Press.

Meyers, Marcia K., and Susan Vorsanger. 2007. "Street-Level Bureaucrats and the Implementation of Public Policy." In *The Handbook of Public Administration*, edited by B. Guy Peters and Jon Pierre, 153–63. Thousand Oaks, CA: Sage.

More, Harry W., and Larry S. Miller. 2015. *Effective Police Supervision*, 7th ed. New York: Routledge.

Muir, William K. 1979. *Police: Streetcorner Politicians*. Chicago: University of Chicago Press.

Muir, William K. 1980. "Power Attracts Violence." *Annals of the American Academy of Political and Social Science* 452 (1): 48–52.

Mutlu, Kayhan. 2000. "Problems of Nepotism and Favouritism in the Police Organization in Turkey." *Policing: An International Journal of Police Strategies & Management* 23 (3): 381–89.

Nathan, Andrew J. 2003. "Authoritarian Resilience." *Journal of Democracy* 14 (1): 6–17.

Ng, Kwai Hang, and Xin He. 2017. *Embedded Courts: Judicial Decision-Making in China*. Cambridge: Cambridge University Press.

O'Brien, Kevin J., and Neil J. Diamant. 2015. "Contentious Veterans: China's Retired Officers Speak Out." *Armed Forces & Society* 41 (3): 563–81.

Ong, Lynette H. 2018. "Thugs and Outsourcing of State Repression in China." *China Journal* 80 (1): 94–110.

Pain, Rachel. 2000. "Place, Social Relations and the Fear of Crime: A Review." *Progress in Human Geography* 24 (3): 365–87.

People's Daily Press. 2009. "Prevention and Disposal of Mass Disturbances" [Yufang yu chuzhi quntixing Shijian dangzheng ganbu duben]. Beijing.

Pérez, Orlando J. 2003. "Democratic Legitimacy and Public Insecurity: Crime and Democracy in El Salvador and Guatemala." *Political Science Quarterly* 118 (4): 627–44.

Powell, Brenna M. 2014. "Policing Post-war Transitions: Insecurity, Legitimacy and Reform in Northern Ireland." *Dynamics of Asymmetric Conflict* 7 (2–3): 165–82.

Qin, Yunfeng, and Luo Jing. 2015. "Research on the Problems of Using Police Dogs to Handle Unexpected Mass Incidents" [Jingquan zai chuzhi quntixing tufashijian zhong de ruogan wenti yanjiu]. *Journal of Guanxi Police Academy* 28 (3): 46–49.

Ritter, Emily Hencken, and Courtenay Conrad. 2016. "Preventing and Responding to Dissent: The Observational Challenges of Explaining Strategic Repression." *American Political Science Review* 110 (1): 85–99.

Scholz, John T., Jim Twombly, and Barbara Headrick. 1991. "Street-Level Political Controls over Federal Bureaucracy." *American Political Science Review* 85 (3): 829–50.

Scoggins, Suzanne E. 2014. "Navigating Fieldwork as an Outsider: Observations from Interviewing Police Officers in China." *PS: Political Science & Politics* 47 (2): 394–97.

Scoggins, Suzanne E. 2018. "Policing Modern China." *China Law and Society Review* 3 (2): 79–117.

Scoggins, Suzanne E. 2021. "Rethinking Authoritarian Resilience and the Coercive Apparatus." *Journal of Comparative Politics*.

Scoggins, Suzanne E. N.d. "Authoritarian Policing under Xi: Continuity Trumps Change." Unpublished manuscript.

Scoggins, Suzanne E. Forthcoming. "Propaganda and the Police: The Softer Side of State Control." *Europe-Asia Studies*.

Scoggins, Suzanne E., and Kevin J. O'Brien. 2016. "China's Unhappy Police." *Asian Survey* 56 (2): 225–42.

Seleti, Yonah. 2000. "The Public in the Exorcism of the Police in Mozambique: Challenges of Institutional Democratization." *Journal of Southern African Studies* 26 (2): 349–64.

Sigley, Gary. 2103. "From Revolution to Government, from Contradictions to Harmony: Urban Community Policing in Post-Deng China." In *Policing Cities: Urban Securitization and Regulation in a 21st Century World*, edited by Randy Lippert and Kevin Walby, 29–42. New York: Routledge.

Sklansky, David A. 2008. *Democracy and the Police*. Stanford, CA: Stanford University Press.

Skocpol, Theda. 1979. *States and Social Revolutions: A Comparative Analysis of France, Russia and China*. Cambridge: Cambridge University Press.

Skogan, Wesley, and Kathleen Frydl. 2004. *Fairness and Effectiveness in Policing: The Evidence*. Washington, DC: National Academies.

Slater, Dan, and Sofia Fenner. 2011. "State Power and Staying Power: Infrastructural Mechanisms and Authoritarian Durability." *Journal of International Affairs* 65 (1): 15.

Smith, Dennis C. 1978. "Dangers of Police Professionalization: An Empirical Analysis." *Journal of Criminal Justice* 6 (3): 199–216.

Smykla, John Ortiz, Matthew S. Crow, Vaughn J. Crichlow, and Jamie A. Snyder. 2016. "Police Body-Worn Cameras: Perceptions of Law Enforcement Leadership." *American Journal of Criminal Justice* 41 (3): 424–43.

Spires, Anthony J. 2011. "Contingent Symbiosis and Civil Society in an Authoritarian State: Understanding the Survival of China's Grassroots NGOs." *American Journal of Sociology* 117 (1): 1–45.

Stern, Rachel E., and Jonathan Hassid. 2012. "Amplifying Silence Uncertainty and Control Parables in Contemporary China." *Comparative Political Studies* 45 (10): 1230–54.

Stockmann, Daniela, and Mary E. Gallagher. 2011. "Remote Control: How the Media Sustain Authoritarian Rule in China." *Comparative Political Studies* 44 (4): 436–67.

Stone, Christopher E., and Heather H. Ward. 2000. "Democratic Policing: A Framework for Action." *Policing and Society: An International Journal* 10 (1): 11–45.

Sun, Ivan Y., Michael A. Cretacci, Yuning Wu, and Cheng Jin. 2009. "Chinese Police Cadets' Attitudes toward Police Role and Work." *Policing: An International Journal of Police Strategies & Management* 32 (4): 758–80.

Sun, Ivan Y., Rong Hu, Daniel F. K. Wong, Xuesong He, and Jessica C. M. Li. 2013. "One Country, Three Populations: Trust in Police among Migrants, Villagers, and Urbanites in China." *Social Science Research* 42 (6): 1737–49.

Sun, Ivan Y., Rong Hu, and Yuning Wu. 2012. "Social Capital, Political Participation, and Trust in the Police in Urban China." *Australian and New Zealand Journal of Criminology* 45 (1): 87–105.

Sun, Ivan Y., Luye Li, Yuning Wu, and Rong Hu. 2018. "Police Legitimacy and Citizen Cooperation in China: Testing an Alternative Model." *Asian Journal of Criminology* 13 (4): 275–91.

Sun, Ivan Y., Jianhong Liu, and Ashley K. Farmer. 2016. "Chinese Police Supervisors' Occupational Attitudes: Role Orientation, Community Policing, and Job Satisfaction." *Policing: An International Journal of Police Strategies & Management* 39 (1): 190–205.

Sun, Ivan Y., James J. Sobol, Michael Cretacci, and Scott W. Phillips. 2010. "A Comparison of Chinese and the US Police Cadets' Occupational Attitudes." *Journal of Criminal Justice* 38 (4): 640–47.

Sun, Ivan Y., and Yuning Wu. 2010. "Chinese Policing in a Time of Transition, 1978–2008." *Journal of Contemporary Criminal Justice* 26 (1): 20–35.

Sun, Ivan Y., Yuning Wu, and Rong Hu. 2013. "Public Assessments of the Police in Rural and Urban China: A Theoretical Extension and Empirical Investigation." *British Journal of Criminology* 53 (4): 643–64.

Sun, Maoli, and Li Wensheng. 2012. *Interpretation of the New Criminal Procedure Law and Police Practice Guide* [Xin xingshi susongfa yu gongan shiwu zhinan]. Beijing: Chinese People's Public Security University Press.

Talmadge, Caitlin. 2015. *The Dictator's Army: Battlefield Effectiveness in Authoritarian Regimes*. Ithaca, NY: Cornell University Press.

Tanner, Harold M. 1999. *Strike Hard! Anti-Crime Campaigns and Chinese Criminal Justice, 1979–1985*. Ithaca, NY: East Asia Program, Cornell University.

Tanner, Murray Scot. 2000. "State Coercion and the Balance of Awe: The 1983–1986 'Stern Blows' Anti-Crime Campaign." *China Journal* 44:93–125.

Tanner, Murray Scot. 2004. "China Rethinks Unrest." *Washington Quarterly* 27 (3): 137–56.

Tanner, Murray Scot. 2005a. "Campaign-Style Policing in China and Its Critics." In *Crime, Punishment, and Policing in China*, edited by Børge Bakken, 171–88. Lanham, MD: Rowman & Littlefield.

Tanner, Murray Scot. 2005b. "Rethinking Law Enforcement and Society: Changing Police Analyses of Social Unrest." In *Engaging the Law in China: State, Society, and Possibilities for Justice*, edited by Neil Diamant, Stanley Lubman, and Kevin O'Brien, 193–212. Stanford, CA: Stanford University Press.

Tanner, Murray Scot. 2014. "The Impact of the 2009 People's Armed Police Law on the People's Armed Police Force." In *The Politics of Law and Stability in China*, edited by Susan Trevaskes, Elisa Nesossi, Flora Sapio, and Sara Biddulph, 202–18. Northampton, MA: Edward Elgar.

Taylor, Brian D. 2006. "Law Enforcement and Civil Society in Russia." *Europe-Asia Studies* 58 (2): 193–213.

Taylor, Brian D. 2007. "Force and Federalism: Controlling Coercion in Federal Hybrid Regimes." *Comparative Politics* 39 (4): 421–40.

Taylor, Brian D. 2011. *State Building in Putin's Russia: Policing and Coercion after Communism*. Cambridge: Cambridge University Press.

Teets, Jessica C., and William Hurst. 2014. *Local Governance Innovation in China: Experimentation, Diffusion, and Defiance*. New York: Routledge.

Trevaskes, Susan. 2003. "Yanda 2001: Form and Strategy in a Chinese Anti-crime Campaign." *Australian and New Zealand Journal of Criminology* 36 (3): 272–92.

Trevaskes, Susan. 2007. "Severe and Swift Justice in China." *British Journal of Criminology* 47 (1): 23–41.

Trevaskes, Susan. 2010. *Policing Serious Crime in China: From "Strike Hard" to "Kill Fewer."* New York: Routledge.

Truex, Rory. 2019. "Focal Points, Dissident Calendars, and Preemptive Repression." *Journal of Conflict Resolution* 63 (4): 1032–52.

Tummers, Lars, and Victor Bekkers. 2014. "Policy Implementation, Street-Level Bureaucracy, and the Importance of Discretion." *Public Management Review* 16 (4): 527–47.

Tyler, Tom R. 1990. *Why People Obey the Law: Procedural Justice, Legitimacy and Compliance*. New Haven, CT: Yale University Press.

Tyler, Tom R., and Jeffrey Fagan. 2008. "Legitimacy and Cooperation: Why Do People Help the Police Fight Crime in Their Communities." *Ohio State Journal of Criminal Law* 6:231–275.

Wakeman, Frederic, Jr. 1995. *Policing Shanghai, 1927–1937*. Berkeley: University of California Press.

Walton, Greg. 2001. *China's Golden Shield: Corporations and the Development of Surveillance Technology in the People's Republic of China*. Montreal: Rights and Democracy.

Wang, Guanglin. 2002. "Sociological Analysis of Police Corruption" [Jjingcha fubai xianxiang de shehuexue fenxi]. *Journal of Jiangsu Public Security College* 16 (2): 176–81.

Wang, Jingping. 2015. "A Discussion on the Chinese Auxiliary Policy Organization and Its Standardization" [Qian tan woguo xiejing zushi ji qi guifanhua]. *Journal of Beijing Police College* 3 (May): 87–90.

Wang, Peng. 2013. "The Rise of the Red Mafia in China: A Case Study of Organised Crime and Corruption in Chongqing." *Trends in Organized Crime* 16 (1): 49–73.

Wang, Peng. 2014. "Extra-Legal Protection in China: How Guanxi Distorts China's Legal System and Facilitates the Rise of Unlawful Protectors." *British Journal of Criminology* 54 (5): 809–30.

Wang, Peng. 2017. *The Chinese Mafia: Organized Crime, Corruption, and Extra-legal Protection*. New York: Oxford University Press.

Wang, Xiaohai. 2014. "Empowering the Frontline Police Officers to Cope with Police Social Service Role Strain in China." *International Journal of Criminology and Sociology* 3:20–45.

Wang, Xiaohai. 2015. "Psychological Empowerment of Frontline Police Officers in Response to Social Service Role Strain in China." *Asian Journal of Criminology* 10 (3): 209–29.

Wang, Xiaohai, and Dennis Sing-wing Wong. 2012. "Police Social Service Work in China: Community Policing with Chinese Characteristics." *Asia Pacific Journal of Police & Criminal Justice* 9 (1): 34–54.

Wang, Yuhua. 2014. "Empowering the Police: How the Chinese Communist Party Manages Its Coercive Leaders." *China Quarterly* 219:625–48.

Way, Lucan A., and Steven Levitsky. 2006. "The Dynamics of Autocratic Coercion after the Cold War." *Communist and Post-Communist Studies* 39 (3): 387–410.

Wei, Guiqing. 2011. "Police Mental Health and Role Conflicts" [Jingcha qunti xinli jiankang yu jiaose chongtu]. *Journal of Chinese People's Public Security University* 151 (3): 108–12.

Westley, William A. 1953. "Violence and the Police." *American Journal of Sociology* 59 (1): 34–41.

Wilson, James Q. 1989. *Bureaucracy: What Government Agencies Do and Why They Do It.* New York: Basic Books.

Wong, Kam C. 2001a. "Community Policing in China: Philosophy, Law and Practice." *International Journal of the Sociology of Law* 29 (2): 127–47.

Wong, Kam C. 2001b. "The Philosophy of Community Policing in China." *Police Quarterly* 4 (2): 186–214.

Wong, Kam C. 2002. "Policing in the People's Republic of China: The Road to Reform in the 1990s." *British Journal of Criminology* 42 (2): 281–316.

Wong, Kam C. 2004a. "Govern Police by Law (yifa zhijing) in China." *Australian and New Zealand Journal of Criminology* 37 (1): b90–106.

Wong, Kam C. 2004b. "Police Legitimacy Crisis and Police Law Reform in China: Part I." *International Journal of Police Science & Management* 6:199–218.

Wong, Kam C. 2005. "Police Legitimacy Crisis and Police Law Reform in China: Part II." *International Journal of Police Science & Management* 7:1–14.

Wong, Kam C. 2009. *Chinese Policing: History and Reform*. New York: Peter Lang.

Wong, Kam C. 2011. *Police Reform in China*. Boca Raton, FL: CRC.

Wu, Yuning. 2010. "College Students' Evaluation of Police Performance: A Comparison of Chinese and Americans." *Journal of Criminal Justice* 38 (4): 773–80.

Wu, Yuning, and Ivan Y. Sun. 2009. "Citizen Trust in Police: The Case of China." *Police Quarterly* 12 (2): 170–91.

Wu, Yuning, and Ivan Y. Sun. 2010. "Perceptions of Police: An Empirical Study of Chinese College Students." *Policing International Journal of Police Strategy and Management* 33 (1): 93–110.

Wu, Yuning, Ivan Y. Sun, and Michael A. Cretacci. 2009. "A Study of Cadets' Motivation to Become Police Officers in China." *International Journal of Police Science & Management* 11 (3): 377–92.

Wu, Yuning, Ivan Y. Sun, and Rong Hu. 2016. "Public Trust in the Chinese Police: The Impact of Ethnicity, Class, and *Hukou*." *Australian Journal of Criminology* 49 (2): 179–97.

Xie, Yue. 2012. "The Political Logic of *Weiwen* in Contemporary China." *Issues & Studies* 48 (3): 1–41.

Xie, Yue. 2013. "Rising Central Spending on Public Security and the Dilemma Facing Grassroots Officials in China." *Journal of Current Chinese Affairs* 42 (2): 79–109.

Xu, Jianhua. 2009. "The Robbery of Motorcycle Taxi Drivers (dake zai) in China: A Lifestyle/Routine Activity Perspective and Beyond." *British Journal of Criminology* 49 (4): 491–512.

Xu, Jianhua. 2012. "Drive-Away Policing and Situational Crime Prevention in China: An Analysis of Motorcycle Ban (jinmo) Policy in Guangzhou." *International Journal of Offender Therapy and Comparative Criminology* 56 (2): 239–64.

Xu, Jianhua. 2013. "Police Accountability and the Commodification of Policing in China: A Study of Police/Business Posters in Guangzhou." *British Journal of Criminology* 53 (6): 1093–1117.

Xu, Jianhua. 2014. "Authoritarian Policing with Chinese Characteristics: A Case Study of Motorcycle Bans in the Pearl River Delta." *Crime, Law and Social Change* 61 (4): 439–60.

Xu, Jianhua. 2015. "Claims-Makers versus Non-Issue-Makers: Media and the Social Construction of Motorcycle Ban Problems in China." *Qualitative Sociology Review* 11 (2): 122–40.

Xu, Jianhua. 2018. "Legitimization Imperative: The Production of Crime Statistics in Guangzhou, China." *British Journal of Criminology* 58 (1): 155–176.

Xu, Youyu, and Hua Ze. 2013. *In the Shadow of the Rising Dragon: Stories of Repression in the New China*. New York: Macmillan.

Xu, Xu. 2020. "To Repress or Co-opt? Authoritarian Control in the Age of Digital Surveillance." *American Journal of Political Science*, April. https://doi.org/10.1111/ajps.12514.

Xu, Yu. 1996. "Computerized Recording System of Police Reports" [Dianxihua de jingcha baogao jilu xitong]. *Public Security Theory and Practice*: 75–76.

Yan, Yunxiang. 1996. "The Culture of *guanxi* in a North China Village." *China Journal* 35:1–25.

Ye, Qing, Xiao Dingdong, and Liu Yan. 2006. "Prevention and Handling of Mass Incidents by Police Public Relations" [Yufang yu chuzhi qunti xing shijian zhong de jingcha gonggong quanxi]. *Political Science and Law* 33 (5): 14–18.

Yin, Jiamei. 2013. "Review of Police Corruption Research in the Reform Era" [Gaige kafang yi lai jingcha fubai yanjiu zongshu]. *Journal of Hubei University of Police* 9 (144): 147–48.

Zenz, Adrian. 2018. "China's Domestic Security Spending: An Analysis of Available Data." *China Brief* 18:4.

Zenz, Adrian, and James Leibold. 2019. "Securitizing Xinjiang: Police Recruitment, Informal Policing and Ethnic Minority Co-optation." *China Quarterly* (July): 1–25.

Zhang, Lening, Steven F. Messner, Jianhong Liu, and Yue Angela Zhuo. 2009. "Guanxi and Fear of Crime in Contemporary Urban China." *British Journal of Criminology* 49 (4): 472–90.

Zhang, Xiaoduo. 2006. "Special Police Equipment Displays New Appearance" [Tezhong jing yong zhuangbei zhanshi shang quanxin liangxiang]. *Police Technology* 1:35–38.

Zhang, Yi, Zou Shaotong, and Tong Gaiyu. 2012. "Psychological Stress Survey of Police Engaged in Stability Maintenance Work in Xinjiang" [Zhu jiang weiwen jingcha xinli ying ji zhuangkuang diaocha]. *China Journal of Health Psychology* 20 (3): 357–59.

Zhong, Lena Y. 2009. "Community Policing in China: Old Wine in New Bottles." *Police Practice and Research: An International Journal* 10 (2): 157–69.

Zhou, Weiqi. 2010. "Forum on Education and New Situations for Police Education and Training" [Luntan shi jiaoxue yu xin xingshi xia de jingcha jiaoyu peixun]. *Journal of Jiangsu Police Officer College* 25 (1): 191–95.

Index

Page numbers followed by letters *f* and *t* refer to figures and tables, respectively.

Studies of the Weatherhead East Asian Institute
Columbia University

Selected Titles

(Complete list at: http://weai.columbia.edu/publications/studies-weai/)

Recovering Histories: Life and Labor after Heroin in Reform-Era China, by Nicholas Bartlett. University of California Press, 2020.
The Chinese Revolution on the Tibetan Frontier, by Benno Weiner. Cornell University Press, 2020.
Making It Count: Statistics and Statecraft in the Early People's Republic of China, by Arunabh Ghosh. Princeton University Press, 2020.
Tea War: A History of Capitalism in China and India, by Andrew B. Liu. Yale University Press, 2020.
Revolution Goes East: Imperial Japan and Soviet Communism, by Tatiana Linkhoeva. Cornell University Press, 2020.
Vernacular Industrialism in China: Local Innovation and Translated Technologies in the Making of a Cosmetics Empire, 1900–1940, by Eugenia Lean. Columbia University Press, 2020.
Fighting for Virtue: Justice and Politics in Thailand, by Duncan McCargo. Cornell University Press, 2020.
Beyond the Steppe Frontier: A History of the Sino-Russian Border, by Sören Urbansky. Princeton University Press, 2020.
Pirates and Publishers: A Social History of Copyright in Modern China, by Fei-Hsien Wang. Princeton University Press, 2019.
The Typographic Imagination: Reading and Writing in Japan's Age of Modern Print Media, by Nathan Shockey. Columbia University Press, 2019.
Down and Out in Saigon: Stories of the Poor in a Colonial City, by Haydon Cherry. Yale University Press, 2019.
Beauty in the Age of Empire: Japan, Egypt, and the Global History of Aesthetic Education, by Raja Adal. Columbia University Press, 2019.
Mass Vaccination: Citizens' Bodies and State Power in Modern China, by Mary Augusta Brazelton. Cornell University Press, 2019.
Residual Futures: The Urban Ecologies of Literary and Visual Media of 1960s and 1970s Japan, by Franz Prichard. Columbia University Press, 2019.
The Making of Japanese Settler Colonialism: Malthusianism and Trans-Pacific Migration, 1868–1961, by Sidney Xu Lu. Cambridge University Press, 2019.
The Power of Print in Modern China: Intellectuals and Industrial Publishing from the End of Empire to Maoist State Socialism, by Robert Culp. Columbia University Press, 2019.
Beyond the Asylum: Mental Illness in French Colonial Vietnam, by Claire E. Edington. Cornell University Press, 2019.
Borderland Memories: Searching for Historical Identity in Post-Mao China, by Martin Fromm. Cambridge University Press, 2019.

Arc of Containment: Britain, the United States, and Anticommunism in Southeast Asia, by Wen-Qing Ngoei. Cornell University Press, 2019.
Sovereignty Experiments: Korean Migrants and the Building of Borders in Northeast Asia, 1860–1949, by Alyssa M. Park. Cornell University Press, 2019.
The Greater East Asia Co-prosperity Sphere: When Total Empire Met Total War, by Jeremy A. Yellen. Cornell University Press, 2019.
Thought Crime: Ideology and State Power in Interwar Japan, by Max Ward. Duke University Press, 2019.
Statebuilding by Imposition: Resistance and Control in Colonial Taiwan and the Philippines, by Reo Matsuzaki. Cornell University Press, 2019.
Nation-Empire: Ideology and Rural Youth Mobilization in Japan and Its Colonies, by Sayaka Chatani. Cornell University Press, 2019.
Fixing Landscape: A Techno-Poetic History of China's Three Gorges, by Corey Byrnes. Columbia University Press, 2019.
The Invention of Madness: State, Society, and the Insane in Modern China, by Emily Baum. University of Chicago Press, 2018.
A Misunderstood Friendship: Mao Zedong, Kim Il-sung, and Sino–North Korean Relations, 1949–1976, by Zhihua Shen and Yafeng Xia. Columbia University Press, 2018.
The Other Milk: Reinventing Soy in Republican China, by Jia-Chen Fu. University of Washington Press, 2018.
Japan's Imperial Underworlds: Intimate Encounters at the Borders of Empire, by David Ambaras. Cambridge University Press, 2018.
Heroes and Toilers: Work as Life in Postwar North Korea, 1953–1961, by Cheehyung Harrison Kim. Columbia University Press, 2018.
Electrified Voices: How the Telephone, Phonograph, and Radio Shaped Modern Japan, 1868–1945, by Kerim Yasar. Columbia University Press, 2018.
Making Two Vietnams: War and Youth Identities, 1965–1975, by Olga Dror. Cambridge University Press, 2018.
Engineering Asia: Technology, Colonial Development, and the Cold War Order, by Hiromi Mizuno, Aaron S. Moore, and John DiMoia. Bloomsbury Press, 2018.
Japan's Occupation of Java in the Second World War: A Transnational History, by Ethan Mark. Bloomsbury Press, 2018.
Navigating Semi-colonialism: Shipping, Sovereignty, and Nation-Building in China, 1860–1937, by Anne Reinhardt. Harvard University Asia Center, 2018.
Playing by the Informal Rules: Why the Chinese Regime Remains Stable Despite Rising Protests, by Yao Li. Cambridge University Press, 2018.
Raising China's Revolutionaries: Modernizing Childhood for Cosmopolitan Nationalists and Liberated Comrades, by Margaret Mih Tillman. Columbia University Press, 2018.
Buddhas and Ancestors: Religion and Wealth in Fourteenth-Century Korea, by Juhn Y. Ahn. University of Washington Press, 2018.
Idly Scribbling Rhymers: Poetry, Print, and Community in Nineteenth Century Japan, by Robert Tuck. Columbia University Press, 2018.
China's War on Smuggling: Law, Economic Life, and the Making of the Modern State, 1842–1965, by Philip Thai. Columbia University Press, 2018.
Forging the Golden Urn: The Qing Empire and the Politics of Reincarnation in Tibet, by Max Oidtmann. Columbia University Press, 2018.
The Battle for Fortune: State-Led Development, Personhood, and Power among Tibetans in China, by Charlene Makley. Cornell University Press, 2018.
Aesthetic Life: Beauty and Art in Modern Japan, by Miya Elise Mizuta Lippit. Harvard University Asia Center, 2018.

Where the Party Rules: The Rank and File of China's Communist State, by Daniel Koss. Cambridge University Press, 2018.

Resurrecting Nagasaki: Reconstruction and the Formation of Atomic Narratives, by Chad R. Diehl. Cornell University Press, 2018.

The Army and the Indonesian Genocide: Mechanics of Mass Murder, by Jess Melvin. Routledge, 2018.

China's Philological Turn: Scholars, Textualism, and the Dao in the Eighteenth Century, by Ori Sela. Columbia University Press, 2018.

Making Time: Astronomical Time Measurement in Tokugawa Japan, by Yulia Frumer. University of Chicago Press, 2018.

Mobilizing without the Masses: Control and Contention in China, by Diana Fu. Cambridge University Press, 2018.

Post-Fascist Japan: Political Culture in Kamakura after the Second World War, by Laura Hein. Bloomsbury, 2018.

China's Conservative Revolution: The Quest for a New Order, 1927–1949, by Brian Tsui. Cambridge University Press, 2018.

Promiscuous Media: Film and Visual Culture in Imperial Japan, 1926–1945, by Hikari Hori. Cornell University Press, 2018.

www.ingramcontent.com/pod-product-compliance
Ingram Content Group UK Ltd.
Pitfield, Milton Keynes, MK11 3LW, UK
UKHW011207260326
469189UK00016BA/135/J